Management for Professionals

The Springer series "Management for Professionals" comprises high-level business and management books for executives, MBA students, and practice-oriented business researchers. The topics cover all themes relevant to businesses and the business ecosystem. The authors are experienced business professionals and renowned professors who combine scientific backgrounds, best practices, and entrepreneurial vision to provide powerful insights into achieving business excellence.

The Series is SCOPUS-indexed.

Klaus Solberg Söilen

Applied Evolutionary Economics

Insights from Biology for Real-World Management

 Springer

Klaus Solberg Söilen
The School of Business, Innovation and Sustainability (FIH)
Halmstad University
Halmstad, Sweden

ISSN 2192-8096   ISSN 2192-810X   (electronic)
Management for Professionals
ISBN 978-3-032-03682-7   ISBN 978-3-032-03683-4   (eBook)
https://doi.org/10.1007/978-3-032-03683-4

This Springer imprint is published by the registered company Springer Nature Switzerland AG
The registered company address is: Gewerbestrasse 11, 6330 Cham, Switzerland

If disposing of this product, please recycle the paper.

In Memory of Nicholas Georgescu-Roegen
(1906–1994)
Economics was fortunate to receive his
genius—unfortunate that so few were ready
to listen.

Preface

This book is written for graduate students, researchers, and reflective practitioners interested in rethinking economic theory from a more dynamic, interdisciplinary perspective. While the tone remains accessible, the concepts are grounded in scientific literature from economics, evolutionary biology, and the philosophy of science.

The impetus for this book isn't a shortage of quality works on evolutionary economics—over the years, I've reviewed close to a hundred, most cited here—but a scarcity of concise, practical ones that are read and applied.

This book then began with a personal urge: to express something complicated in a brief and practical way. The initial goal was simple—yet ambitious: to explain evolutionary theory and its relevance for economics in 100-something pages. The idea was loosely inspired by the structure of the *A Short Introduction* series and similar formats that aim to make complex ideas accessible without sacrificing substance. Naturally, this approach comes with limitations—trade-offs, simplifications, and a lack of in-depth explanations were unavoidable.

In part, the motivation came from recalling a common phrase in both academic and everyday contexts: that when something remains unclear, it's often because the speaker or author has not fully mastered the topic. That idea stayed with me: Could evolutionary economics become clearer—not by oversimplifying it, but by distilling it? By making its essence accessible, applicable, and grounded in real-world dynamics—something useful for practitioners? I believe so. After all, my students were not economics majors; they were taking courses in economics but were unlikely to ever read a long book on the topic. What they needed was something theoretical, but also practical—and something they could devour fast.

One of the key arguments made in this book, though not a new one, is that the study of economics must move beyond rigid assumptions such as perfect rationality, perfect information, and equilibrium. These assumptions, while useful for mathematical modeling, fail to capture the messy, adaptive, and emergent behaviors that characterize real-world economies. By becoming interdisciplinary and integrating concepts from evolutionary biology, sociology, and anthropology, we can start to develop economic models that are not only more realistic but also more useful for addressing complex challenges like inequality, sustainability, and technological disruption.

Moreover, evolutionary economics can provide tools for understanding long-term processes, such as the coevolution of technologies and institutions or the cultural transmission of economic practices.

Just as species evolve in response to environmental pressures, economies evolve in response to technological innovations, policy changes, and shifts in consumer behavior. For example, the rapid adoption of renewable energy technologies in response to the degradation of the climate can be seen as an adaptive response to both environmental and economic pressures. It is only when humanity begins to see itself as part of the broader evolution of living organisms—alongside other beings in nature—that we start to recognize the finite resources of our planet.

The maximizing and selfish individual, by contrast, is often unrestrained by such considerations. Thus, the evolutionary approach is not only the scientifically accurate way to study humans and their environment but also a perspective essential for guiding humanity to avoid overexploiting resources, ensuring enough remains for future generations and social cohesion. In other words, evolutionary thinking fosters awareness of our limitations, our role in the natural world, and our responsibilities. This perspective on economics, grounded in balance and sustainability, is needed today.

This book also explores the historical reasons behind the dominance of the physics paradigm in economics—especially in the post-World War II era, when the United States emerged as a global superpower and heavily influenced the development of all social sciences, including economics. The resulting focus on mathematical formalism, while often well-intentioned and elegant, has produced models that are frequently detached from empirical realities and practical applications.

The aim here is to open your mind to the possibility of studying economics as an evolutionary science—one grounded in real-world dynamics, historical trajectories, and adaptive processes. By revisiting the evolutionary paradigm, we can develop a more comprehensive and relevant understanding of how economies actually function and change over time. This perspective not only enriches economic analysis but also provides practical tools for meaningful societal transformation.

Just as Darwin (1859) transformed biology by revealing the dynamic interplay of variation, adaptation, and selection, I hope to show you, dear reader, that economics too can benefit from returning to its evolutionary roots. Yes—*returning*—for we have been here before, notably at the close of the nineteenth century.

I wish I could thank my first economics teachers for this book—but I can't. They kept babbling about Robinson Crusoe on some island making choices, and we never really shared many ideas after that. Instead, it was—as so often—the statistician and my PhD supervisor, Klaus Lange in Leipzig, who quietly set me on the right track many years later.

I'd also like to express my gratitude to a few individuals who helped shape the ideas in this book, beyond those already recognized in the main text. My fascination with dynamic systems began with Carl Brønn, an American engineer from a lineage of aviation and engine enthusiasts, during his tenure at BI Norwegian Business School in Oslo. At the time, I was an auditor at KPMG, grappling with a PhD proposal. Brønn's refusal to accept the prevailing assumption of linearity in his academic circles ignited a curiosity that has guided my work in economics ever since.

I also want to thank all the students who, over the years, contributed to our discussions and helped sharpen my perspective. For many years, I have taught the course *History of Economic Thought*—a class focused on the evolution of economic ideas, where I also made it a point to highlight who won the Nobel Prize and why, both as part of the historical narrative and for the students' broader education. Still, I could never entirely keep my own convictions about evolutionary thinking in the background, as most textbooks seem to require. One notable exception has been Morgen Witzel's *History of Management Thought*, which I have long admired—not least because he manages to present economic thinking from a truly global perspective rather than one centered solely on Europe or the United States. This book serves as an extended companion to that book—a way to share with my students a perspective I believe aligns most closely with the economic and social realities we face today, and indeed, have faced yesterday as well.

As I began teaching and publishing more actively, new colleagues helped encourage and shape my thinking. Mikael Sandberg (now retired) from Halmstad University—who has published extensively on evolutionary thinking in the social sciences—and Charlie Karlsson (also retired), a former colleague at Blekinge Institute of Technology (BTH) and one of Sweden's leading economists in entrepreneurship, innovation, and regional economics, became good conversational partners on the intersection of evolution and economics.

Thanks to Ron Boschma for visiting our research group CIEL and sharing his insights on Economic Geography during his time as head of CIRCLE at Lund University in 2014. I'm also grateful for the occasional contact with the Schumpeterian Society and the editors of the *Journal of Evolutionary Economics*—sources of inspiration over the years. I often wished I had more time to engage deeply with your institution, but my focus on teaching and various projects in microeconomics kept me from doing so.

This book was also written as part of an ongoing conversation with my wife, Professor Oksana Mont. Fragments of its ideas often surface whenever we discuss the challenges of finite natural resources and the environment. Her deep commitment to environmental issues—which I share—inspired me to return again and again to evolutionary economics and to the work of Nicholas Georgescu-Roegen. Although I never met him, his writings became something of an intellectual companion over the years. I was intrigued by his remarkable life story: from his early education in a Romanian monastery to his studies in Paris, where he distinguished himself as a brilliant statistician, to his visits to England and eventual recruitment to the United States by Joseph Schumpeter.

For those who see economics as part of the problem, I believe Georgescu-Roegen's groundbreaking ideas still offer tools and insights worth recovering—though, as this book will show, they also require adjustment.

Finally, my editor at Springer, Felix Torres, has been—as ever—a steadfast ally. His insightful feedback and encouragement helped refine this manuscript, making it clearer and more compelling.

Rosenhill, Svedala   Klaus Solberg Söilen
May 2025

Contents

List of Figures

List of Tables

Introduction

Have you ever wondered why the study of economics often feels disconnected from real life, or maybe even why parallels to evolutionary theory are so rarely drawn in economics education? After all, humans and the societies we form—whether families, organizations, or nations—are *living systems* not so different from other species like ants or whales, which also display complex social and adaptive behaviors. If this seems puzzling to you, you're not alone.

The aim of this short book is not only to demonstrate that economics can and should draw deeply from evolutionary theory, bridging the gap between abstract economic models and the description of dynamic realities of human behavior, but to show you how.

The current state of mainstream economics, heavily reliant on static, physics-inspired paradigms, is not without its merits, but it falls short of capturing the dynamic and adaptive nature of real-world economic systems.

This shift away from the *evolutionary perspective*, which dominated much of nineteenth-century economic thought, was not due to a grand conspiracy but rather stemmed from a strong desire to make the social sciences more rigorous by applying mathematics—an unintended consequence of broader scientific trends. Sciences, much like economies, are evolutionary themselves, exploring various paradigms and shifting focus as new methods and tools emerge. Truths are not always eternal; they evolve as new and better evidence emerges. However, as we will show later in this book, economics abandoned the *biological paradigm* for the physics-based approach prematurely and for reasons more historical and political than scientific.

A neoclassical economist might argue that the primary focus of economics is to address practical, day-to-day problems and that while evolution is an intriguing concept, it primarily influences human behavior over the long term. They would contend that assuming a static world is necessary to construct mathematical models that are both usable and predictive. Moreover, they might question the practicality of evolutionary economics by pointing out that it has yet to produce robust mathematical models capable of solving real-world issues. Much of this critique is valid. However, the core problem remains: what Georgescu-Roegen referred to as "standard economics"—and what is commonly called neoclassical economics today—has not delivered realistic results. We simply need a study of economics that works better.

Proponents may claim that many economic models address important social issues—often earning their creators Nobel Prizes—but, at the risk of sounding disrespectful, these models are rarely practical or effective in solving real-world problems. When laureates receive their awards, they often emphasize the noble problems they seek to address. Yet they seldom show how—or to what extent—those problems have actually been solved. Nor do practitioners often use their theories in daily work. That alone should make us question the scientific paradigm. But somehow, it doesn't. And therein lies the deeper issue: many of these theories are frequently cited, but rarely applied in the real world of business.

In this book, therefore, I will not only explore why and how the *evolutionary paradigm* provides a richer, more realistic framework for understanding economic systems but, more importantly, show how it can be done. Moreover, I will present you with a toolbox you can start using right away—whether you're an economist or a manager.

From Micro to Macro: Constructing an Evolutionary Framework

I have spent most of my academic life addressing micro-questions—problems faced by individuals and organizations that fall within the realm of microeconomics. For macro-level questions, I have preferred to draw on current events, history, and, in my case, geopolitics—particularly its economic strain, geoeconomics—supplemented by an evolutionary approach to economics when analyzing macro factors. Moreover, I want to show you that economics and business studies should not be treated as two disconnected spheres—as is too often the case today—but as two levels of a single, integrated field of inquiry grounded in evolutionary theory: economics offering the macro-level perspective and business providing the micro-level application. Thus, this book.

This is a book about theory—*economic theory*. One of the major shortcomings of the social sciences, including economics, is the insufficient attention paid to theoretical foundations. Too much contemporary research consists of a long series of empirical studies clustered around trendy or policy-relevant topics, often with only vague and superficial connections to the underlying theory. Theoretical references, when they appear, tend to be incidental rather than guiding frameworks—leaving studies vulnerable to context specificity and difficult to replicate.

Unlike the natural sciences, where replication is central to progress, the social sciences undervalue it. This undermines the reliability of findings and weakens the field's ability to accumulate lasting knowledge. Without strong theoretical anchors, empirical research risks becoming fragmented and directionless.

Foundational contributions such as Veblen's (1898) early call for an evolutionary approach, Aruka's (2014) epistemological reflections, and Dopfer's (2005) theoretical synthesis laid the groundwork for what this book builds on. Likewise, Hanusch (1988) emphasized the relevance of Schumpeter's insights, Witt (2003) explored how economic evolution can be modeled systematically, and Hodgson (2002) provided a comprehensive collection of institutional and evolutionary perspectives. If these efforts have not yet succeeded in convincing the broader public or academic mainstream, it may be for two main reasons: first, that evolutionary thinking has not been applied concretely enough to both macroeconomic systems and micro-level behavior, and second, that the field has struggled to present a coherent and unified framework that could serve as common ground for researchers across disciplines.

Evolutionary theory emphasizes adaptation, variation, competition, and selection—all concepts that resonate deeply with the processes of innovation, market competition, and institutional change in economics. For instance, Schumpeter's idea of "*creative destruction*," where new innovations disrupt and replace existing market structures, is a clear example of economic evolution in action (Schumpeter, 1934). Similarly, the rise and fall of industries or the adaptive strategies of firms in response to crises can be understood as evolutionary processes. Another approach to addressing *dynamic models*, as suggested by Georgescu-Roegen, is through the *dialectical model*.

These works demonstrate that evolutionary theory is not a vague metaphor but a coherent and cumulative research tradition. It deserves far more centrality in economic thinking than it currently enjoys.

Beyond Equilibrium: Toward a Dynamic and Evolutionary Economics

One of the most fundamental shortcomings of economics as currently practiced is its *static nature*. Many widely used models assume conditions of equilibrium or rational choice that ignore the realities of a constantly changing world. In doing so, they risk becoming elegant abstractions with limited relevance to real-world challenges. If economics is to become more applicable—more useful—it must become more dynamic.

Integrating the element of change into standard economics requires moving beyond static models and embracing systems that account for innovation, adaptation, feedback loops, and human-caused non-innovative changes. These elements are central to *evolutionary theory*, which provides a framework for understanding how systems evolve over time—not just in biology, but in culture, technology, institutions, and markets.

This shift can also be formalized mathematically. For example, equations modeling innovation can incorporate differential dynamics to reflect how new technologies spread and influence behavior:

Equation (1) Modeling the Rate of Technological Change Using Differential Equations

$$I^{\cdot} = \alpha \cdot I \cdot (1 - I) \tag{1}$$

where I represents innovation (as a normalized measure, $I \in [0,1]$) and α is the innovation rate.

Alternatively, in applied economics or business modeling contexts, a more flexible formulation may be preferred:

$$I' = aI\left(1 - \frac{I}{I_{\max}}\right)$$

where $I_{\max}$ denotes the maximum innovation capacity or available investment resources.

Similarly, human-caused non-innovative changes can be modeled using simple feedback loops to capture both positive and negative effects:

Equation (2) Modeling Non-Innovative, Human-Induced Changes

$$C_t = \beta \cdot P_t - \delta \tag{2}$$

where C_t represents environmental change, P_t is population pressure, and δ denotes mitigation efforts such as regulation or technology offsets.

Equation (3) Standard Utility and Production Functions in Comparative Context

$$U = \ln(C) - \gamma P_t \tag{3}$$

where C is consumption and P_t is pollution, with γ representing the weight or perceived cost of pollution in the utility calculation.

These types of models are used in fields such as *endogenous growth theory* (e.g., Romer, 1990), *environmental economics* (e.g., Nordhaus, 1994), and *innovation diffusion studies* (e.g., Bass, 1969). They serve to connect micro-level behaviors and constraints with macroeconomic dynamics and long-term outcomes, especially where feedback, adaptation, and externalities are central to system evolution.

Game theory can analyze cooperation versus competition in addressing global challenges like environmental stress and degradation. Moreover, *agent-based modeling* can simulate the impact of innovation and societal behaviors over time, offering a granular view of how systems evolve under different policies.

Mathematical models must incorporate stochastic elements to reflect uncertainty, especially in innovation and environmental responses. These advancements would align economic theory better with real-world complexities, making it more adaptable to change while retaining analytical rigor.

So, it's not that we cannot model this mathematically, but doing so often results in more complex mathematical models that are harder to use. As we will show in this book, the "cool factor" of evolutionary economics does not lie in its mathematical models, but rather in the applicability of key concepts from biology that can be used to understand both animals and humans. This toolbox of concepts, underpinned by theories forming the backbone of evolutionary thinking, is highly valuable for scholars in fields like economics and sociology, as well as practitioners such as managers.

What the Book Covers: A Chapter-by-Chapter Guide

The purpose of this book, then, is to reimagine economics as an evolutionary science, bridging theoretical insights with practical applications to address complex, adaptive systems. It begins by establishing evolutionary principles and aligning them with economic dynamics and then traces the historical evolution of economic systems to highlight their adaptive nature. The book integrates interdisciplinary insights and critiques, offering a robust framework for policymaking (Fig. 1).The diagram logically structures the book's ideas to build a comprehensive framework for evolutionary economics. Chapter 1 establishes the need to rethink economics as a discipline by highlighting its disconnection from dynamic, real-world phenomena. Chapter 2 introduces evolutionary theory as a natural and scientifically robust framework, setting the stage for its application to economics. Building on this, Chap. 3 aligns the principles of evolution—adaptation, variation, selection, and competition—with economic dynamics, creating a foundational theoretical lens.Chapter 4 extends this framework historically, showing how economic systems have evolved in response to shocks like wars and technological breakthroughs. With this historical perspective in place, Chap. 5 focuses on methodologies, emphasizing rigorously integrating qualitative and quantitative approaches to study dynamic economic processes. Chapter 6 highlights core concepts such as innovation, competition, and cooperation, deepening the reader's understanding of the mechanisms that drive economic evolution.Chapter 7 then grounds these ideas in practice through case studies illustrating how industries and policies adapt to changing environments. Chapter 8 addresses critiques, ensuring that the evolutionary framework is robust and able to accommodate real-world economics' complexities. Building on this refined framework, Chap. 9 transitions to policy implications, offering adaptive strategies for managing crises, fostering innovation, and addressing systemic inequalities.Chapter 10 expands the framework's relevance by integrating insights from disciplines such as sociology, anthropology, and biology, demonstrating how collaboration enriches economic models. Chapter 11 looks ahead, proposing areas for future research, such as the application of evolutionary principles to digital economies and global trade networks. Finally, Chap. 12 concludes with a call for educational reforms, equipping future economists with the tools to understand and engage with complex, adaptive systems.The tables in this book follow a deliberate sequence, moving from foundational critique to applied insight. Table 1 sets the structure by outlining the chapters and their contributions across theory, application, and methodology. Tables 1.1, 1.2, 1.3 and 1.4 critique the assumptions of mainstream economics and introduce alternative schools of thought, laying the groundwork for an evolutionary approach. Tables 1.5, 1.6, 1.7 and 1.8 explore the biological and cultural foundations of human behavior, drawing on the bioeconomic tradition to deepen our understanding of economic life.Tables 2.1 and 2.2 classify types and frequencies of change in social systems. Tables 2.3 and 2.4 present theoretical frameworks that support evolutionary analysis, linking them to economic dynamics. Tables 3.1 and 4.1 connect core principles like adaptation, selection, and coevolution to long-term transformations in economic systems. Tables 5.1, 6.1 and 7.1

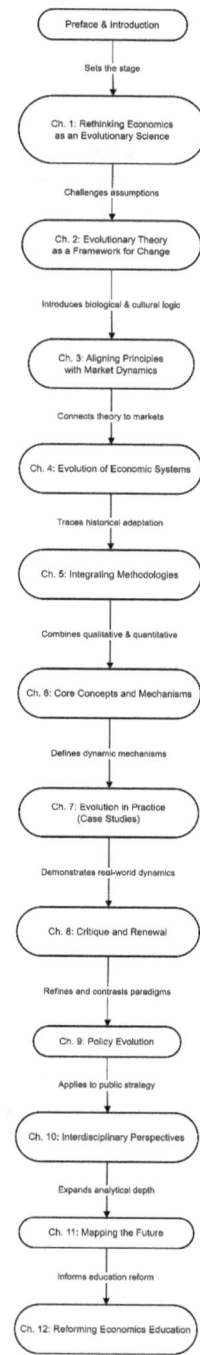

Fig. 1 Chapter structure and thematic progression of the book

focus on methodology and empirical illustration, demonstrating how evolutionary processes manifest in real-world industries and decision-making contexts.

Tables 8.1 and 9.1 introduce key policy implications grounded in evolutionary thinking. Table 9.2 builds on this foundation by contrasting traditional and evolutionary policy paradigms across dimensions such as failure, institutional logic, and adaptation—highlighting the distinctive contributions of the evolutionary framework. Tables 10.1 and 11.1 extend the discussion to interdisciplinary integration and the future of social science education, while Tables 12.1 and A.1 provide practical toolkits for applying biological concepts to economic analysis and policymaking.

Together, these 25 tables guide the reader from critique to conceptual development, from methodological design to policy application—reinforcing the book's core argument that economics must embrace its evolutionary potential to remain capable of addressing today's complex and dynamic challenges.

The intention behind this structure was to build a coherent argument—one that equips the reader with actionable insights and a forward-looking perspective, hopefully making the book useful. But it is, of course, for you, dear reader, to judge to

Table 1 Overview of chapters and their contribution

Chapter	Focus	Contribution	Type
1	Rethinking economics	Establishes the need to reconsider economics by highlighting its disconnection from real-world dynamics	T
2	Evolutionary theory	Introduces evolutionary theory as a scientifically grounded framework for understanding economic change	T
3	Core principles	Aligns adaptation, variation, selection, and competition with economic processes	T
4	Historical evolution	Illustrates how economic systems have evolved in response to shocks and disruptions	A
5	Methodology	Advocates integrating qualitative and quantitative methods to study economic evolution	M
6	Key concepts	Explores core evolutionary dynamics such as innovation, competition, and cooperation	T
7	Case studies	Demonstrates real-world examples of industries and institutions adapting to change	A
8	Critiques and refinement	Addresses major criticisms of evolutionary economics and refines the framework	T
9	Policy implications	Applies evolutionary thinking to policymaking for resilience, adaptability, and equity	A
10	Interdisciplinary integration	Shows how insights from sociology, anthropology, and biology enrich economic models	T/A
11	Future research	Proposes future directions for evolutionary economics, including digital economies and sustainability	T
12	Educational reform	Calls for reforming economics education to incorporate complexity and adaptive systems thinking	A

(T = Theory, A = Application, M = Methodology)

what extent I have succeeded. I am deeply humbled that you are giving me your attention—especially in a time like ours when there is too much to read and so many distractions.

References

Aruka, Y. (2014). *Evolutionary foundations of economic science: How can scientists study evolving economic doctrines from the last centuries?* Springer Japan.

Bass, F. M. (1969). A new product growth for model consumer durables. *Management Science, 15*(5), 215–227.

Dopfer, K. (2005). *The evolutionary foundations of economics.* Cambridge University Press.

Hanusch, H. (1988). *Evolutionary economics: Applications of Schumpeter's ideas.* Cambridge University Press.

Hodgson, G. M. (2002). *A modern reader in institutional and evolutionary economics: Key concepts.* Edward Elgar Publishing.

Leydesdorff, L., & Van den Besselaar, P. (Eds.). (1994). *Evolutionary economics and chaos theory: New directions in technology studies.* Pinter Publishers.

Marshall, A. (1920). *Principles of economics* (8th ed.). Macmillan.

Nelson, R. R., Dosi, G., Helfat, C. E., Pyka, A., Saviotti, P. P., Lee, K., Dopfer, K., Malerba, F., & Winter, S. G. (2018). *Modern evolutionary economics: An overview.* Cambridge University Press.

Nordhaus, W. D. (1994). *Managing the global commons: The economics of climate change.* MIT Press.

Romer, P. M. (1990). Endogenous technological change. *Journal of Political Economy, 98*(5, Part 2), S71–S102.

Schumpeter, J. A. (1959). *Capitalism, socialism, and democracy.* Harper & Row.

Veblen, T. (1898). Why is economics not an evolutionary science? *The Quarterly Journal of Economics, 12*(4), 373–397.

Veblen, T. (1898/2013). *Why is economics not an evolutionary science?* Timeless Books. (Original work published 1898). https://doi.org/10.2307/1882952

Witt, U. (2003). *The evolving economy: Essays on the evolutionary approach to economics.* Edward Elgar Publishing.

Witt, U. (2008). What is specific about evolutionary economics? *Journal of Evolutionary Economics, 18*(5), 547–575.

Rethinking Economics: Toward an Evolutionary Science

Abstract

This chapter introduces the core premise of the book: that economics, like all studies of living systems, should be grounded in evolutionary theory. It lays out the foundational logic for rethinking economics as an evolutionary science by exploring both historical precedents and contemporary applications. The chapter distinguishes between macro-level approaches to evolutionary economics and the proposed micro-level extensions—Biological Behavioral Economics and Physiology Economics—which integrate physiological and evolutionary insights into decision-making theory. It discusses how these frameworks improve our understanding of real-world behavior, from consumer decisions to public policy, and compares them with mainstream economic schools and heterodox alternatives. Drawing on developments in evolutionary game theory, neuroeconomics, and ecological economics, the chapter argues for a reintegration of economics with the life sciences. This shift, we argue, will produce more realistic, adaptable, and human-centered economic models that better reflect the complexity of contemporary economic life.

Keywords

Evolutionary economics · Biological Behavioral Economics · Physiology Economics · Evolutionary game theory · Economic paradigms · Adaptive behavior · Decision-making · Historical schools of thought · Georgescu-Roegen · Bioeconomics · Complexity economics · Cultural evolution · Economic modeling · Interdisciplinary economics · Economic adaptation

So, let's begin by approaching economics simply as evolutionary economics. The study offers foundational insights into how economics operates as a dynamic, adaptive system.

For anyone seeking an early introduction to the topic, Cantner and Hanusch (2002) offer an accessible and insightful entry point to these concepts.[1] Ulrich Witt's framework for understanding the diversity in evolutionary economics provides a useful starting point for examining its theoretical underpinnings: at the *heuristic level*, the focus is on the tools and methods selected to frame economic problems, which can vary widely depending on the emphasis placed on particular models, analogies, or methodologies. The *agenda level* addresses what is studied within evolutionary economics, ranging from subjective factors like individual preferences and beliefs to broader systems involving environmental interactions or societal patterns. Finally, the *ontological level* delves into foundational assumptions about whether economics is a distinct sphere of human behavior or intrinsically connected to natural and biological processes, such as evolution, environmental constraints, or genetic influences.[2]

Building on Witt's structure, a pragmatic approach can help demonstrate the relevance of evolutionary theory to economics. By explicitly linking economic behavior to biological and evolutionary mechanisms, we can ground the field in observable, scientific principles. For instance, mechanisms like *natural selection* can explain competitive market behaviors, while *cooperation and altruism* in social groups offer insights into collective economic actions. Similarly, *adaptation* helps clarify how firms and industries evolve in response to environmental and market pressures. Concepts like *fitness landscapes* can model optimization strategies, and *niche formation* can illustrate specialization in industries.

One of the clearest examples of an evolutionary process in human society is the *market mechanism* itself. Here, buyers and sellers meet under conditions of variation and selection: those who fail to meet demand go out of business, and more adaptive actors take their place. This dynamic is not dictated by *natural law*, but it operates with *Darwinian logic* in most of today's societies. As long as economies remain structured in this way, evolutionary economics will remain essential—not only for understanding economic behavior but also for grasping how our societies adapt, compete, and evolve over time. Economics is, in turn, central to the social sciences, because so much of what we do depends on how we use natural resources and apply our abilities to shape both our lives and the societies we live in.

This link between evolutionary mechanisms and economic phenomena also has strong implications for practical domains: for instance, understanding firm competition through the lens of selection and adaptation can guide industrial strategy, innovation policy, and even antitrust regulation.

Almudi and Fatas-Villafranca (2021) emphasize the *coevolution of firms, technologies, and institutional environments*, showing how adaptive feedback loops shape long-term economic outcomes. At the organizational level, Levinthal (2021)

---

[1] Cantner and Hanusch (2002).

[2] Witt (2008), and Witt and Chai (2018).

draws on Mendelian and evolutionary principles to explain how firms adapt to changing environments through strategic variation and selective retention of successful practices. These ideas are also finding application in the field of leadership and organizational change, where scholars like Santa Anna (2025) argue for *evolutionary leadership*—adaptive strategies that align organizational decision-making with complex, dynamic challenges. Together, these contributions underscore the growing relevance of evolutionary thinking for guiding policy and managerial decisions in uncertain and competitive environments.

This practical approach has the advantage of demonstrating the tangible ways evolutionary mechanisms manifest in economic behavior, making evolutionary economics more accessible to a broader group of users but also scientifically grounded. Instead of engaging in abstract debates about the nature of economics or quibbling over differences between certain approaches—topics largely confined to ivory-tower discussions—this framework focuses on drawing actionable parallels between biological processes and economic phenomena. By incorporating these mechanisms, this book aims to show that economics is not merely inspired by evolution but is deeply rooted in its principles, offering new ways to analyze and predict economic behaviors. This focus bridges the gap between theory and application, making evolutionary economics a more cohesive and impactful field.

As any reader who has picked up this book and held it in their hands can imagine, this thin volume does not aim to present a fully formalized model of evolutionary economics. Rather, it offers a conceptual scaffolding upon which such models may eventually be constructed—ideally through interdisciplinary collaboration and empirical development.

1.1 Evolutionary Game Theory (EGT)

The *evolutionary game theory (EGT)* complements rather than conflicts with this agenda by extending traditional game theory to include the dynamics of strategy evolution over time. Introduced by John Maynard Smith and George R. Price in the 1970s, EGT emphasizes concepts like *evolutionary stable strategies* (ESS) and draws inspiration from biological processes such as natural selection. What makes EGT distinctly "evolutionary" is its emphasis on population dynamics and the gradual adaptation of strategies over time. Unlike *classical game theory*, which typically focuses on rational decision-making by isolated individuals, EGT seeks to understand how behaviors and strategies evolve within populations under varying conditions.

In many ways, EGT is a natural extension of the foundational work of von Neumann and Morgenstern, who introduced the mathematical frameworks underlying game theory in their seminal *Theory of Games and Economic Behavior*.[3] While their model emphasized static, rational equilibrium strategies, evolutionary game theory incorporates dynamic and adaptive elements—modeling how strategies shift

---

[3] von Neumann and Morgenstern (1944).

over time through feedback and selection. This dynamic perspective has become increasingly influential in economics, especially in understanding competitive inter-actions such as pricing strategies among airlines or tech firms, where competitors adapt incrementally based on observed outcomes rather than optimizing in a vacuum.

A number of key contributions have further developed this quantitative field. Weibull (1995) offered one of the most comprehensive formal treatments of EGT in economics, establishing rigorous foundations for its application. Schecter and Gintis (2016) provided an accessible yet robust introduction that bridges classical and evolutionary models. Saglam (2025) expands the field with a pedagogical guide for strategic decision-making under evolutionary constraints. Tanimoto (2018) introduced interdisciplinary extensions through *sociophysics*, demonstrating how EGT can model collective behavior in traffic and epidemics. Tokumaru (2016) explored the intersection of social preferences and institutions, highlighting the philosophical underpinnings of evolving strategies in distributive settings. Together, these works underscore the value of EGT as a versatile and evolving framework that continues to enrich both theoretical and applied economic analyses. However, due to its quantitative and formal nature, it tends to be less frequently adopted in the broader social sciences.

1.2   From Macro Patterns to Micro Mechanisms

Most approaches to evolutionary economics focus on macro-level phenomena, such as the evolution of industries, institutions, or markets, often emphasizing broad pat-terns like adaptation or competition over time. These approaches offer valuable insights into systemic dynamics but rarely address the detailed mechanisms behind individual behavior in specific situations.

In contrast, what we could call *Biological Behavioral Economics* and *Physiology Economics* concentrates on the micro-level factors that directly shape decision-making, such as innate behavioral tendencies or physiological states like hunger or stress. These micro-level drivers are highly relevant for areas like consumer behav-ior, labor productivity, and even public policy design, where momentary physiologi-cal states—such as fatigue or blood sugar levels—can significantly alter choices.

Shiozawa et al. (2019) lay the groundwork for understanding how *evolutionary microfoundations* help explain this kind of individual-level variability in economic action. Potts (2001) similarly emphasizes complexity and adaptive behavior in his formulation of evolutionary microeconomics, extending it to areas like innovation and market dynamics. Later, Potts (2011) and Horsman (2013) demonstrate how these insights apply to creative industries and inequality, showing how evolution-based models can address both structural and behavioral dimensions of eco-nomic life.

Evolutionary theory provides the overarching framework for understanding long-term trends, but it does not predict how a specific individual will act in a par-ticular context by itself—something the more detailed, biology-driven approaches aim to explore.

Table 1.1 Comparing emerging evolutionary subfields in economics

Approach	Level of analysis	Focus	Example question	Key methods	Applications
Evolutionary Economics	Macro	Analyzes economic systems through principles like adaptation, competition, and coevolution	How do industries evolve and adapt in response to technological change?	Agent-based modeling, evolutionary game theory, historical analysis	Understanding long-term market dynamics, e.g., the rise of renewable energy industries; explaining firm survival after economic shocks
Biological Behavioral Economics (suggested)	Micro	Studies human and animal behavior in economic contexts using evolutionary and biological insights	How do resource-sharing strategies in primates inform human cooperation?	Behavioral experiments, comparative studies, ecological modeling	Explaining fairness preferences, cooperation in markets, and social decision-making in organizations
Physiology Economics[a]	Micro	Examines how physiological states (e.g., hunger, fatigue, stress) influence economic choices	How does hunger affect financial risk-taking?	Neuroeconomic studies, experimental psychology, biomarker analysis (e.g., cortisol)	Designing decision environments (e.g., workplaces, financial platforms) to reduce stress-related biases

[a] While *physioeconomics* focuses primarily on measuring physiological responses during economic decision-making—typically in controlled, experimental settings—*Physiology Economics* takes a broader view. It examines how underlying physiological states such as hunger, stress, or fatigue systematically influence economic behavior in real-world contexts. The emphasis is less on biometric measurement itself and more on understanding the causal role of the body in shaping preferences, risk tolerance, and decision quality. This approach opens up practical applications in areas like workplace design, financial decision environments, and public policy

In Table 1.1 not only differentiates theoretical focus but also points to distinct practical applications across fields—ranging from consumer policy to firm strategy and from *neuroeconomics* to *sustainable planning*.

1.2.1 Introducing Applied Evolutionary Economics and Behavior

Together, these approaches form what this book refers to as *Applied Evolutionary Economics and Behavior*. This umbrella term captures the shared evolutionary logic across macroeconomic systems, individual behavior, and physiological influences. It highlights a unified framework grounded in adaptation, selection, and coevolution—applied at multiple levels of analysis. The aim is to reconnect economics to its biological and behavioral foundations without fragmenting the field further.

While *Biological Behavioral Economics* and *Physiology Economics* share a concern for how the body and brain shape economic behavior, the two approaches differ in scope and emphasis. In this book, I suggest the term *Biological Behavioral Economics* to describe a subfield that integrates insights from evolutionary biology, psychology, and neuroscience to understand human (and in some cases animal) behavior in economic contexts. It focuses on long-term adaptive traits—such as fairness, cooperation, and risk aversion—shaped by natural and sexual selection over evolutionary time. In contrast, what I propose as *Physiology Economics* centers on short-term physiological states like hunger, fatigue, or hormonal fluctuations and how these moment-to-moment conditions influence decision-making in real-world contexts.

Biological Behavioral Economics, as defined here, builds on and differs from traditional behavioral economics by addressing a deeper question: not just how people deviate from rational choice models, but why such deviations exist in the first place. It links economic behavior to evolutionary pressures, suggesting that many observed "biases" may actually reflect adaptive strategies.

Scholars such as Saad (2007), Wilson (2007), and Shermer (2007) have contributed to this perspective by connecting consumption patterns,[4] market behavior, and social decision-making to evolved cognitive and emotional traits. This framing situates economic decisions within the broader context of human evolution, emphasizing instincts like reciprocity, in-group preference, and competition, which continue to influence behavior in modern markets.

A distinctive feature of *Biological Behavioral Economics* is its attention to physiological inputs—yet viewed through an evolutionary lens. Rather than treating hunger, stress, or hormonal changes as mere noise, it sees these factors as functionally significant variables with evolutionary roots. Shermer (2007) demonstrates how emotions and stress hormones like cortisol can influence financial behavior and market volatility, while Wilson (2007) emphasizes the role of evolved social structures in shaping altruism and decision-making. Saad (2007) similarly highlights how consumption preferences can be linked to reproductive signaling and mate selection cues.

This approach expands the scope of economic modeling by integrating physiological, psychological, and evolutionary dimensions. For example, research shows that hunger increases impulsivity and shortens time horizons—a finding relevant not only for marketing but also for the design of public assistance programs. Hormonal fluctuations, such as those related to the menstrual cycle, have been shown to affect risk tolerance and social preferences, with implications for financial planning and workplace design.[5] Even nutritional intake, such as creatine consump-

---

[4] Loewenstein (1996).
[5] Pearson and Schipper (2013).

tion, has measurable effects on cognitive performance, which may influence decision-making in high-stakes environments like trading or crisis response.[6]

By accounting for such biological variables, *Biological Behavioral Economics* offers a more granular understanding of behavior—grounded not just in *cognitive psychology* but in the body itself. It moves beyond surface-level patterns to explore the evolutionary and physiological mechanisms underlying economic decisions.

1.2.2 Microeconomic Applications and Interdisciplinary Connections

Much of my own research has been in the fields of *marketing* and *intelligence studies*—particularly how organizations gain competitive advantage through the use of information.[7] These microeconomic domains stand to benefit significantly from the perspectives offered by Biological Behavioral Economics and Physiology Economics. In marketing, for instance, understanding how evolved preferences, emotional triggers, and physiological states influence consumer behavior can lead to more precise models and more ethical interventions. Similarly, intelligence studies can draw on these insights to better predict competitor behavior and decision-making under stress or uncertainty. These approaches also have the potential to bridge the long-standing divide between micro- and macroeconomics, offering a more integrated view of how individual behavior scales into institutional patterns and systemic outcomes. Today, it is not uncommon for *marketing professionals* to work entirely without reference to economic theory—an indication of just how disconnected economics has become from practical business contexts, especially on the micro-level.

This disconnection also highlights the need to draw on adjacent branches of economics that, while sometimes overlooked in mainstream theory, offer valuable insights for grounding an evolutionary approach. *Cultural economics*, for example, helps explain how norms, values, and collective meaning systems shape economic behavior—closely aligned with the sociocultural mechanisms discussed earlier in this book. *Information economics* is another critical strand, particularly relevant in light of my own background in intelligence studies, where the role of asymmetrical knowledge and signaling is central to understanding real-world competition and strategy. Likewise, *experimental economics* shares important methodological affinities with what I refer to as Physiology Economics, particularly in its use of laboratory settings to explore the effects of stress, fatigue, and environmental triggers on economic decision-making. *Economic psychology* also deserves renewed attention, as it sits at the intersection of behavioral traits and physiological states, offering tools to understand the emotional and cognitive variability that shapes human action. Finally, *financial economics*—especially through the adaptive markets hypothesis proposed by Lo and others—has already begun to incorporate

---

[6] Rae et al. (2003).

[7] Söilen (2024).

evolutionary logic, suggesting a broader readiness for paradigms that account for change, uncertainty, and biological constraint.[8]

1.2.3 Mapping Evolutionary Subfields within Economics

These connections reinforce that what I am proposing here is not a rupture with established traditions, but an invitation to reweave economics with the disciplines it once drew freely from—biology, psychology, and anthropology among them. Evolutionary theory offers a way to reunify these perspectives and help economics return to what it once aspired to be: a truly integrative social science (Table 1.2).

The table shows how the proposed subfields relate to existing branches of economics, showing where they extend or complement current thinking. It positions Biological Behavioral Economics and Physiology Economics within the broader disciplinary landscape. The relationships between these branches can also be illustrated using a Venn diagram, which offers examples of how the proposed subfields intersect with existing areas of economics (Fig. 1.1).

Definitions of the Venn diagram circles:

- A—Biological Behavioral Economics (red): focuses on long-term evolved traits such as cooperation, fairness, and competition, shaped by natural and sexual selection.
- B—Physiology Economics (green): concentrates on short-term physiological states like hunger, fatigue, and hormonal fluctuations and their influence on decision-making.
- C—existing economic subfields (blue): includes behavioral economics, neuro-economics, cultural economics, experimental economics, and others that inform or relate to micro-level behavior.

Examples of overlaps:

- A ∩ B (red + green): *embodied decision-making*—how evolved instincts interact with physiological states to guide behavior under stress or urgency.
- A ∩ C (red + blue): *evolutionary frameworks in established theory*—such as fairness models in behavioral economics or adaptive preferences in cultural economics.
- B ∩ C (green + blue): *experimental and neuroeconomic methods*—studies exploring how hormones, stress, or physical states affect risk-taking and cognition.
- A ∩ B ∩ C (red + green + blue): *a unified human-centered economic science*—integrating biological, physiological, and behavioral insights into a coherent framework for understanding real-world decision-making.

---

[8] Lo (2004).

Table 1.2 Positioning subfields of evolutionary economics within the broader economic landscape

Branch of Economics	Primary focus	Connection to evolutionary economics	Related to proposed subfields
Neoclassical Economics	Rational choice, utility maximization, equilibrium	Often critiqued by evolutionary economics for its static assumptions	Contrasts with both subfields
Behavioral Economics	Cognitive biases, heuristics	Highlights deviations from rationality	Foundational for Biological Behavioral Economics
Economic Psychology	Emotion, cognition, decision-making	Explores emotional/ cognitive processes in economic contexts	Strongly linked to both subfields
Neuroeconomics	Brain mechanisms in decision-making	Adds physiological detail, but often lab-based and narrow	Related to Physiology Economics
Experimental Economics	Controlled experiments, incentive-based behavior	Important for testing biologically informed hypotheses	Methodological tool for both subfields
Cultural Economics	Cultural norms, preferences, symbolic value	Supports cultural transmission models of evolution	Deepens Biological Behavioral Economics
Information Economics	Asymmetric information, signaling, incentives	Helps explain strategic behavior and bounded rationality	Relevant to both, esp. intelligence studies context
Ecological Economics	Environmental limits, sustainability	Shares concern for long-term constraints	Shares values, but less applicable to micro behavior
Financial Economics	Asset pricing, risk, market behavior	Adaptive markets hypothesis embraces evolutionary logic	Related to Biological Behavioral Economics
Bioeconomics	Biological constraints on growth and consumption	Georgescu-Roegen's contribution; macro and energy-focused	Complementary but distinct from proposed micro focus
Proposed: Biological Behavioral Economics	Evolutionary roots of behavior, cooperation, and fairness	Synthesizes biology and behavior in economic contexts	New, grounded in long-term traits and instincts
Proposed: Physiology Economics	Bodily states (hunger, stress, hormones) and decisions	Focus on short-term variation in physical and psychological states	New, connects physiology to economic behavior

Biological Behavioral Economics   Physiology Economics

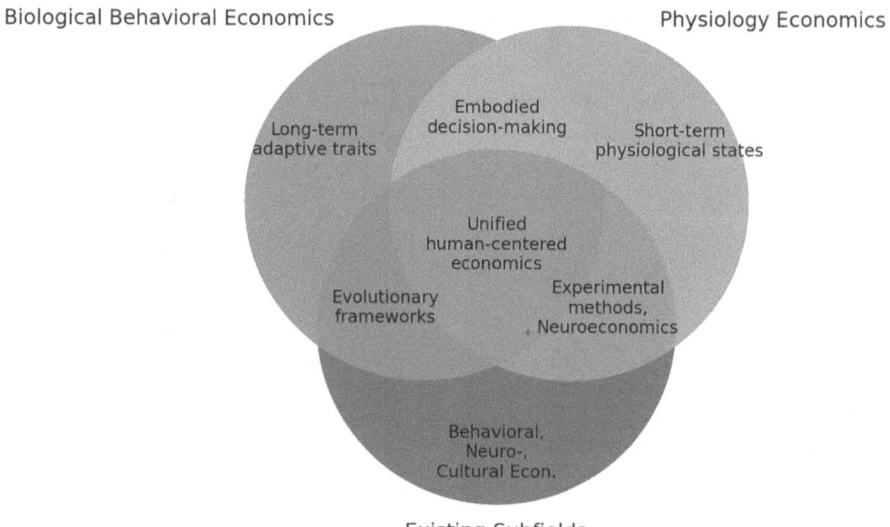

Existing Subfields

Fig. 1.1 Conceptual overlaps between the proposed evolutionary subfields and existing economic branches

The Venn diagram visualizes conceptual overlaps between the proposed and existing subfields. It highlights how the new areas integrate long-term evolutionary traits and short-term physiological dynamics with insights from established economic theories. Together, they offer a more comprehensive, human-centered economic framework.

Today, students often attend university to study either macroeconomics—referred to simply as "economics"—or micro-level subjects under labels such as business, management, or marketing. This separation has fragmented the field and weakened the broader identity of economics as a unified discipline. By reintegrating macro with micro, we restore economics to its rightful position as an all-encompassing framework for understanding human behavior, institutions, and systemic change.

In this way, *Biological Behavioral Economics* provides a richer complement to behavioral economics. While behavioral economists might observe that consumers respond positively to "limited-time offers," a biologically informed perspective would examine why sensitivity to scarcity cues exists in the first place—and how it may be modulated by individual differences in stress levels or hormonal states. The integration of evolutionary thinking allows for more robust theories of behavior that hold across time, cultures, and contexts.

In practical terms, this perspective can guide the design of public policy and institutional structures that better align with evolved human tendencies. Tax compliance campaigns, for example, might appeal to fairness instincts rather than abstract civic duty. Resource-sharing schemes might succeed when they reflect reciprocity norms rather than strictly rational incentives. Hartmann (2018) also notes that embracing economic complexity and social interdependence can enhance agency and welfare—goals that evolutionary frameworks are well suited to address.

Ultimately, these proposed distinctions between *Biological Behavioral Economics* and *Physiology Economics* are not rigid, but rather intended as a conceptual contribution to deepen and broaden the conversation. Together, they reflect a growing recognition that to understand economic behavior in full, we must attend not only to minds but also to bodies—and not only to the present moment but also to the deep past that shaped us.

While some may argue that these areas are already covered under existing branches of economics, much of that coverage remains fragmented, narrow, or purely theoretical. For example, *behavioral economics* documents decision biases but rarely explores their biological or evolutionary origins. *Neuroeconomics* investigates brain activity during choices, yet often overlooks how bodily states like hunger or hormonal fluctuations shape those decisions. *Health economics* studies the economic effects of illness but typically ignores how short-term physiological changes influence everyday economic behavior. Meanwhile, *evolutionary game theory* and *physioeconomics* offer useful tools, but they remain either too abstract or too limited in scope to fully capture the dynamic interplay between biology, physiology, and economic decision-making.

My intention is not to claim entirely new territory, but to offer clearer conceptual distinctions that integrate biological and physiological insights more explicitly into economic thinking. These proposed labels serve as organizing tools to highlight underexplored connections and encourage interdisciplinary research, rather than to compete with or displace established subfields.

Economics as a discipline has long benefited from borrowing from other sciences—mathematics, physics, and psychology—so there is no reason it should not now learn from biology and physiology as well. Furthermore, naming and framing new areas of inquiry is essential for drawing attention to gaps in the literature and clarifying research agendas for the next generation. In this light, these contributions should be seen not as redundant, but as an invitation to expand the boundaries of what economics can explain.

Applications of Biological Behavioral Economics
Real-world domains impacted by Biological Behavioral Economics:

- *Public policy*: Understanding how stress and fatigue impair financial decisions can improve welfare program design.
- *Workplace management*: Recognizing hormonal and physiological cycles can inform productivity and well-being strategies.
- *Consumer behavior*: Physiological triggers like hunger or dopamine sensitivity shape purchase behavior and ad response.
- *Financial services*: Biological rhythms may affect short-term risk tolerance—useful for credit scoring or investment apps.
- *Education and training*: Tailoring learning environments based on circadian or hormonal patterns may boost retention and performance.

If the conclusion holds, then treating economic actors as *biological organisms* opens new pathways for intervention—such as recognizing stress-driven irrationality in fiscal planning or using evolutionary stable behaviors to guide sustainable consumption.

1.3   Making the Case for Evolutionary Economics

Now, let's take a step back and look at the key argument.

The central idea of this book is fairly straightforward—and if memory serves, it first came to me in the late 1980s:

Premise 1: A(x).
If x is a living organism, then x is studied scientifically using evolutionary theory.
Premise 2: B(x).
Humans are living organisms.
Conclusion: C(x).
Humans must be studied scientifically using evolutionary theory.

Or, as a symbolic representation:
Equation (1.1) Logical syllogism representing the core argument

$$\forall x \big(A(x) \Rightarrow C(x) \big)$$

$$B(x) \Rightarrow A(x)$$

$$\therefore B(x) \Rightarrow C(x) \tag{1.1}$$

This is a *valid syllogism*, as I later learned during a preparatory course in Logic at the University of Oslo, which I attended while serving in the military. It follows the basic structure of *modus ponens*, a valid form of *deductive reasoning*, but is it true?

If this is true—and I welcome anyone to challenge it—then why isn't economics studied as a branch of evolutionary theory?

As I will suggest, the short answer lies more in historical circumstances than in scientific reasoning.

1.4   How the Argument Unfolds: From Foundations
to Application

While the Introduction has already presented the diagram and logic behind the book's structure, it may help to restate briefly how the argument unfolds. Chapters 1–3 lay the conceptual groundwork, beginning with the case for rethinking

economic paradigms and introducing evolutionary theory as a natural framework. Chapters 4–6 extend this foundation through historical analysis, methodological tools, and key evolutionary concepts such as innovation, competition,
and cooperation. Chapters 7–12 move into practical terrain, covering case studies, policy implications, interdisciplinary enrichment, research frontiers, and
educational reform. Each chapter builds upon the last, gradually shaping a comprehensive evolutionary framework for economics. The aim is to show—not just
argue—that such a framework is both scientifically grounded and practically
useful.

Key Contributions
To understand the relevance—and, at least in part, the attempted originality—
of this book, it helps to clarify its core contributions. These contributions
reflect the book's dual ambition: to build a stronger theoretical foundation for
economics and to make that foundation more applicable to real-world
dynamics.

1. The book reintroduces evolutionary theory as a scientific basis for understanding economic behavior and systemic change.
2. It proposes and defines Biological Behavioral Economics as a new subfield linking physiology, biology, and economic decision-making.
3. It offers a historical analysis of why economics diverged from evolutionary thinking and critiques the assumptions of mainstream models.
4. It advances dialectics as a method for modeling dynamic change in
   economics.
5. It compares bioeconomics and ecological economics, highlighting
   Georgescu-Roegen's influence and limits.
6. It presents practical implications for policy, interdisciplinary research, and
   education in the context of evolutionary economics.

This progression will allow the reader—especially graduate students,
researchers, and practitioners—to trace a clear line from conceptual foundations to actionable insights, I think.

With this orientation in place, we now turn to the set of assumptions that continue to shape much of economic modeling today—and to the critiques that evolutionary approaches help us formulate in response.

To facilitate this transition, the social sciences, particularly those examining
human actions and behavior, adopted a series of stringent restrictions in the form of
assumptions. These assumptions imposed rigid constraints on how human behavior
could be analyzed, ensuring it conformed to the new theoretical framework. Without
these simplifying assumptions, the resulting models and theories would simply fail
to function.

1.5   Foundational Assumptions of the Discipline

The well-known ceteris paribus assumption—"all else being equal," though it never is—has dominated much of economic theory, especially since the Second World War. Rooted in a physics-inspired paradigm, this simplification has rendered many economic models unrealistic and of limited practical value.

These models, while often mathematically elegant, often fail to reflect the dynamic and evolving nature of real-world economies. As a result, they serve more as theoretical exercises than as tools for practical application. This approach has come to define what we commonly refer to as *mainstream economics* since the post-war era (Table 1.3):

To take only the last example here, the assumption of the *neutrality of money*—that money affects only nominal variables and not real outcomes like employment or production—is deeply flawed. In practice, the Unites States now spends about

Table 1.3 Key ceteris paribus assumptions and critiques

Assumption	Why it is unrealistic	Critics and references
Rationality of agents	Assumes that individuals always act rationally to maximize utility, ignoring cognitive biases, heuristics, and emotional influences	Simon (1955), Kahneman and Tversky (1979)
Perfect information	Assumes that all agents possess complete and accurate information, disregarding real-world asymmetries and uncertainty	Akerlof (1970), Stiglitz (2000)
No transaction costs	Assumes costless exchange, ignoring the time, negotiation, legal enforcement, and institutional barriers involved in real transactions	Coase (1937), Williamson (1981)
Constant preferences	Assumes individual preferences are stable over time, neglecting the influence of context, learning, and socialization on decision-making	Sen (1977), Bowles (1998)
Market equilibrium	Assumes that markets tend toward stable equilibrium, ignoring frequent disequilibria, volatility, and path dependence	Keynes (1936), Kirman (1992)
Perfect competition	Assumes many small actors with no market power, ignoring monopolies, oligopolies, and firm strategies that distort pricing and output	Schumpeter (1942), Chamberlin (1933)
Exogenous technological change	Assumes innovation occurs outside the economic system, failing to account for internal drivers such as firm behavior and institutional incentives	Romer (1990), Nelson and Winter (1982)
Homogeneous products	Assumes identical products within markets, overlooking product differentiation, branding, and subjective value creation	Lancaster (1966), Stiglitz (1987)
Independence of economic agents	Assumes that agents act in isolation, ignoring social influence, feedback loops, and contagious behaviors like herding and imitation	Granovetter (1978), Schelling (1971)
Neutrality of money	Assumes that money only affects nominal variables, not real outcomes like employment or production—Especially in the short run	Keynes (1936), Minsky (1986)

one-third of its income just to service the interest on government debt, primarily through Treasury notes, which drastically limits spending on education, infrastructure, and long-term investment. The same logic applies to households: when people are heavily indebted—as is the case for much of the working class in the Western world, not only in the United States—they have far less capacity to buy a home, start a family, or invest in their future. Debt is not neutral—it directly constrains real choices—and this is just one reason why the neoclassical framework has proven disastrous for the US economy and any other that follows its advice.

1.5.1 The Historical Origins of an Assumption that Misguided Neoclassical Economics

To begin with, there is nothing truly "classical" about *neoclassical economics*. Instead, this can be considered almost cheeky marketing.[9] The frequent attempt to associate it with Adam Smith is misguided on several levels. First, Smith was not the first economist; schools of thought such as the French *Physiocrats* came before him and deserve more credit than they are usually given—though they, like many heterodox traditions, have been unfairly dismissed for falling outside the mainstream.[10] More importantly, Smith's approach to economics differs significantly from what is now called the neoclassical or marginalist school. While both discuss broad topics like labor, money, profit, stock, rent, and wages, Smith—like Ricardo after him[11]—was far more focused on the dynamics of production and the structural sources of a nation's competitiveness. This deeper analysis of production and real economic processes has been largely abandoned by the marginalists, who shifted attention to utility, equilibrium, and individual choice at the expense of structural understanding.

The dynamic and static methodological approaches to the study of economics have a long history. They are rooted in the challenge of satisfactorily addressing dynamic aspects of economic systems. This limitation explains why most well-developed theories focus primarily on static models.

As Schumpeter explains, this distinction traces back to the Norwegian economist and statistician Ragnar Frisch, who defined *static analysis* as "a method of dealing with economic phenomena that tries to establish relations between elements of the economic system—prices and quantities of commodities—all of which have the same time subscript, that is to say, refer to the same point of time" (p. 963).[12] Static

---

[9] The term *neoclassical economics* was coined by Thorstein Veblen in his 1900 article *Preconceptions of Economic Science*, where he grouped together marginalist thinkers like Alfred Marshall with the Austrian School. His aim was primarily classificatory: to distinguish these schools from fundamentally different approaches, such as the Marxist and historical traditions, which he considered too divergent to include in the same analytical frame (Veblen, 1900).

[10] Smith (1776).

[11] Ricardo (1817).

[12] Frisch (1933a).

models, by their nature, involve a higher degree of abstraction and rely on numerous assumptions, many of which may not convincingly reflect *realism*. Schumpeter also references contributions by Marshall, Cassel,[13] Walras,[14] and Böhm-Bawerk,[15] stating that while these thinkers significantly advanced the field, "they had no explicit dynamic schema or method to help them, [and] they failed to realize the severe limitations of their static scheme or method" (p. 967). This highlights the enduring gap in effectively integrating dynamic methods into economic theory.

As Schumpeter reminds us at the end of his book, "dynamic" does not necessarily mean an evolutionary process but refers to "quantities pertaining to different points of theoretical time" (p. 1160). It is practically coextensive with sequence analysis and includes period analysis as a special case. However, it is not synonymous with the theory of economic growth, development, or "progress."

Significant contributions to *macrodynamics* emerged in the 1930s, including Ragnar Frisch's *Macrodynamics* (*Economic Essays in Honor of Gustav Cassel*, 1933).[16] Later, Jan Tinbergen advanced the field with *Statistical Testing of Business-Cycle Theories* (1939),[17] and Trygve Haavelmo (another Norwegian economist) furthered the probabilistic approach with his work *The Probability Approach in Econometrics* (Supplement to Econometrica, July 1944).[18] The intersection between macrodynamics and business-cycle research was also explored by Wesley Clair Mitchell and the National Bureau of Economic Research (p. 1166, Schumpeter).[19] Schumpeter concludes his analysis by recognizing that the future of economic theory lies in adopting more dynamic and, if possible, biological approaches. Yet he acknowledges that he lacked the time and resources to fully pursue this direction. As we shall see, this is a familiar pattern—economists who envisioned a more evolutionary approach to economics but never completed the work. I suspect this was partly because the ideas were controversial and funding for such research was hard to come by.

This raises an important question: why does the marginalist school continue to dominate, despite decades of criticism challenging its core assumptions? One explanation may be the limited progress made in developing dynamic, especially biologically inspired, models. I remember this being a recurring topic during my PhD studies. Some scholars recognized its importance—some even saw it as the key unresolved issue—but few concrete advances were made, despite notable interest in certain academic circles, above all in Germany and Japan, as I would later discover. In hindsight, I realize this may have been due, at least in part, to how difficult it was to secure funding or institutional support for such a complex and unconventional approach.

---

[13] Cassel (1918).

[14] Walras (1874).

[15] Böhm-Bawerk (1889).

[16] Frisch (1933b).

[17] Tinbergen (1939).

[18] Haavelmo (1944).

[19] Mitchell (1927).

The persistence of the dominance of the marginalist school, even despite such criticism, warrants further investigation, possibly through the lens of historians, sociologists, and psychologists, to uncover deeper insights into the institutional, cultural, and cognitive factors that sustain it. Another partial reason may simply be poor luck: several brilliant minds working on the problem—such as Marshall, Georgescu-Roegen, and Schumpeter—passed away before they could properly address it.

Back to the assumptions and the methodology used in this chapter of the book.

1.5.2 Comparing Economic Paradigms: Assumptions and Methods

To assess how different economic schools of thought rely on core assumptions, I use here—just as I do with my students in the *History of Economic Thought* course—the classification of schools provided by the *History of Economic Thought* website, created through the tireless efforts of Gonçalo L. Fonseca, a Portuguese economist and scholar. His work, made freely available online since the early days of the Internet, offers a comprehensive and extensive overview of the major traditions in economic thought. This framework has allowed us to systematically examine which schools depend on these core assumptions—and which do not.

For this book I reviewed a broad spectrum of schools, starting with the *Schools of Political Economy (Ancient–1871)*, including the *Pre-Classical* era with traditions such as the *Ancients*, *Islamic Economics*, the *Scholastics*, the *Salamanca School*, and the *Mercantilists*—a school of thought we will return to later in the book. I also included the Marginalist or *Classical Schools*, such as the *Classical Ricardian School*, the *Manchester School*, and the *Marxian School*.[20] These schools shaped the foundations of modern economic theory, focusing on different aspects of production, distribution, and societal wealth.

For the *Marginalist* or *Neoclassical Schools (1871–Today)*, I examined both Anglo-American and Continental traditions. Examples include the *Chicago School*, which strongly emphasizes rationality and market equilibrium, and the *Neo-Walrasian School*, which integrates mathematical formalism into its models. These schools represent the mainstream trajectory of economic thought, particularly after the Second World War.

I also explored *Alternative Schools*, including *Heterodox Traditions* like the *German Historical School* and *Evolutionary Economics*, as well as various *Keynesian Schools* such as the *Cambridge Keynesians* and the *New Keynesians*. These schools often critique mainstream assumptions, focusing on systemic instability, institutional influences, and dynamic economic processes.

---

[20] Note here that Fonseca classifies the Marxian School within the broader classical tradition, alongside Ricardian and Physiocratic thought, reflecting a historical grouping based on shared pre-marginalist concerns with production and value. As we recall, Veblen (1900) used the term to group marginalist economists like Marshall and the Austrian School, explicitly distinguishing them from Marxian and historical approaches, which he viewed as fundamentally different.

This short review highlights the diversity in economic thought and sheds light on the extent to which various schools rely on assumptions like rationality, perfect information, and equilibrium. By examining these traditions, we see more clearly the theoretical divides and the ongoing debates within the study of economics (Table 1.4).

In practical terms, assuming perfect rationality has led to no end of flawed economic policies that ignore how stress or scarcity affects judgment—seen, for example, in welfare program designs that presume consistent, optimal decision-making among low-income populations.

Similarly, policies built on the assumption of perfect information typically fail in healthcare markets, where patients often lack the data or capacity to make informed decisions about complex treatments.

Among the various economic schools, *Neoclassical Schools* such as the *Chicago School*, the *New Classical School*, and the *Neo-Walrasian School* rely heavily on the core assumptions, including rationality, perfect information, and market equilibrium. These schools emphasize mathematical formalism and often use these assumptions as foundational to their models, focusing on idealized markets and predictive efficiency.

Close behind are the *Anglo-American Marginalist Schools*, like the *English Marginalists* and *Cambridge Neoclassicals*, which also adopt many of these assumptions, particularly rational behavior and perfect competition, as central to their theoretical frameworks. Their work laid the groundwork for later Neoclassical developments.

Continental Neoclassical Schools, such as the *Lausanne School* and *Paretian Revival*, similarly depend on these assumptions but sometimes integrate unique methodological approaches, such as general equilibrium models, which provide a slightly different perspective on how these assumptions function in economic systems.

In contrast, *Keynesian Schools* like the *Neo-Keynesian Synthesis* and *New Keynesians* selectively adopt some assumptions, such as rationality and market equilibrium, but often critique or relax others. For example, they emphasize market imperfections, sticky wages, and incomplete information, making their models more flexible and less reliant on the rigidities of earlier Neoclassical traditions.

Yet what these Keynesian approaches often gain in flexibility, they may lack in theoretical rigor and internal consistency. Few schools of thought offer such a wide range of interpretations and applications, making it difficult to generalize or build cumulative theoretical foundations. While J.M. Keynes himself was a towering intellect, his work was deeply rooted in the English pragmatic tradition, where political science and economics were seen as inseparable. That spirit of practical engagement remains valuable, but the lack of formal cohesion in many later Keynesian models has limited their broader applicability and coherence.

What Keynes achieved, above all, was to rescue economic policy from the paralyzing grip of neoclassical orthodoxy during the Great Depression. In a time when the prevailing wisdom insisted that markets would naturally self-correct—no matter the human cost—Keynes introduced a pragmatic framework grounded in real-world

Table 1.4 Use of core assumptions across economic schools of thought

Assumption	Marginalist/ Neoclassical Schools	Classical Schools	Alternative Schools
Rationality of agents	Central assumption in all strands, particularly in the Chicago, English Marginalist, Monetarist, and New Classical Schools	Present but less formalized in Ricardian, Manchester, and French Liberal Schools	Critiqued by Marxians, Neo-Marxians, and Evolutionary economists; New Keynesians use it narrowly for microfoundations
Perfect information	Assumed in New Classical, Chicago, and Neo-Walrasian models as a foundation for equilibrium	Rarely stated explicitly; less applicable in pre-mathematical frameworks	Challenged by Keynesians and Historical Schools; Evolutionary Economics stresses uncertainty and bounded rationality
No transaction costs	Implicit in many models, especially in Neo-Walrasian and Cowles Commission approaches	Seldom addressed explicitly	Highlighted by Institutional Economics as a major limitation of standard theory
Constant preferences	Assumed across most neoclassical models, especially in Edgeworthian and New Classical theory	Informal assumption; less central due to simpler behavioral modeling	Rejected by Keynesians and Evolutionary Economics, which emphasize preference formation and change over time
Market equilibrium	Core to Monetarist, New Classical, and Walrasian frameworks, often mathematically formalized	Central to Physiocrats and Ricardians focusing on production and distribution balance	Rejected by Marxians, Keynesians, and Historical Schools, which emphasize disequilibrium and systemic instability
Perfect competition	Foundational in Chicago and New Classical theories; used to explain efficiency and pricing	Mentioned in Classical thought (e.g., Manchester School), but not rigorously defined	Critiqued by Evolutionary and Institutional Economics, which highlight firm heterogeneity and market power
Exogenous technological change	Embedded in neoclassical growth models like Solow's; innovation treated as external to the model	Present but undeveloped; innovation viewed as external or historical	Replaced by endogenous innovation in Schumpeterian and Evolutionary Economics, emphasizing firm behavior and competition
Homogeneous products	Standard in perfect competition models, simplifying markets for analytical clarity	Implied in Ricardian and Physiocratic models; goods treated as uniform	Rejected by Marxian and Evolutionary economists; focus on product variety and quality dynamics
Independence of economic agents	Assumed across neoclassical theory, including Edgeworth and Walrasian frameworks	Less emphasized; focus on macro or class-based aggregates	Critiqued by Keynesians, Marxians, and socio-institutional schools for ignoring interdependence and feedback
Neutrality of money	Core principle in Monetarist and New Classical models, especially in the long run	Largely irrelevant or undefined	Rejected by Keynesians and Post-Keynesians, who view money as central to real activity and instability

observation. His emphasis on aggregate demand, fiscal stimulus, and state intervention not only challenged the dominant laissez-faire assumptions, but arguably helped save the world economy from further collapse. For this reason, Keynes is rightly remembered not as much as a theorist, but as a practitioner who reshaped the role of economics in public life.

Finally, *Alternative Schools*, such as *Evolutionary Economics* and the *German Historical School*, largely reject these assumptions, focusing instead on institutional dynamics, historical processes, and adaptive behaviors. These schools challenge the universality of rationality and equilibrium, advocating for a more dynamic and context-dependent understanding of economic systems.

Both Evolutionary Economics and the German Historical School rely on certain foundational assumptions, though these differ from the rigid abstractions of neoclassical economics. Evolutionary Economics assumes that economic systems are dynamic and adaptive, shaped by processes such as competition, innovation, and institutional change, mirroring biological evolution. The German Historical School, on the other hand, assumes that economic behavior and systems are deeply embedded in cultural, historical, and institutional contexts, requiring a case-by-case analysis rather than universal laws. These assumptions, while more flexible and context-sensitive, provide the theoretical scaffolding necessary to analyze and interpret economic phenomena within their respective frameworks.

The strength of both Evolutionary Economics and the German Historical School lies in their shared ability to reflect the complexity and variability of real-world human behavior. Unlike the rigid, abstract assumptions of neoclassical economics, these approaches do not filter out inconvenient aspects of human conduct to fit tidy mathematical models. Instead, they embrace the messiness of actual economic and social dynamics, aligning more closely with how people perceive and act in everyday life. What unites the evolutionary and historical traditions is their emphasis on context, process, and change—recognizing that economic systems are not static or universal, but embedded in specific biological, cultural, and institutional environments. This orientation toward realism requires us to move beyond equilibrium thinking and into a more nuanced exploration of how human behavior evolves over time. It is in this spirit that we turn to the biological and cultural foundations of economic life and the role of cultural propensity in shaping long-term outcomes.

While biological and cultural factors are deeply intertwined, they are not mutually dependent; each operates within its distinct domain. Biological influences are grounded in the natural sciences, focusing on the physiological and evolutionary mechanisms that drive behavior. On the other hand, cultural influences belong to the humanities, exploring the shared values, norms, and practices that shape human societies over time. Together, these perspectives offer complementary insights, enriching our understanding of economic and social systems without necessitating that one subsumes the other.

1.6   The Biological and Cultural Foundations of Economic Behavior

To assume that all cultures are alike in terms of human behavior—such that a specific case will yield the same outcome regardless of cultural context—is perhaps the most significant assumption of all and one that risks rendering any results meaningless. Of course, achieving that would not only be desirable but brilliant, as it would bring us one step closer to universal theories—but reality tends to demand otherwise.

On that note, according to Georgescu-Roegen, the *Methodenstreit* was essentially about the claim that it is possible to construct a universally valid economic theory (Georgescu-Roegen, 1976, p. 111).[21]

Many authors have highlighted that the study of humans is not easily approached through mathematics due to the complexity of social life or, as Schrödinger puts it, "the role that cultural propensity plays in the economic process" (Schrödinger, pp. 8–9).[22] In other words, all human actions are influenced by cultural factors, which vary significantly across societies—with no indication that these differences will disappear or converge anytime soon, despite being, for some, a part of a globalist ideal. People generally value their cultural differences, and this need not conflict with *humanist values* such as human rights. What's required is respect—and maybe also appreciation—for those differences.

Understanding the interplay between social identity and entrepreneurial activity is critical. Thus, for example, the work by Obschonka et al. (2012) bridges *cultural psychology* and *economic behavior*.[23]

To predict human behavior, it is essential to account for how each culture shapes individuals and communities. One approach, as demonstrated by Hofstede and others, is to analyze how cultures differ and how these differences influence behavior. Another way is to examine the biological characteristics that contribute to behavior—or, ideally, to combine both perspectives, as shown in Table 1.5.

These distinctions matter in practice: marketing strategies, public education campaigns, and entrepreneurship policy all benefit greatly from a clearer understanding of which human motives are biologically constrained and which are shaped by culture. From an economic standpoint, companies often aim to streamline *global advertising* in order to reduce costs, hoping that a universal message will suffice. However, they frequently discover that such standardization is suboptimal—especially in competitive markets where cultural variation influences consumer behavior. As a result, many firms accept the higher costs of differentiation and even go so far as to hire local advertising agencies to ensure their messaging resonates with local values, norms, and expectations.

This tension between biological and cultural influences becomes especially evident when we look at how entire disciplines have approached human behavior. A telling example from the social sciences is criminology. Although genetic research

---

[21] Georgescu-Roegen (1976).

[22] Schrödinger (1951).

[23] Obschonka et al. (2012).

Table 1.5 The biological and cultural foundations of human behavior

Category	Type of motive	Description	Examples	Key influences
Biological motives	Physiological needs	Basic biological drives necessary for survival	Hunger, thirst, sleep, shelter, reproduction	Evolutionary adaptation, bodily homeostasis, genetic imperatives
	Homeostasis	Tendency to maintain internal physical and chemical balance	Regulation of body temperature, thirst when dehydrated	Autonomic nervous system, metabolic control, feedback regulation
	Fight-or-flight response	Instinctive reaction to perceived threats	Escaping danger, defensive aggression	Sympathetic nervous system, hormonal surges (e.g., adrenaline)
	Desires	Aspirations linked to pleasure or comfort beyond basic survival	Seeking pleasure in food, relaxation after work	Dopaminergic reward systems, limbic system activation
	Restlessness	Subconscious impulses to act, driven by physical or mental discomfort	Pacing, tapping fingers, seeking novelty	Psychological arousal, need for stimulation, physical discomfort
Cultural motives	Cultural adherence	Actions influenced by societal norms, traditions, and shared values	Celebrating holidays, language use, respecting authority	Socialization, education, collective norms
	Social desires	Motivations to gain social acceptance, status, or belonging	Seeking approval, participating in group activities, networking	Peer influence, group dynamics, status hierarchies
	Ethical/ religious values	Behavior guided by moral principles or spiritual beliefs	Acts of charity, prayer, ethical consumption	Religious teachings, moral philosophy, community traditions
	Fashion and trends	Following societal trends to align with group identity or personal expression	Wearing trendy clothes, using popular gadgets	Media exposure, cultural signaling, consumer culture
	Intelligence (trained)	Skills and knowledge developed through education and cultural exposure	Analytical skills, problem-solving, cultural literacy	Formal education, mentorship, cultural capital

(continued)

Table 1.5 (continued)

Category	Type of motive	Description	Examples	Key influences
Mixed influences	Personal identity	Combination of biological and cultural factors shaping self-concept	Career choices, lifestyle preferences, hobbies	Genetic predispositions, cultural narratives, life experiences
	Restlessness (cultural)	Unease influenced by societal pressures or norms rather than physical causes	Changing careers, dissatisfaction with social status	Social comparison, cultural dissonance, internalized expectations
	Aesthetic appreciation	Seeking beauty or art for emotional or intellectual satisfaction	Enjoying music, visiting art galleries	Neural pattern recognition, emotional processing, exposure to art and culture

has demonstrated that certain traits linked to criminal behavior—such as impulsivity or aggression—have a heritable component, mainstream criminology has often underplayed or dismissed these insights. As a result, the field has struggled to develop fully integrated models that reflect the complex interplay between biological predispositions and environmental conditions.

The table highlights the multifaceted nature of human behavior, driven by both biological and cultural motives, often with overlapping influences. Biological motives, such as physiological needs and the fight-or-flight response, are rooted in survival instincts and automatic processes, while cultural motives, like adherence to societal norms and ethical values, stem from shared traditions and learned behaviors. Mixed influences, such as personal identity and aesthetic appreciation, showcase the interplay between biological predispositions and cultural education. Together, these factors demonstrate that human behavior cannot be reduced to simplistic models, as it is shaped by a complex web of innate drives and societal contexts.

This complexity underscores the limitations of static frameworks in capturing the dynamic nature of human actions and societal evolution. To address this, we turn again to Georgescu-Roegen's suggestions, this time of studying human change through the method of dialectics—a long-standing approach that embraces the fluid and evolving character of human systems.

1.7 Dialectical Reasoning and the Neuroscience of Adaptive Economic Thinking

One approach then, suggested by Georgescu-Roegen, is to study the dynamics of human change, much as we have always done—since Socrates, at least—through the method of "*dialectics*" (Table 1.6).

Table 1.6 Different approaches to the dialectic method

Thinker	Approach to dialectics	Key focus	Differences from others
Plato	Dialectics as a method of inquiry and dialogue to uncover universal truths	Pursuit of ideal forms beyond sensory experience	Emphasizes metaphysical ideals; lacks material or empirical grounding
Aristotle	Dialectics as logical reasoning and debate to refine understanding	Practical investigation of reality using logic and observation	More empirical and pragmatic; avoids metaphysical abstraction
Hegel	Idealistic dialectics: ideas evolve through contradiction (thesis-antithesis-synthesis)	Development of consciousness and the Absolute through unfolding historical logic	Abstract, focused on thought itself; not rooted in material or economic realities
Marx	Dialectical materialism: historical progress through class conflict and material forces	Transformation of society via class struggle and ownership relations	Grounded in economics and material conditions; rejects idealist dialectics
Engels	Extended dialectical materialism to the natural sciences	Application of dialectics to physical, biological, and social processes	Applied Marx's ideas to natural systems; emphasized continuity between society and nature
Georgescu-Roegen	Biophysical dialectics: applied to energy, resources, and human systems	Interplay between entropy, finite resources, and economic behavior	Integrates thermodynamics with economics; moves beyond social or philosophical dialectics
Herman Daly	Dialectics of economy and ecology, especially sustainability vs. growth	Reconciling economic activity with ecological boundaries; steady-state economics	Builds on Georgescu-Roegen's framework; applies dialectics to sustainability policy
Adorno	Negative dialectics: contradiction without resolution	Persistent contradictions in society, resisting totalizing explanations	Rejects synthesis; critiques systems that claim coherence or closure
Habermas	Communicative dialectics: resolving contradictions through rational discourse	Achieving mutual understanding via dialogue and public reasoning	Focuses on language and deliberation; not on material or metaphysical synthesis

The concept of *dialectics* has evolved significantly over time, ranging from Plato's open and flexible approach to Marx's more rigid framework. Plato viewed dialectics as a method of inquiry through dialogue, where the exchange of ideas could lead to discoveries that none of the participants might have anticipated on their own. This process was not constrained by strict rules but thrived on the fluid interplay of perspectives. In contrast, Marx's dialectics adopted a more structured form, rooted in material conditions and class struggle, where historical change was driven by a predictable pattern of conflict and resolution.

Dialectics, however, need not conform to a single formula, such as Hegel's widely recognized thesis-antithesis-synthesis model. It can take on various forms, reflecting the complexity of the subject matter it seeks to address. For instance, Nicholas Georgescu-Roegen applied dialectics to economic and *biophysical systems*, focusing on the interplay between energy, resources, and human behavior, without adhering to any fixed structure. Similarly, Jürgen Habermas employed dialectics in the form of *communicative action*, emphasizing rational discourse to resolve societal contradictions. This diversity demonstrates that dialectics can be both a flexible tool for discovery and a structured method for analyzing processes of change.

Another important question is what drives the emergence of the new element—the synthesis—in dialectical processes. It is unlikely to arise purely from reason or well-constructed arguments. More often, it is shaped by *power structures*, where each party seeks to assert their influence and ensure their interests are included in the outcome. When participants are allowed to contribute, the synthesis often becomes a compromise, reflecting the competing wills of those involved. Misunderstandings also play a crucial role, as differing interpretations or incomplete communication can inadvertently lead to unexpected resolutions.

In economic policymaking, dialectical reasoning allows us to navigate between competing goals—such as growth and sustainability, or efficiency and equity. But this logic extends beyond institutions and negotiation tables. From an evolutionary standpoint, the dialectic may be embedded in how the human brain itself works. When we try a strategy and it fails, we often don't refine it incrementally—we swing to something quite different, sometimes even its opposite. If that fails too, we recalibrate again. This pattern of oscillation, trial and error, and contrast-seeking appears to be part of our evolved *cognitive architecture*.

Neuroscientific research supports this interpretation. The anterior cingulate cortex (ACC), a region crucial for error monitoring, is activated when individuals experience failure or conflict. It acts as a signal to modify behavior in response to negative outcomes (Shenhav et al., 2013).[24] This system underpins a feedback loop where unsuccessful decisions prompt the search for alternative strategies—an adaptive trait for navigating complex environments.

Moreover, the brain's reinforcement learning pathways, particularly those involving dopaminergic signaling, have been shown to adjust expectations and promote strategy switching following negative feedback (Holroyd & Coles, 2002).[25] This dynamic is observable in the phenomenon known as *post-error slowing*, where individuals instinctively pause after an error to reorient and prevent repeat failure—effectively embodying the evolutionary principle of *adaptive correction* (Danielmeier & Ullsperger, 2011).[26]

These patterns are not limited to conscious reflection. They occur even in fast-paced decision-making under stress, indicating that the dialectical rhythm of failure,

---

[24] Shenhav et al. (2013).

[25] Holroyd and Coles (2002).

[26] Danielmeier and Ullsperger (2011).

inversion, and synthesis is a built-in feature of *adaptive cognition* (Tervo et al., 2014).[27] In social species like ours, survival depends not only on consistent strategy but also on cognitive flexibility—on the ability to shift course, question assumptions, and revise beliefs in real time.

From this perspective, dialectics may not merely be a philosophical tool. They reflect how adaptive minds function: integrating reason, emotion, social feedback, and memory to adjust to changing environments. Evolution did not equip us with perfect *foresight*—it equipped us with feedback systems to adapt when foresight fails, which it often does. Humans tend to exhibit *systematic optimism*, a cognitive bias believed to have evolved to encourage risk-taking and persistence (Sharot, 2011; Haselton et al., 2005).[28] This bias appears particularly strong in males, where evolutionary pressures have historically favored competitive and *risk-prone behaviors*, especially in the context of *status-seeking* and *reproductive strategies* (Wilson & Daly, 1985).[29]

1.8   The Bioeconomic Project: Toward Integration of Biology and Economics

Georgescu-Roegen himself did not fully complete the practical application of dialectics, merely noting that his perspective differed from that of Hegel and, consequently, Marx. He coined his approach "bioeconomics," which he described in eight points in an article published in 1976:

> One of the most important ecological problems for mankind, therefore, is the relationship of the quality of life of one generation with another, more specifically, the distribution of mankind's dowry among all generations. Economics cannot even dream of handling this problem.[30]

Below is a table placing the eight factors Nicholas Georgescu-Roegen suggested for inclusion in a minimal bioeconomic program, the schools of economic thought that would support them, and examples of the social scientists who come closest to agreeing with these ideas, in my view (Table 1.7).

Georgescu-Roegen's eight factors represent a highly logical and scientifically grounded extension of his *Entropy Law*, which itself is an extraordinary theoretical contribution to the social sciences. However, implementing these suggestions reveals significant practical challenges, many of which stem from human behavior, societal structures, and political realities. Here are some counterarguments:

Point 1—the prohibition of all instruments of war—while morally compelling, is largely unrealistic and, some would argue, even dangerous. History and human

---

[27] Tervo et al. (2014).

[28] Sharot (2011), Haselton et al. (2005).

[29] Wilson and Daly (1985).

[30] Georgescu-Roegen (1976, p. 374).

Table 1.7 The eight factors in Nicholas Georgescu-Roegen's bioeconomic program

Factor	Supporting schools of economic thought	Social scientists/economists in agreement
1. Prohibition of all instruments of war	Institutional Economics, Post-Keynesian Economics, Ecological Economics	Thorstein Veblen (critique of militarism), Kenneth Boulding (peace economics)
2. Aid to underdeveloped nations for a good, non-luxurious life	Development Economics, Keynesian Economics, Ecological Economics	Amartya Sen (capabilities approach), Herman Daly (sustainable development)
3. Reduction of global population to a level sustainable by organic agriculture	Ecological Economics, Bioeconomics, Malthusian Theory (revised)	Paul Ehrlich (population control), Herman Daly (steady-state economy)
4. Elimination of energy waste until renewable energy is viable	Ecological Economics, Environmental Economics, Green Economics	E.F. Schumacher (*Small Is Beautiful*), Donella Meadows (*Limits to Growth*)
5. Abandonment of extravagant gadgets and unnecessary consumer goods	Behavioral Economics, Ecological Economics, Degrowth Movement	Tim Jackson (*Prosperity Without Growth*), Juliet Schor (consumerism critique)
6. Elimination of fashion-driven consumption	Institutional Economics, Behavioral Economics, Degrowth Movement	Thorstein Veblen (*Conspicuous Consumption*), Juliet Schor (*The Overspent American*)
7. Design durable, repairable goods to reduce waste	Circular Economy, Ecological Economics, Degrowth Movement	Walter Stahel (circular economy), Donella Meadows (sustainability advocacy)
8. Reduction of the "circumdrome" of efficiency for efficiency's sake	Institutional Economics, Behavioral Economics, Degrowth Movement	Ivan Illich (*Tools for Conviviality*), E.F. Schumacher (*Small Is Beautiful*)

nature have consistently shown that disarmament by a major country risks leaving it vulnerable to invasion. The idea assumes a level of global cooperation and trust that human societies have not yet achieved, and there is little evidence to suggest we are close to such a state.

On foreign aid (Point 2), while progress has been made, its effectiveness is often undermined by corruption, as aid money frequently ends up in the hands of elites who misuse it for luxury consumption rather than poverty alleviation. Moreover, foreign aid has often served as a strategic instrument of soft power for Western nations—more a tool of political influence than a reflection of genuine commitment to supporting underdeveloped countries.

Point 3—the reduction of global population—is a theoretically sound proposal for aligning human activity with environmental limits. However, it remains a taboo topic in many parts of the social sciences, also among degrowth scholars. Addressing this issue—which I have attempted to tackle myself on several occasions, though so far without success in getting published—would require extensive research and targeted policy interventions, both of which remain largely absent.

Point 4—the elimination of energy waste—is one area where we *are* making measurable progress. Advancements in energy efficiency and renewable technologies demonstrate that this goal, while challenging, is achievable with sustained effort and innovation.

The suggestion to abandon extravagant gadgets and unnecessary consumer goods (Point 5) is idealistic but faces resistance from human desires. People—especially in consumer-driven societies like our own—will likely continue to pursue beautiful and luxurious things as long as they are within reach. As I often half-joke with my wife, who is a professor of Sustainable Consumption, the only thing that would truly change our behavior on this point is a mandatory salary cut. As humans, we seem wired to adapt our consumption to match whatever we earn—no matter how much. There's always a bigger house, a superyacht, or even a private island to aspire to. Similarly, eliminating fashion-driven consumption (Point 6), though a sensible idea in principle, is difficult to enforce as fashion remains a powerful cultural and personal expression—especially among women, as consumer behavior trends demonstrate.

Point 7—designing durable, repairable goods—is both strong and realistic. However, current consumer preferences still tend to favor low prices over long-term quality, resulting in an economy of increasingly disposable products. Even when consumers are shown that it's far cheaper, in the long run, to invest in a quality pair of shoes, most still opt for the latest fashion in poor materials—despite the eventual higher cost. Reversing this trend would require not just better products, but a broader cultural and economic shift in how we value longevity, sustainability, and cost over time.

Lastly, Point 8, reducing the "circumdrome" of efficiency for efficiency's sake, offers a clear opportunity for progress by encouraging sustainable practices and mindful consumption instead of relentless technological escalation. Some steps have been taken in this direction, particularly within sustainability movements—such as within sustainable consumption—and in the growing interest in slow living trends.

In summary, while Georgescu-Roegen's suggestions are theoretically sound and address critical global challenges, most are extremely difficult to implement due to entrenched cultural habits, economic incentives, and political realities. In other words, and to put it bluntly, his program was never realistic. This argument by itself is likely why his program has not been carried forward as such and why other research directions, such as *ecological economics* and *degrowth*, have emerged as more pragmatic directions of research. Nonetheless, his insights remain an essential foundation for addressing the limits of growth and the need for systemic change.

A comparison of Nicholas Georgescu-Roegen's Bioeconomics and the broader field of *Ecological Economics* is presented in a table format to highlight their differences (Table 1.8):

In summary, *Bioeconomics* is more narrowly focused on the physical laws (especially entropy) and critiques of growth, calling for a paradigm shift in how we view economic processes. Ecological economics, on the other hand, adopts a broader and more interdisciplinary approach, focusing on sustainability and integrating ecological and social considerations. For instance, while bioeconomics pushes us to consider resource constraints as absolute, ecological economics offers transitional policies more digestible for policymakers.

As we have shown, the primary criticism of Georgescu-Roegen's bioeconomics lies in its perceived lack of practicality and feasibility in addressing real-world economic and environmental challenges. While his ideas were groundbreaking in integrating thermodynamics and economics, the radical nature of his proposals—such as population reduction and abandoning entire industries—was and is still seen as

Table 1.8 A comparison of Bioeconomics to Ecological Economics

Aspect	Bioeconomics (Georgescu-Roegen)	Ecological Economics
Foundational focus	Rooted in the entropy law (thermodynamics) and the finite nature of Earth's resources	Explores the relationship between ecological systems and economic systems, emphasizing sustainability
Primary concern	Emphasizes the irreversibility of resource depletion and the need to reduce throughput	Focuses on achieving sustainable development by balancing ecological, economic, and social needs
Key principles	– Entropy law governs economic processes	– Views the economy as a subsystem of the biosphere
	– Advocates for a degrowth or steady-state economy	– Promotes sustainable resource use
	– Critiques mainstream economics for ignoring physical limits	– Uses interdisciplinary approaches, including systems theory
Interdisciplinary approach	Strongly influenced by physics (thermodynamics) and natural limits. Limited integration with social sciences	Combines economics, ecology, and social sciences, aiming for holistic understanding
Practical applications	Calls for fundamental shifts in consumption patterns and economic systems to align with biophysical limits	Suggests policies like ecological pricing, green technology, and renewable energy adoption for sustainability
Reception	Seen as radical, with limited mainstream acceptance. Influential in early ecological economics but considered niche	Broader acceptance and integration into policymaking and sustainability discourse
Focus on growth	Critically opposes economic growth, advocating for degrowth and reduced material throughput	Critiques unchecked growth but often works within frameworks of sustainable growth or steady-state economy
Temporal scope	Long-term perspective emphasizing the irreversible consequences of current practices	Focuses on short- and medium-term policies for sustainable management of resources
Core works/ founders	– Nicholas Georgescu-Roegen (*The Entropy Law and the Economic Process*, 1971)	– Herman Daly (strongly influenced by Georgescu-Roegen)
		– Robert Costanza (*Ecological Economics*, 1991)

utopian and difficult to implement politically and socially. This, we must assume, led to limited mainstream acceptance, as policymakers and economists have found it challenging to translate his theoretical framework into actionable policies.

Moreover, bioeconomics' focus on entropy and resource limits, while scientifically valid, lacked the interdisciplinary flexibility needed to engage broader social, ecological, and economic dynamics. Critics also argued that its emphasis on degrowth and steady-state economies, though idealistic, did not account sufficiently for the immediate socioeconomic needs of developing countries or the complexities of globalized markets.

As a result, other frameworks emerged to fill the gap. Ecological economics built on several of Georgescu-Roegen's insights but largely set aside the evolutionary theoretical strand, opting instead for a more pragmatic and interdisciplinary orientation. It incorporated insights from ecology, sociology, and systems theory to create actionable policies like ecological pricing, renewable energy adoption, and sustainable development. Similarly, fields like *sustainable consumption* and *circular economy* focused on practical strategies for reducing waste and promoting long-term resource efficiency.

Movements such as the *degrowth group* and *behavioral economics* provided alternative critiques of growth-oriented models while being more accessible to mainstream discourse. These approaches emphasized shifting consumption patterns, addressing inequality, and fostering cultural change, all while avoiding the more radical elements of bioeconomics. Horsman (2013) contributes to this discussion by highlighting how evolutionary economics can offer a normative framework for promoting equality within adaptive economic systems, bridging critical concerns with pragmatic policy thinking.

Ultimately, we may say that, while bioeconomics laid the intellectual groundwork for many of these movements, its limitations in practical applicability meant it was often overshadowed by frameworks that were more adaptable to the complexities of modern economic systems. They also abandoned most serious scientific and theoretical ambitions, evolving instead into more applied managerial functions with limited theoretical depth.

Nonetheless, Georgescu-Roegen's pioneering work remains a critical reference point for discussions on sustainability and the intersection of economics and the environment.

1.9 Wrapping Up: Key Insights and Transition to Evolutionary Perspectives

This chapter questioned the assumptions underlying all major schools of economic thought—but particularly those of the neoclassical tradition, which has long dominated the field. We argued that economic behavior is not universally rational, predictable, or reducible to equilibrium models. While neoclassical economics rests on highly formalized, often unrealistic premises, most alternative schools—including various strands of Keynesianism—suffer from a different weakness: they lack a coherent theoretical foundation altogether. Despite offering valuable insights, they often fail to explain systemic change in a consistent and scientifically grounded way. In contrast, we introduced an evolutionary perspective rooted in variation, adaptation, and selection—an approach that treats economic systems as dynamic, historically contingent, and shaped by cultural and institutional evolution.

Still, one might reasonably ask: is theory even necessary? After all, many subfields within the social sciences—including parts of economics and management—seem to function without a coherent theoretical core. Practical success, not theoretical elegance, often drives real-world relevance. From a pragmatic standpoint, solving concrete problems can be more valuable than abstract consistency. But this raises a deeper question: if a field is primarily oriented toward solving ad hoc problems without theoretical ambition, can it still be considered a science? If economics wants to operate as a consultancy profession—focused on local fixes, industry trends, and short-term strategy—that is perfectly legitimate. What becomes problematic, however, is when consultancy-style work masquerades as *theoretical science*. In many business school departments, for example, "theory" is reduced to the act of citing other people's frameworks—more akin to a literature review than a coherent, testable system of explanation. Worse still, it is often mistaken for a two- or three-dimensional diagram—the ubiquitous "model" that simply visualizes what has already been said in text. But theory is not a collage of citations, nor a decorative schematic. It is a structured attempt to explain, predict, or at least clarify causal relationships and systemic patterns. If the goal is merely to offer practical advice or frameworks for action, that is entirely valid—but then it is more honest to follow the lead of consultancy firms and dispense with theory altogether. The pretense of doing science—without its clarity, rigor, or epistemic ambition—does more damage than openly acknowledging one is not attempting science in the first place.

Against this backdrop, we revisited the often-neglected lineage of thought that links cultural evolution to economic behavior—demonstrating how values, norms, and collective habits coevolve with institutions, influencing everything from labor participation to national competitiveness. Cultural change operates on a slower timescale than individual behavior, but its impact is profound. Societies that internalize adaptive traits like cooperation, discipline, or fairness tend to produce more resilient economies over time. This deeper layer of explanation—too often ignored in economic theory—sets the stage for the work ahead.

While bioeconomics offered a bold vision for integrating biological limits into economics, it ultimately stalled due to the unrealistic scenarios proposed by Georgescu-Roegen. What followed—movements like degrowth and local economics—shifted focus toward more pragmatic and managerial goals. In doing so, they largely abandoned the scientific ambition of building a general theoretical framework. What was gained in practicality was too often lost in conceptual coherence.

To move forward, we need frameworks that connect macro-level evolution with micro-level behavior. Concepts like Biological Behavioral Economics and Physiology Economics help us do that, by grounding economic action in both long-term adaptation and short-term physiological states.

In Chap. 2, we turn to the theoretical foundations of this approach. Drawing directly from evolutionary biology, we explore how key principles like variation, selection, coevolution, and niche formation can help us understand not just how markets behave—but how cultures, institutions, and preferences evolve over time.

References

Akerlof, G. A. (1970). The market for "lemons": Quality uncertainty and the market mechanism. *Quarterly Journal of Economics, 84*(3), 488–500. https://doi.org/10.2307/1879431

Almudi, I., & Fatas-Villafranca, F. (2021). *Coevolution in economic systems*. Cambridge University Press.

Böhm-Bawerk, E. von. (1889). *Positive Theorie des Kapitals*. Verlag der Wagner'schen Universitäts-Buchhandlung.

Bowles, S. (1998). Endogenous preferences: The cultural consequences of markets and other economic institutions. *Journal of Economic Literature, 36*(1), 75–111.

Cantner, U., & Hanusch, H. (2002). 11 evolutionary economics, its basic concepts and methods. *Journal of Evolutionary Economics, 1991*, 96.

Cassel, G. (1918). *Theoretische Sozialökonomie [The theory of social economy]*. C.F. Winter.

Chamberlin, E. H. (1933). *The theory of monopolistic competition*. Harvard University Press.

Coase, R. H. (1937). The nature of the firm. *Economica, 4*(16), 386–405. https://doi.org/10.1111/j.1468-0335.1937.tb00002.x

Danielmeier, C., & Ullsperger, M. (2011). Post-error adjustments. *Frontiers in Psychology, 2*, 233. https://doi.org/10.3389/fpsyg.2011.00233

Frisch, R. (1933a). Propagation problems and impulse problems in dynamic economics. In *Economic essays in honour of Gustav Cassel* (pp. 171–205). George Allen & Unwin.

Frisch, R. (1933b). Macrodynamics. In *Economic essays in honour of Gustav Cassel* (pp. 171–205). George Allen & Unwin.

Georgescu-Roegen, N. (1976). *Energy and economic myths: Institutional and analytical economic essays*. Pergamon Press.

Granovetter, M. (1978). Threshold models of collective behavior. *American Journal of Sociology, 83*(6), 1420–1443. https://doi.org/10.1086/226707

Haavelmo, T. (1944). The probability approach in econometrics. *Econometrica, 12*(Suppl), 3–115. https://doi.org/10.2307/1906935

Hartmann, D. (2018). *Economic complexity and human development: How economic diversification and social networks affect human agency and welfare*. Routledge.

Haselton, M. G., Nettle, D., & Andrews, P. W. (2005). The evolution of cognitive bias. In D. M. Buss (Ed.), *The handbook of evolutionary psychology* (pp. 724–746). Wiley.

Holroyd, C. B., & Coles, M. G. (2002). The neural basis of human error processing: Reinforcement learning, dopamine, and the error-related negativity. *Psychological Review, 109*(4), 679–709. https://doi.org/10.1037/0033-295X.109.4.679

Horsman, G. (2013). *Evolutionary economics and equality: An age of enlightenment*. CreateSpace Independent Publishing Platform.

Kahneman, D., & Tversky, A. (1979). Prospect theory: An analysis of decision under risk. *Econometrica, 47*(2), 263–291. https://doi.org/10.2307/1914185

Keynes, J. M. (1936). *The general theory of employment, interest, and money*. Macmillan.

Kirman, A. (1992). Whom or what does the representative individual represent? *Journal of Economic Perspectives, 6*(2), 117–136. https://doi.org/10.1257/jep.6.2.117

Lancaster, K. J. (1966). A new approach to consumer theory. *Journal of Political Economy, 74*(2), 132–157. https://doi.org/10.1086/259131

Levinthal, D. A. (2021). *Evolutionary processes and organizational adaptation: A Mendelian perspective on strategic management*. Cambridge University Press.

Lo, A. W. (2004). The adaptive markets hypothesis: Market efficiency from an evolutionary perspective. *The Journal of Portfolio Management, 30*(5), 15–29. https://doi.org/10.3905/jpm.2004.442611

Loewenstein, G. (1996). Out of control: Visceral influences on behavior. *Organizational Behavior and Human Decision Processes, 65*(3), 272–292. https://doi.org/10.1006/obhd.1996.0028

Minsky, H. P. (1986). *Stabilizing an unstable economy*. Yale University Press.

Mitchell, W. C. (1927). *Business cycles: The problem and its setting*. National Bureau of Economic Research.

Nelson, R. R., & Winter, S. G. (1982). *An evolutionary theory of economic change*. Harvard University Press.

Obschonka, M., Goethner, M., Silbereisen, R. K., & Cantner, U. (2012). Social identity and the transition to entrepreneurship: The role of group identification. *Journal of Vocational Behavior, 80*(1), 137–147.

Pearson, M., & Schipper, B. C. (2013). Menstrual cycle and competitive bidding. *Games and Economic Behavior, 78*, 1–20.

Potts, J. (2001). *The new evolutionary microeconomics: Complexity, competence and adaptive behaviour*. Edward Elgar Publishing.

Potts, J. (2011). *Creative industries and economic evolution*. Edward Elgar Publishing.

Rae, C., et al. (2003). Oral creatine monohydrate supplementation improves brain performance: A double-blind, placebo-controlled, cross-over trial. *Proceedings of the Royal Society B: Biological Sciences, 270*(1529), 2147–2150. https://doi.org/10.1098/rspb.2003.2492

Ricardo, D. (1817). *On the principles of political economy and taxation.* John Murray.

Romer, P. M. (1990). Endogenous technological change. *Journal of Political Economy, 98*(5), S71–S102. https://doi.org/10.1086/261725

Saad, G. (2007). *The evolutionary bases of consumption.* Lawrence Erlbaum Associates.

Saglam, C. (2025). *Evolutionary game theory and strategic decision-making.* [Manuscript in preparation].

Santa Anna, A. D. (2025). *Evolutionary leadership applied: Transforming organizations with adaptive strategies for 21st century success.* Independently published.

Schecter, S., & Gintis, H. (2016). *Game theory in action: An introduction to classical and evolutionary models.* Princeton University Press.

Schelling, T. C. (1971). Dynamic models of segregation. *Journal of Mathematical Sociology, 1*(2), 143–186. https://doi.org/10.1080/0022250X.1971.9989794

Schrödinger, E. (1951). *Wissenschaft und Humanismus: Physik in unserer Zeit.* Cambridge University Press.

Schumpeter, J. A. (1942). *Capitalism, socialism, and democracy.* Harper & Brothers.

Sen, A. K. (1977). Rational fools: A critique of the behavioral foundations of economic theory. *Philosophy & Public Affairs, 6*(4), 317–344.

Sharot, T. (2011). The optimism bias. *Current Biology, 21*(23), R941–R945. https://doi.org/10.1016/j.cub.2011.10.030

Shenhav, A., Botvinick, M. M., & Cohen, J. D. (2013). The expected value of control: An integrative theory of anterior cingulate cortex function. *Neuron, 79*(2), 217–240. https://doi.org/10.1016/j.neuron.2013.07.007

Shermer, M. (2007). *The mind of the market: Compassionate apes, competitive humans, and other tales from evolutionary economics.* Henry Holt.

Simon, H. A. (1955). A behavioral model of rational choice. *Quarterly Journal of Economics, 69*(1), 99–118. https://doi.org/10.2307/1884852

Smith, A. (1776). An inquiry into the nature and causes of the wealth of nations. In E. Cannan (Ed.). Methuen & Co., Ltd.

Söilen, K. S. (2024). *Intelligence studies in business: A guide to navigating the competitive landscape.* Springer.

Stiglitz, J. E. (1987). The causes and consequences of the dependence of quality on price. *Journal of Economic Literature, 25*(1), 1–48.

Stiglitz, J. E. (2000). The contributions of the economics of information to twentieth-century economics. *Quarterly Journal of Economics, 115*(4), 1441–1478. https://doi.org/10.1162/003355300555015

Tanimoto, J. (2018). *Evolutionary games with sociophysics: Analysis of traffic flow and epidemics.* Springer Japan. https://doi.org/10.1007/978-981-13-2859-2

Tervo, D. G. R., Proskurin, M., Manakov, M., Kabra, M., Vollmer, A., Branson, K., & Karpova, A. Y. (2014). Behavioral variability through stochastic choice and its gating by anterior cingulate cortex. *Cell, 159*(1), 21–32. https://doi.org/10.1016/j.cell.2014.08.037

Tinbergen, J. (1939). *Statistical testing of business-cycle theories.* League of Nations Economic Intelligence Service.

Tokumaru, N. (2016). *Social preference, institution, and distribution: An experimental and philosophical approach.* Springer Japan.

Veblen, T. (1900). Preconceptions of economic science. *The Quarterly Journal of Economics, 14*(2), 240–269.

von Neumann, J., & Morgenstern, O. (1944). *Theory of games and economic behavior.* Princeton University Press.

Walras, L. (1874). *Éléments d'économie politique pure, ou théorie de la richesse sociale.* Corbaz.

Weibull, J. W. (1995). *Evolutionary game theory.* MIT Press.

Williamson, O. E. (1981). The economics of organization: The transaction cost approach. *American Journal of Sociology, 87*(3), 548–577. https://doi.org/10.1086/227496

Wilson, D. S. (2007). *Evolution for everyone: How Darwin's theory can change the way we think about our lives*. Delacorte Press.
Wilson, M., & Daly, M. (1985). Competitiveness, risk-taking, and violence: The young male syndrome. *Ethology and Sociobiology, 6*(1), 59–73. https://doi.org/10.1016/0162-3095(85)90041-X
Witt, U. (2008). What is specific about evolutionary economics? *Journal of Evolutionary Economics, 18*(5), 547–575. https://doi.org/10.1007/s00191-008-0095-7
Witt, U., & Chai, A. (Eds.). (2018). *Understanding economic change*. Cambridge University Press.

Further Reading

Aoyama, H., Aruka, Y., et al. (2020). Complexity. In *Heterogeneity, and the methods of statistical physics in economics: Essays in memory of Masanao Aoki*. Springer Japan.
Auyang, S. Y. (1999). Foundations of complex-system theories: In *Economics, evolutionary biology, and statistical physics*. Cambridge University Press.
Avşar, R. (2019). *The evolutionary origins of markets: How evolution*. Routledge. https://doi.org/10.4324/9780429276759
Bohr, N. (1913). On the constitution of atoms and molecules. *Part I. Philosophical Magazine, 26*(151), 1–25. https://doi.org/10.1080/14786441308634955
Comte, A. (1830–1842). *Cours de philosophie positive* [The course of positive philosophy] (Vols. 1–6). Bachelier.
Condorcet, M. J. A. N. C. (1795). *Esquisse d'un tableau historique des progrès de l'esprit humain* [Sketch for a historical picture of the progress of the human spirit]. Agasse.
Cuvier, G. (1812). *Recherches sur les ossements fossiles de quadrupèdes*. Dufour & D'Ocagne.
Darwin, C. (1859). *On the origin of species by means of natural selection*. John Murray.
Einstein, A. (1905). Zur Elektrodynamik bewegter Körper [On the electrodynamics of moving bodies]. *Annalen der Physik, 17*(10), 891–921. https://doi.org/10.1002/andp.19053221004
Hegel, G. W. F. (1837). *Die Vernunft in der Geschichte* [The reason in history]. Duncker & Humblot.
Hildebrand, B. (1848). *Die Nationalökonomie der Gegenwart und Zukunft* [The National Economy of the present and future]. Verlag von Heinrich Hoff.
Lamarck, J.-B. (1809). *Philosophie zoologique*. Dentu.
List, F. (1841). *Das nationale system der politischen Ökonomie* [The National System of political economy]. G. Reimer.
Marshall, A. (1890). *Principles of economics* (8th ed.). Macmillan.
Marx, K. (1867). *Das Kapital: Kritik der politischen Ökonomie* [Capital: Critique of political economy] (Vol. 1). Verlag von Otto Meisner.
Maynard Smith, J., & Price, G. R. (1973). The logic of animal conflict. *Nature, 246*(5427), 15–18. https://doi.org/10.1038/246015a0
Mayr, E. (1942). *Systematics and the origin of species*. Columbia University Press.
Malthus, T. R. (1798). *An essay on the principle of population*. J. Johnson.
Roscher, W. (1854). *Grundriss zu Vorlesungen über die Staatswirtschaft nach geschichtlicher Methode* (Outline of lectures on political economy according to the historical method). J.G. Cotta.
Schumpeter, J. A. (1954). *History of economic analysis*. Oxford University Press.
Shiozawa, Y., Morioka, M., et al. (2019). *Microfoundations of evolutionary economics*. Springer Japan.
Söilen, K. S. (2025). *The researcher's journey: A guide to methodology and academia in social sciences* (1st ed.). Springer Cham.
Spencer, H. (1876). *The principles of sociology*. Williams and Norgate.
von Schmoller, G. (1900). *Grundriss der allgemeinen Volkswirtschaftslehre* [Outline of General Economics]. Duncker & Humblot.

Evolutionary Theory as a Framework for Change

2

Abstract

This chapter provides a conceptual foundation for understanding change through the lens of evolutionary theory. It challenges the notion of universal behavioral models in economics and instead emphasizes context-dependent adaptation shaped by both biological and cultural evolutions. The discussion draws on key thinkers including Darwin, Veblen, Schumpeter, and Georgescu-Roegen to build a theoretical framework for evolutionary economics. Through a classification of different types of societal change, the chapter highlights how innovations, human-caused transformations, and worldviews interact to shape economic systems. It further explores how key concepts from biology—such as selection, drift, speciation, and inclusive fitness—can be mapped to economic behavior, offering a more dynamic and empirically grounded approach to theory development and policy analysis. This chapter serves as a bridge between foundational ideas and the applied modeling strategies developed in later parts of the book.

Keywords

Evolutionary theory · Evolutionary economics · Economic adaptation · Innovation · Cultural evolution · Weltanschauung · Natural selection · Inclusive fitness · Punctuated equilibrium · Schumpeter · Georgescu-Roegen · Evolutionary psychology · Institutional change · Complexity economics · Historical economics

The question of how societies change—whether gradually or through abrupt transformation—has long preoccupied both economists and social theorists. In this chapter, we develop an evolutionary framework for interpreting such change. Rather than beginning with abstract assumptions about human rationality or universal economic laws, we look to evolution for its capacity to explain adaptation, variety, and systemic transformation across time and cultures.

We draw on a range of intellectual traditions—biological, historical, and institutional—to examine why traditional economic models struggle with real-world complexity. In contrast, evolutionary thinking allows for richer explanations that account for both inherited constraints and emergent possibilities. The typologies and theoretical mappings that follow (including Tables 1.8 and 2.1) serve as tools to help conceptualize the many different kinds of change shaping economic systems today.

Table 2.1 Types of change in social life

Type of change	Description	Key scholars	Relevant disciplines
Very long-term changes (evolutionary)	Changes shaped by evolutionary processes over millennia, influencing human biology and psychology	Charles Darwin (natural selection), Konrad Lorenz (behavioral evolution), Thorstein Veblen (cultural evolution)	Evolutionary biology, anthropology, evolutionary psychology
Innovations	Human-created ideas, technologies, or practices that reshape social life through diffusion and disruption	Joseph Schumpeter (creative destruction), Everett Rogers (diffusion of innovations)	Economics, sociology, innovation studies
Human-caused non-innovative changes	Transformations caused by human activity not rooted in innovation—e.g., resource depletion or pollution	Jared Diamond (ecological collapse), Nicholas Georgescu-Roegen (entropy and economic limits)	Environmental science, political economy
Natural changes	External natural phenomena that shape societies through disruption or long-term influence	–	–
– Climate change	Gradual or abrupt shifts in climate affecting ecosystems, livelihoods, and migration	James Lovelock (Gaia theory), Naomi Oreskes (climate communication and policy)	Climatology, environmental studies
– Geological events	Physical disruptions like earthquakes or volcanic eruptions that alter human settlement patterns	Alfred Wegener (plate tectonics)	Geology, disaster management
– Biological changes	Pandemics and biodiversity shifts that influence health, survival, and behavior	Charles Rosenberg (history of disease), Jared Diamond (germs and conquest)	Epidemiology, ecology
– Cosmic events	Rare extraterrestrial events (e.g., asteroid impacts, solar flares) with potential large-scale effects	Carl Sagan (cosmic systems and risk)	Astronomy, planetary science

2.1   Theories of Change in Evolutionary Economics

A *theory* is a systematic framework for explaining and predicting phenomena, based on evidence, principles, and reasoning. It provides a foundation for understanding relationships between variables and generates testable hypotheses to guide further inquiry. For the social sciences, this systematic framework should ideally describe mechanisms that consistently influence behavior due to fundamental aspects of human nature, remaining stable over time.

For most scientists studying living organisms in general, it is evident that this structure can be rooted in evolutionary theory, offering a dynamic yet universal lens for understanding societal and economic processes. This connection between biological and economic systems invites a broader reflection: if evolution offers such a powerful explanatory framework for life itself, why shouldn't it also serve as a foundation for understanding economic behavior?

The idea that economics should be treated as an evolutionary science is, as we have seen, far from new. Early proponents include Thorstein Veblen (1898) in his article "Why Is Economics Not an Evolutionary Science?,"[1] Alfred Marshall (1920) when he stated that "the Mecca of the economist lies in economic biology,"[2] and Joseph Schumpeter (1959), who argued that "in dealing with capitalism we are dealing with an evolutionary process."[3] We also note that Veblen did not delve deeply into the matter of evolutionary economics, and while Georgescu-Roegen made a significant contribution with his work *The Entropy Law and the Economic Process*, he wanted to do much more. Schumpeter, who knew Georgescu-Roegen well and was rumored to have considered co-authoring a book with him on the subject, only alluded to the idea toward the end of his *History of Economic Analysis*. For Marshall, one of the earliest to recognize its significance, the concept remained even more ambiguous. Marshall's biological metaphors were suggestive but underdeveloped, and the idea did not take root in mainstream theory. This left a gap that later generations attempted to fill, often without a shared language or methodological core.

Although a substantial body of work on evolutionary economics has emerged since the Second World War, much of it remains either theoretically fragmented or lacking in practical applicability. A widely acknowledged problem is the absence of consensus on what evolutionary economics actually is, resulting in a fragmented field marked by competing approaches. This fragmentation is both unfortunate and, at a broader level, unnecessary. One clear example is the limited integration between evolutionary game theory and the wider body of evolutionary economic research—each often developing in parallel with little mutual engagement.[4] Such intellectual siloing diminishes opportunities for theoretical refinement and empirical relevance, ultimately weakening both the field's coherence and its perceived legitimacy.

---

[1] Veblen (1898).

[2] Marshall (1920).

[3] Schumpeter (1959).

[4] Witt (2008).

The limited integration between evolutionary game theory and broader evolutionary economics stems largely from differences in methodological training and disciplinary background—EGT's mathematical rigor and biological roots often make it inaccessible to many social scientists. Bridging this gap will require more interdisciplinary translation, with simplified modeling frameworks, shared case studies, and curricula that foster mutual literacy across quantitative and qualitative traditions.

Another influential perspective is presented by Nelson and Winter,[5] who assert that "evolutionary economics is Schumpeterian" (p. 3) and argue that change is predominantly driven by innovation, which "ought to be built into the core of the basic economic theory" (p. 3). Other contributions within this field have focused on understanding and modeling technological change as a central component of evolutionary economics.[6]

A possible solution is to reframe innovation as one among several evolutionary drivers—alongside ecological, biological, and cultural change—thus situating Schumpeterian dynamics within a broader framework of adaptive processes, as illustrated in Table 2.1.

While innovation plays a crucial role in shaping economic and social development, it is just one of the many forces driving change. Societal evolution results from the interplay of multiple processes—biological, ecological, cultural, technological, and even cosmic—each contributing to adaptation and transformation in distinct ways. Overemphasizing innovation risks overlooking this broader complexity.

To capture the full spectrum of evolutionary dynamics, it is useful to classify the different types of change that shape economic and social systems and examine how they interact over time. The following table offers one such framework.

All of these categories of change—ranging from the evolutionary to the cosmic—offer valuable insights for social scientists. However, some have a more immediate and frequent impact on human behavior and economic systems than others. In particular, innovations and human-caused non-innovative changes stand out, as they shape daily decision-making, social norms, and institutional evolution.

These are the types of change most directly influenced by cultural, political, and regulatory shifts rather than by natural forces or rare global events. While all types of change are relevant, focusing on those that occur regularly and influence everyday economic life allows us to better understand, anticipate, and design for the dynamics that most consistently shape society (Table 2.2).

The table highlights how innovations and human-driven non-innovative changes are especially influential in shaping everyday life—not just through technology or policy, but by reshaping how societies view progress, organize institutions, and adapt to challenges. These frequent changes do more than alter behaviors—they shape expectations, shift norms, and ultimately influence the underlying worldviews of different cultures.

---

[5] Nelson et al. (2018).
[6] Leydesdorff et al. (1994).

Table 2.2 Categories of frequent changes to social life

Category	Impact	Examples	Authors	References	Disciplines
Innovations	Positive	Renewable energy technologies, vaccines, digital communication tools like the internet	Joseph Schumpeter	Schumpeter, J. (1942). *Capitalism, Socialism, and Democracy.* Harper & Row	Economics, Innovation Studies, Public Health
			Everett Rogers	Rogers, E. M. (1962). *Diffusion of Innovations.* Free Press	Sociology, Technology Studies
	Negative	Fossil fuel technologies, nuclear weapons, social media causing misinformation	Langdon Winner	Winner, L. (1986). *The Whale and the Reactor: A Search for Limits in an Age of High Technology*	Philosophy of Technology, Political Economy
			Neil Postman	Postman, N. (1992). *Technopoly: The Surrender of Culture to Technology*	Media Studies, Sociology
Human-caused non-innovative changes	Positive	Reforestation, conservation efforts, cleanup of polluted areas	Elinor Ostrom	Ostrom, E. (1990). *Governing the Commons: The Evolution of Institutions for Collective Action*	Environmental Science, Political Economy
			Rachel Carson	Carson, R. (1962). *Silent Spring*	Ecology, Environmental Policy
	Negative	Deforestation, overfishing, industrial pollution, urban sprawl	Jared Diamond	Diamond, J. (2005). *Collapse: How Societies Choose to Fail or Succeed*	Environmental History, Sociology
			Nicholas Georgescu-Roegen	Georgescu-Roegen, N. (1971). *The Entropy Law and the Economic Process*	Environmental Economics, Bioeconomics

In the next section, we explore how such worldviews—what the German tradition calls *Weltanschauung*—are central to understanding how economic behavior varies across societies and over time.

2.2   Why Universal Theories of Man Fail: Culture, Worldviews, and Change

Georgescu-Roegen sharply critiques what he calls "standard economics"—effectively the neoclassical school—for ignoring insights from the German Historical School. At the same time, he observes that the German economists often failed to grasp the mechanistic models favored by their Anglo-Saxon counterparts. This mutual misunderstanding reveals a deeper intellectual rift: one school prioritized empirical, cultural-historical understanding; the other sought elegant mathematical formalisms.

At the end of *Analytical Economics*, Georgescu-Roegen calls for a synthesis that includes the German concepts of *Geist* (spirit) and *Weltanschauung* (worldview). He argues that economic thought must consider not only measurable variables but also the cultural and philosophical frames through which societies perceive and act. For instance, he points to efforts throughout history to create "a new man" by replacing outdated worldviews—and cites Japan's economic success as an outcome partly rooted in its distinct Weltanschauung.

Geist refers to the collective intellectual and cultural character of a people, while Weltanschauung denotes the broader worldview that shapes how a society interprets and engages with the world. Together, they inform economic behavior, expectations, and institutional forms. These cultural lenses are not merely background variables; they actively shape institutional success, innovation capacity, and long-term economic trajectories.

A telling illustration comes from the post-Cold War period, when the collapse of the Soviet Union led many in the United States to view their own model—rooted in liberal democracy, free markets, and individualism—as the optimal and inevitable path to economic success. Some even declared "the end of history," expecting that the world would converge around this American worldview. Yet this perception soon proved misguided. The rapid rise of China, with a markedly different political system and cultural orientation, demonstrated that alternative Weltanschauungen could also produce sustained economic growth. In doing so, it became clear that worldviews are not interchangeable—and that they play a fundamental role in shaping economic development.

One useful distinction is that between "do" and "be" cultures—terms explored by Hall and Hall (1990), Stewart and Bennett (1991), and Trompenaars and Hampden-Turner (1997). "Do" cultures emphasize work, productivity, and structure, while "be" cultures may prioritize relationships, harmony, or presence in the moment. These orientations profoundly affect institutional behavior, labor force participation, and competitiveness.

This is not a moral judgment; "be" cultures are no less human or valuable. But within the context of global economic systems, some cultural traits align more effectively with modern production, innovation, and governance. Yet *globalist thinkers*—who promote international cooperation, open markets, and transnational governance—often fail to acknowledge that different cultures vary in their compatibility with modern capitalism, preferring instead to assume that all societies adapt equally to its demands.

Even more telling was the disappearance of serious discussions around virtues in Western discourse. While values remained, virtues—understood as internalized behavioral standards like discipline, duty, or respect—were increasingly dismissed. But it is virtues, not values alone, that sustain a culture. They are the evolutionary glue that enables trust, cooperation, and long-term planning. A society that neglects to cultivate its core virtues through upbringing and formal education will inevitably witness the erosion of its institutions. This blindness—particularly prevalent in universities and elite circles—has been a key factor in the decline of Western performance and resilience.

Globalization made this oversight visible. By opening markets indiscriminately, it gave structurally disciplined and industrious cultures—especially in Asia—a competitive edge. This shift did not merely relocate manufacturing; it transferred technological know-how, capital, and long-term strategic vision to regions that maintained a focus on industrial development. Western economies, by contrast, bet their futures on services and abstract intellectual labor, under the illusion that production could be outsourced indefinitely without societal or strategic cost. As argued in Söilen (2012), the glorification of the service economy obscured the material foundations of national strength and competitiveness, leading to a *deindustrialization* that hollowed out not only economic capacity but also long-term resilience.[7] This wasn't just naïve—it was the outcome of economic theories that systematically ignored culture, undervalued strategic foresight, and misunderstood the structural importance of production.

This assumption—that all cultural systems would produce the same economic results—has been one of the significant misjudgements of our time.

To be clear, all cultures deserve respect and appreciation. But they do not yield the same material or institutional outcomes. Cultural frameworks shape how people learn, organize, innovate, and plan. Some promote intergenerational thinking and cooperation; others emphasize hierarchy, fatalism, or individual expression. These differences affect everything from education to policy to national strength.

The Fig. 2.1 offers a visual guide to how different worldviews generate different paths of economic adaptation and performance.

This diagram illustrates the layered nature of reality in *social systems*. The three blue layers represent different levels at which we live and interact:

1. Cultural worldviews (top layer)—the beliefs, values, and ideas that shape how a society understands reality.

---

[7] Søilen (2012b).

2. Policy and institutions (middle layer)—the rules, structures, and systems created to operationalize those worldviews.
3. Lived reality (bottom layer)—the material and social consequences that emerge in daily life, including economic performance.

The dotted downward arrows represent the influence of ideas on institutions and of institutions on everyday life: beliefs shape policies, and policies shape behavior. The dotted upward arrows reflect the feedback loop from outcomes back to ideas—how real-world experiences and results may challenge, reinforce, or reshape the cultural worldview over time.

The green box at the bottom emphasizes the global competitive context: different societies, operating with different worldviews, produce different results. Some ideas—by virtue of how well they align with adaptability, innovation, or cooperation—create more competitive societies and higher standards of living. The figure highlights how these differences are not merely abstract but have real economic and social consequences.

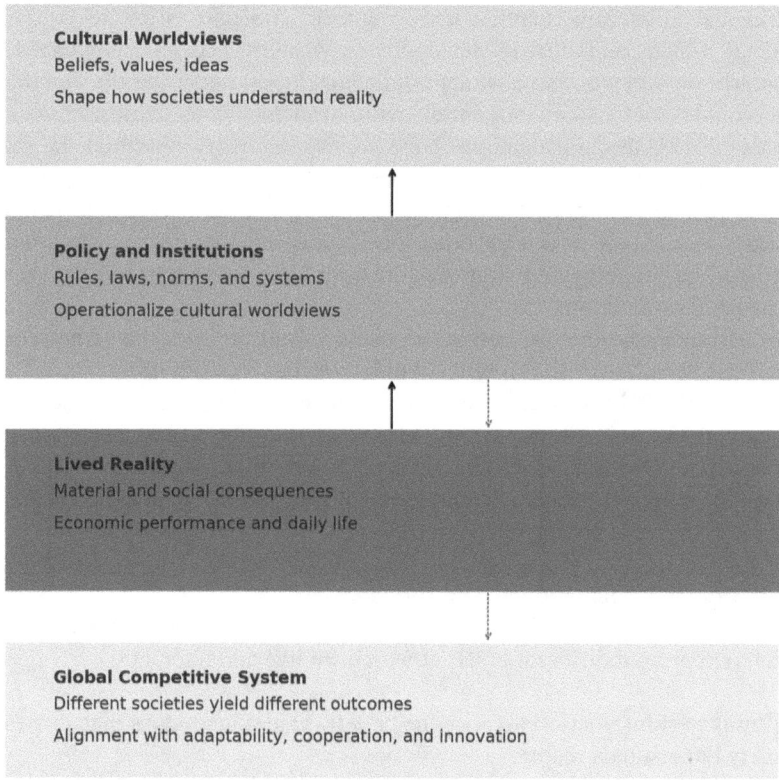

Fig. 2.1 From cultural worldviews to economic outcomes in a competitive global system

What we call *cultural evolution* is, in many ways, the gradual adaptation to the most successful virtues—those that foster cooperation, productivity, and resilience. Societies that align their institutions with such traits tend to outperform others over time. This adaptive dynamic is not random but patterned, and evolutionary economics offers a framework for understanding it systematically. It allows us to track how virtues become embedded in policy and practice. In this way, virtues become not only ethical ideals but also drivers of competitive advantage.

This idea is not new, nor is it particularly radical. In fact, what's striking is not its novelty but how easily it has been forgotten. For centuries, it was taken for granted that virtues played a central role in the health of communities and institutions. That our modern social sciences have, at times, set aside this wisdom in pursuit of *value-neutral analysis* may be understandable—but it also reminds us of the importance of reconnecting with what was once considered common sense.

There is a historical parallel here. The *culturalist view*—where success depends on the internal virtues and norms of a society—echoes, in parts, the principles of *mercantilism*. According to that economic school, nations sought to strengthen domestic production, protect their own markets through customs barriers, and project competitiveness outward through exports. Mercantilism valued cultural cohesion and national strategy, arguing that ideas, discipline, and structure mattered. In contrast, the *universalist logic* underpinning, among other directions, neoclassical economics assumes frictionless exchange, rational agents, and global convergence—omitting how different cultures interpret and act upon economic incentives. In this sense, evolutionary economics reintroduces a longstanding perspective: that economic outcomes are shaped not only by market dynamics but also by the broader social context—including ideas, institutions, and collective identities.

The *universalist assumption* in the study of human behavior is understandably tempting. After all, materials like zinc or hydrogen behave the same whether in the northern or southern hemisphere, and the natural sciences have advanced precisely because they deal with phenomena that are, by and large, universal and predictable. The error arises when we extend this logic to human beings—assuming that, because we all belong to the species *Homo sapiens*, we must also think, act, and respond in much the same way. Anyone who has ever hosted or attended a dinner party—with an apéritif to start, wine flowing through the meal, and perhaps a pousse-café to finish—knows how alcohol can shift behavior in ways no economic model fully predicts. Culture, context, and history all shape how we act, especially under the subtle influence of altered states, revealing just how far from mechanistic rationality real behavior often is. While natural laws may govern chemistry and physics, the social world runs on something far messier: personalities, interpretation, meaning, contradiction—and yes, even alcohol. That's what makes social life so endlessly fascinating, but also why universal theories of man so often miss the mark.

While individuals do change, especially in response to new environments or incentives, such changes often occur within the boundaries of deeply rooted cultural norms. People from the same society are shaped by shared histories, values, and behaviors—many of which have been reinforced over centuries or even millennia of coexistence.

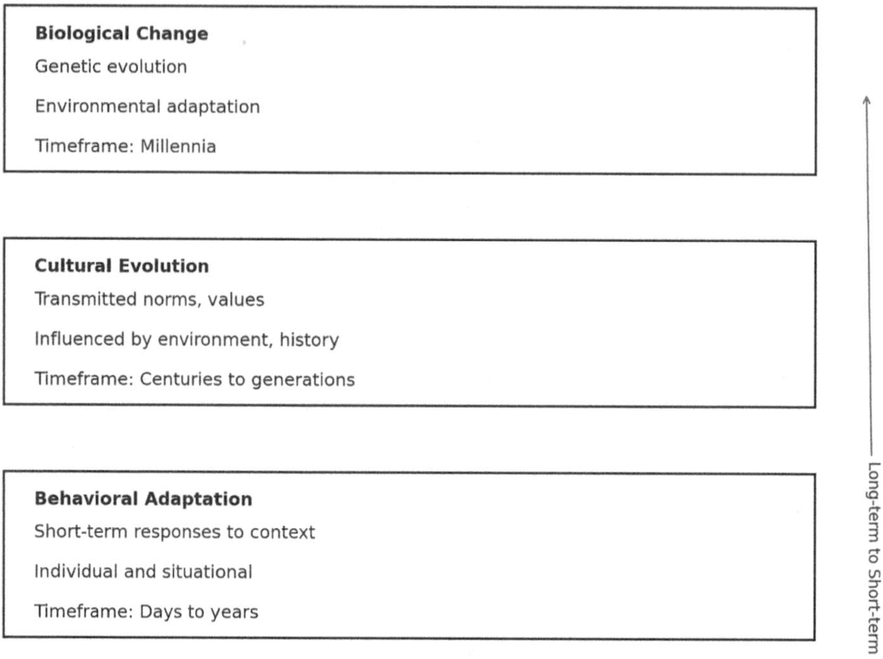

```
┌─────────────────────────────────────────────────────────┐
│  Biological Change                                       │
│                                                          │
│  Genetic evolution                                       │
│                                                          │
│  Environmental adaptation                                │
│                                                          │
│  Timeframe: Millennia                                    │
└─────────────────────────────────────────────────────────┘

┌─────────────────────────────────────────────────────────┐
│  Cultural Evolution                                      │
│                                                          │
│  Transmitted norms, values                               │
│                                                          │
│  Influenced by environment, history                      │
│                                                          │
│  Timeframe: Centuries to generations                     │
└─────────────────────────────────────────────────────────┘

┌─────────────────────────────────────────────────────────┐
│  Behavioral Adaptation                                   │
│  Short-term responses to context                         │
│                                                          │
│  Individual and situational                              │
│                                                          │
│  Timeframe: Days to years                                │
└─────────────────────────────────────────────────────────┘
```

Long-term to Short-term

Fig. 2.2 Levels of human change: long-term cultural evolution vs. short-term behavioral adaptation

These patterns are not only social but also, to some extent, biological, transmitted through both cultural learning and genetic selection. It is this long-term molding that distinguishes cultural change between nations from short-term behavioral shifts within them. Environmental factors—particularly climate—have also played a formative role: for example, populations in colder climates historically had to cooperate more closely to survive harsh winters and food shortages, which likely contributed to the development of more collectivist, future-oriented norms.[8] At the same time, colder regions have also been associated with greater tendencies toward social withdrawal or isolation, a trade-off that may reflect both environmental adaptation and psychological cost (Fig. 2.2).[9]

The failure to grasp the role of culture then—how different cultures perceive the world, organize their societies, and influence their capacity for competition—may be the single greatest reason why the economic project developed after the Second World War never became truly useful beyond the confines of academia. As a result, it remains largely confined to academic ivory towers and is primarily utilized by banking institutions and large international organizations, which appear to value, not least, the rigor of economics as a means of asserting authority.

---

[8] Van de Vliert (2013), Hofstede (2001).
[9] Ijzerman et al. (2018).

The issue of theoretical irrelevance is not unique to economics—it is equally visible in business studies. Much of the literature in international business, for instance, feels disconnected from practice. One major reason is its failure to adequately account for cultural differences.[10] That insight was central to the very first courses I taught at Copenhagen Business School more than 25 years ago.

This realization led me to outline, in my book *Geoeconomics*, why economics is better understood as a branch of evolutionary theory.[11] That book marked an early attempt to develop a more realistic framework—one capable of explaining not just static comparative advantage, but dynamic shifts in global competitiveness.

Evolutionary theory offers six key advantages:

1. *It emphasizes dynamic processes* such as adaptation, variation, and continuous change, which align more closely with real-world economic behavior than the static equilibrium models that dominate neoclassical theory.
2. *It challenges the mechanical analogies inherited from physics*, which have shaped much of mainstream economics. Traditional models rely on assumptions of balance and predictability, but real economies evolve through complexity, nonlinearity, and feedback—features better captured by evolutionary frameworks. As Lipsey (2018) has noted, scale effects and non-constant returns challenge the foundational assumptions of neoclassical thought.
3. *It draws on historical methods*, allowing for the study of cumulative change, institutional evolution, and long-term adaptation—elements often ignored by marginalist approaches.
4. *It is behaviorally realistic*, rejecting perfect rationality and instead incorporating bounded rationality, institutional embeddedness, and actual human decision-making under uncertainty.
5. *It grounds its models in observable mechanisms*, such as niche formation, selection pressures, and adaptive behavior, making them more directly applicable to real-world problems.
6. *It integrates cultural and biological evolution*, providing a richer foundation for understanding economic behavior as socially and biologically embedded, not just utility-driven.

These insights eventually led me to part ways with the standard textbooks used in international business education—particularly in how they approach macro-level factors such as institutions, culture, and long-term systemic change. But, while *Geoeconomics* offered a first framework for these ideas, it was not the right place to fully develop the theoretical underpinnings of evolutionary economics. That required a different book—this one.

The book *Geoeconomics* focused on helping students understand the geopolitical and economic shifts of the twenty-first century. It was a response to the question I

---

[10] Hofstede (1983), Shenkar (2004), Rugman and Verbeke (2004), Mintzberg (1994), and Bartlett and Ghoshal (1989).

[11] Söilen (2012).

kept asking myself: why was the West declining while Asia—and especially China—was rising? I needed a framework that could explain what I was observing, both in global developments and in my own experiences.[12]

This book, then, is an attempt to pick up where *Geoeconomics* left off. It develops the evolutionary perspective more systematically, showing how it offers a more realistic, dynamic, and interdisciplinary foundation for understanding economic change. To sum up the main distinctions between evolutionary and conventional economics:

- *Dynamic vs. static*: Evolutionary theory models change over time, not equilibrium at a moment in time.
- *Realistic assumptions*: It accepts bounded rationality, uncertainty, and adaptive learning.
- *Cultural and biological grounding*: Behavior is shaped by evolutionary history and social transmission, not just incentives.
- *Historical depth*: Institutions and technologies coevolve through path-dependent trajectories.
- *Practical relevance*: It helps explain innovation, crisis response, and institutional adaptation.
- *Interdisciplinary openness*: It integrates insights from biology, anthropology, sociology, and systems theory.

For these reasons, we must approach evolutionary theory not as a decorative appendix to economic thought but as a core foundation. If we are to rethink economics seriously, we must revisit its most basic assumptions. That is the work of this book—starting in earnest with the next section, where we begin to lay the theoretical groundwork for understanding change through the lens of evolutionary theory.

2.3   The Evolution of Evolutionary Theory: From Biology to Social Science

Evolutionary theory is the overarching framework that explains how organisms change over generations through processes like natural selection, genetic drift, mutation, and gene flow. It emphasizes the adaptation of species to their environments, leading to the diversity of life forms observed today.

Charles Darwin (1859)[13] introduced the foundation of evolutionary theory through natural selection, highlighting how traits that increase survival and repro-

---

[12] My experiences—including work in China and a visiting scholarship at Stanford—revealed the limits of prevailing models. I completed the first draft of *Geoeconomics* there in 2009 and chose an open-access publisher funded by embedded ads to make it freely available. I still feel for students paying high prices for textbooks, but that's the incentive structure under major publishers.

[13] Darwin (1859).

duction become more common in a population over time. Modern evolutionary synthesis integrates Darwin's ideas with genetics, providing a unified explanation for biological diversity and speciation (Mayr, 1942).[14]

Darwin was not the first to explore ideas in this direction; similar concepts had already been circulating for a few generations, particularly in France. However, he elevated these ideas to a new level, primarily because he could substantiate his claims with compelling evidence. His systematic approach and meticulous observations set his work apart, solidifying the foundation of evolutionary theory.

Jean-Baptiste Lamarck's theory of *inheritance of acquired characteristics* predates Darwin and differs fundamentally in its mechanism.[15] Lamarck suggested that traits developed during an organism's lifetime, such as a giraffe stretching its neck to reach leaves, could be passed to offspring. Darwin, by contrast, proposed that variation and selection—not acquired traits—drive evolution, relying on heritable genetic changes rather than environmental modifications of individuals. However, Lamarck's ideas—even though he was on the right track—lacked empirical support for inheritance mechanisms, which Darwin's natural selection later addressed.

Georges Cuvier, while opposing Lamarck, also contrasts sharply with Darwin. Cuvier's *catastrophism* dismissed gradual species change, positing instead that extinctions occurred due to sudden, divine catastrophes, followed by new creations.[16] Darwin rejected this episodic view, emphasizing slow, continuous processes shaped by natural selection as explained by geological principles from Charles Lyell.[17] While Cuvier focused on extinction and stasis, Darwin's theory highlighted gradualism and adaptation through variation and survival advantages.

I suppose we could argue that evolutionary economics aligns with both Darwin's definition, focusing on long-term changes at the species level, and Lamarck's perspective, emphasizing gradual changes at the individual level in the short term. Alternatively, one might even invoke Cuvier's ideas to suggest that humanity occasionally undergoes rapid transformations, prompted by events akin to a "divine conviction" or other life-altering occurrences that drive drastic changes in behavior or systems.

One example might be the global shift in behavior and policy following the COVID-19 pandemic. In line with Cuvier's model, the pandemic acted as a sudden shock that catalyzed rapid transformation across societies—accelerating digitalization, reshaping labor markets, and altering consumer behavior almost overnight. At the same time, ongoing changes in dietary habits, such as the rise of plant-based diets, reflect more gradual, Lamarckian-style adaptations at the individual level. Meanwhile, the broader evolution of economic systems—from agrarian societies to industrial and now digital economies—illustrates the kind of long-term species-level adaptation that Darwin's framework helps explain.

---

[14] Mayr (1942).

[15] Lamarck (1809).

[16] Cuvier (1812).

[17] Lyell (1830–1833).

These predecessors illustrate the paradigm shift Darwin achieved by synthesizing evidence and providing a unifying, testable framework for evolution. Many more studies would follow which confirm his theory (Table 2.3):

The table highlights eight foundational theories supporting evolutionary understanding. Darwin's *natural selection* emphasizes survival and reproduction advantages for better-adapted organisms, illustrated by antibiotic resistance in bacteria.

Sewall Wright's *genetic drift* explains random allele frequency changes in populations, as seen in isolated animal groups with unique traits. Motoo Kimura's *molecular evolution* attributes molecular-level evolutionary changes to genetic drift rather than selection, exemplified by neutral mutations in DNA.

Gould and Eldredge's *punctuated equilibrium* introduces the concept of long stasis periods disrupted by rapid evolutionary changes, as demonstrated in trilobite fossils. Darwin's *sexual selection* explores how traits increasing mating success, like a peacock's feathers, evolve even when survival disadvantages exist. Hamilton's *inclusive fitness* accounts for altruistic behaviors benefiting relatives, such as worker bees protecting the hive.

Schluter's *ecological speciation* details how species adapt to environmental pressures, resulting in *niche differentiation*, like Darwin's finches. Lastly, Kimura's *neutral theory* suggests much genetic variation arises from random, neutral changes rather than selective pressures, evident in DNA synonymous mutations. These theories collectively offer a multifaceted framework for understanding evolutionary dynamics.

Still, humanity and society do not yet seem mentally prepared to fully accept the implications of DNA differences on group characteristics, which is one reason why evolutionary economics encounters more political and psychological barriers than scientific ones. This was evident when *James Watson*, co-discoverer of the DNA double helix, faced backlash for his controversial comments on genetics and had to sell his Nobel Prize medal in 2014. Society remains deeply rooted in the belief that differences among humans are primarily shaped by environmental factors, often sidelining the potential role of genetic influences in shaping behavior and abilities. In other words, we embrace—and prefer to live in—a world where we believe we can shape our own future through rational choices (*free will*), even as a growing body of research suggests otherwise.

Sooner or later, however, this contradiction will have to be confronted. As evidence continues to mount from fields such as behavioral economics, neuroscience, and evolutionary theory, the prevailing image of the rational, autonomous decision-maker will become increasingly difficult to sustain. The shift may be gradual or abrupt, but eventually, our models—and perhaps even our institutions—will need to adapt to a more accurate understanding of how decisions are made and understood.

Ironically, the process of this transformation itself offers evidence in favor of evolutionary theory. We do not change our minds, our methods, or the way we organize society simply because better arguments emerge. Change is often met with resistance—especially from those who hold power and benefit from the existing system. Ideas evolve not just through logic, but through selection pressures, conflict, and time.

Table 2.3 Major theories supporting evolutionary theory

Theory	Author(s)	References	Explanation	Example
Natural selection	Charles Darwin	Darwin, C. (1859). *On the Origin of Species*	Organisms better adapted to their environment are more likely to survive and reproduce	Antibiotic-resistant bacteria thriving after exposure to medication
Genetic drift	Sewall Wright	Wright, S. (1931). *Evolution in Mendelian Populations*	Random fluctuations in allele frequencies occur in small populations due to chance events	A small, isolated animal population showing unexpected traits not found in larger groups
Molecular evolution	Motoo Kimura	Kimura, M. (1968). *Evolutionary Rate at the Molecular Level*	Most evolutionary changes at the molecular level occur through drift, not selection	Mutation rates of neutral DNA segments across species
Punctuated equilibrium	Stephen J. Gould and Niles Eldredge	Gould, S. J., & Eldredge, N. (1972). *Punctuated Equilibria*	Evolution occurs in rapid bursts following long periods of stasis	Fossil records of trilobites showing long stability followed by sudden morphological change
Sexual selection	Charles Darwin	Darwin, C. (1871). *The Descent of Man, and Selection in Relation to Sex*	Traits that increase mating success evolve, even if they reduce survival	Male peacocks with elaborate tails attracting mates despite being more vulnerable to predators
Inclusive fitness	W. D. Hamilton	Hamilton, W. D. (1964). *The Genetical Evolution of Social Behaviour*	Altruistic behavior can evolve if it increases the reproductive success of close relatives	Worker bees defending the hive and sacrificing themselves to protect the queen
Ecological speciation	Dolph Schluter	Schluter, D. (2000). *The Ecology of Adaptive Radiation*	New species emerge due to adaptation to different ecological niches	Variation in finch beak shapes on the Galápagos Islands based on food source specialization
Neutral theory	Motoo Kimura	Kimura, M. (1983). *The Neutral Theory of Molecular Evolution*	Most genetic variation is due to neutral mutations that drift randomly rather than adaptive selection	Synonymous DNA mutations that spread despite having no effect on protein function

Having established the biological underpinnings of evolutionary theory, we now turn to explore how these principles apply to economic systems, firm behavior, and policy dynamics.

2.4   Applying Biological Insights to Social Systems

The main argument in this book is that the principles of evolutionary theory not only offer insights into biological systems but also provide a practical framework for understanding economic phenomena. By mapping these theories into economic contexts, we can start to explore how competition, innovation, and market dynamics reflect evolutionary processes.

The following table illustrates how major evolutionary theories apply to economics, offering practical examples and an assessment of their relevance (Table 2.4).

The level of relevance is simply estimated by the author as a conceptual example on a scale from 0 to 10, based on personal judgment and experience. On this scale, 10 indicates the highest level of applicability—where the concept or method is fully relevant and effective in the given context—while 0 denotes complete non-applicability. Although these initial estimates are subjective, the same scale can be systematically applied to a representative sample of respondents within a given group using statistics. This allows for the aggregation of diverse perspectives into a quantifiable measure, enabling comparative analysis and the identification of broader patterns or trends.

In this example, the application of evolutionary theories to economics reveals striking parallels between natural and market systems. *Natural selection* explains the survival of adaptable firms like Amazon, demonstrating how market competition mirrors evolutionary survival dynamics. *Genetic drift* captures the role of chance events, such as unexpected consumer shifts, in shaping market outcomes. Meanwhile, *punctuated equilibrium* reflects how industries experience long stability periods disrupted by rapid innovations, as with digital photography replacing traditional film.

Sexual selection aligns with marketing strategies where firms invest in visibility and desirability, akin to luxury brands enhancing their appeal. These business cases illustrate a combination of evolutionary mechanisms—primarily variation, selection, and niche formation. Innovation-driven sectors like electric vehicles and streaming exemplify how new strategies emerge and are filtered by competitive pressure. These dynamics can be effectively explored through *agent-based modeling* (ABM) to simulate market responses to innovation, or network analysis to trace the diffusion of new technologies across firms and consumers.

Inclusive fitness translates into collaborative behaviors that benefit networks, such as open-source contributions in the tech industry. Similarly, *ecological speciation* highlights how businesses adapt to niche markets, tailoring products to specific demands. The lower applicability of *neutral theory* to economics underscores the reduced significance of random variations compared to competitive pressures. Together, these theories demonstrate the potential for interdisciplinary approaches,

Table 2.4 Applying core evolutionary theories to economics

Theory	Author(s)	Explanation in economics	Example in economics	Practical relevance (1–10)[a]
Natural selection	Charles Darwin	Explains how firms better adapted to market conditions outcompete and displace less adaptive rivals	Amazon thriving by adapting to e-commerce trends, while Sears fails due to rigid business models	9
Genetic drift	Sewall Wright	Describes random changes in market position not driven by performance but by chance, especially in small firms or markets	A small startup gains unexpected market share due to viral attention or unpredictable consumer shifts	6
Molecular evolution	Motoo Kimura	Highlights how cumulative, small-scale innovations evolve over time without strong selection pressure	Continuous minor updates in search engine algorithms that eventually reshape online business behavior	7
Punctuated equilibrium	Stephen J. Gould and Niles Eldredge	Suggests markets remain stable for long periods and then shift dramatically due to crises or breakthrough innovations	The rapid decline of film cameras and rise of digital photography disrupted an entire industry within a few years	8
Sexual selection	Charles Darwin	Explains how firms invest in branding, design, or signaling to attract attention and customers, even at high cost	Louis Vuitton uses prestige and aesthetic appeal to command premium pricing, despite cheaper functional alternatives	7
Inclusive fitness	W. D. Hamilton	Explains strategic altruism where firms support their ecosystem to ensure long-term collective success	Red Hat contributing to open-source software while monetizing support and enterprise solutions	8
Ecological speciation	Dolph Schluter	Describes how firms adapt to specific environments, leading to specialization and market segmentation	Independent cafés tailoring offerings to local culture, differentiating from global chains like Starbucks	9
Neutral theory	Motoo Kimura	Suggests much economic variation results from non-selective, neutral changes—noise rather than strategy	Stock prices fluctuating due to random trades or herd behavior, not fundamental business shifts	5

[a] *Practical relevance (1–10)*: a subjective estimate of how directly and usefully the theory applies to understanding real-world economic dynamics
10 = high relevance (widely applicable in business, policy, and strategic contexts)
1 = low relevance (primarily theoretical or limited in scope)

enriching our understanding of economic systems through evolutionary perspectives.

Real-World Applications of Evolutionary Theory in Economics
- *Industry adaptation*: The rapid collapse of physical video rental services (e.g., Blockbuster) and rise of streaming platforms (e.g., Netflix) is a textbook example of punctuated equilibrium and ecological speciation.
- *Policy design*: Welfare programs can be restructured using insights from evolutionary psychology—for instance, by recognizing how stress and scarcity affect short-term decision-making (relevant for timing benefits or designing choice architecture).
- *Innovation ecosystems*: Natural selection and inclusive fitness concepts help explain how firms in clusters (like Silicon Valley) coevolve through cooperation, competition, and knowledge spillovers.
- *Marketing strategies*: Sexual selection theories can help explain why luxury brands invest in high-cost, high-visibility marketing tactics that signal prestige rather than price efficiency.
- *Organizational behavior*: Concepts from group selection and kin altruism are increasingly used to model employee loyalty, workplace cooperation, and even organizational culture in adaptive firms.
- *Sustainability and resilience, strategic foresight*: Adaptive responses to climate crises—such as shifts to renewable energy or regenerative agriculture—can be interpreted through ecological speciation and evolutionary adaptation lenses.

These examples demonstrate that the principles of evolution are not merely metaphors, but practical and powerful tools for understanding the real-world phenomena we encounter and seek to navigate in everyday life.

However, despite clear parallels between evolutionary theories and economic systems, these applications are not really adopted in the social sciences and for several reasons:

First, traditional economic models prioritize mathematical precision and equilibrium analysis, which often clash with the dynamic and probabilistic nature of evolutionary frameworks.

Second, evolutionary concepts, such as natural selection or genetic drift, require interdisciplinary thinking that challenges the siloed structure of academic disciplines.

Third, the social sciences often focus on short-term, policy-driven outcomes, whereas evolutionary processes emphasize long-term adaptation and change, making them less immediately actionable.

Fourth, integrating evolutionary theories into economics demands complex modeling that can be difficult to formalize mathematically or empirically test.

Lastly, resistance to change within established paradigms discourages the exploration of alternative frameworks, even when they offer richer, more realistic insights into economic and social systems.

The truth is it doesn't have to be this way. By simply beginning to apply these theories, their practical usefulness will naturally drive broader adoption and integration into the social sciences.

Conversely, if one chooses *not* to apply evolutionary theory, it becomes crucial to explain—clearly and rigorously—why human behavior should be exempt from its principles. Simply rejecting it due to discomfort with its biological roots or personal preferences is not a scientifically defensible position. Statements like "biology makes me feel less human" or "I just don't like it" may be emotionally understandable, but they fall far short of the standards required for serious academic inquiry.

To ignore evolutionary theory without a sound justification is a major intellectual oversight. It discards one of the most robust frameworks we have for understanding complex behavior—thereby weakening our ability to make sense of societies, organizations, and markets, or to compete effectively in a global economy.

2.5   A Forward Path: The Evolutionary Roadmap for Economics

The rest of this book will demonstrate, through specific examples and frameworks, how economics can be studied as an evolutionary science by addressing key aspects of this approach. It will begin by establishing the theoretical foundations, aligning core principles of evolutionary theory, such as adaptation, variation, selection, and competition, with economic phenomena. For instance, *economic agents* can be viewed as analogous to organisms, while *market forces* represent environmental pressures.

We will explore the historical context of economic systems, tracing their evolution over time and showing how institutional, cultural, and technological changes have shaped economic behaviors. Using historical data, the book will highlight how economies adapt to shocks like wars, pandemics, or technological breakthroughs, emphasizing the dynamic and adaptive nature of these systems.

The book will also delve into methodological considerations, advocating for a combination of qualitative and quantitative approaches to capture the dynamic processes at work. Techniques such as evolutionary game theory, agent-based modeling, and network analysis will be introduced to simulate adaptive behaviors, complemented by historical and comparative analyses for depth.

Focusing on central themes like innovation, competition, cooperation, and the emergence of new markets and institutions, the book will demonstrate how evolutionary dynamics drive these processes. Through case studies, we will illustrate how industries rise and fall, how technological revolutions reshape economies, and how economic policies adapt over time.

Additionally, the book will also address critiques and limitations of the evolutionary approach, comparing it to mainstream economic theories. This comparative analysis will reveal both the strengths of evolutionary economics in explaining real-world phenomena and its areas for improvement.

The policy implications of evolutionary economics will also be explored, highlighting how it can inform innovation, crisis management, and strategies to address systemic inequalities. Adaptive strategies and long-term planning will be central to this discussion.

Finally, the book will propose future research directions and educational reforms, advocating for the integration of evolutionary principles into economic curricula. By doing so, it seeks to equip future economists with the tools needed to understand complex, adaptive systems and contribute to a more realistic and impactful study of economics.

References

Bartlett, C. A., & Ghoshal, S. (1989). *Managing across borders: The transnational solution.* Harvard Business School Press.

Cuvier, G. (1812). *Recherches sur les ossements fossiles de quadrupèdes* [Researches on the fossil bones of quadrupeds]. Dufour & D'Ocagne.

Darwin, C. (1859). *On the origin of species by means of natural selection, or the preservation of favoured races in the struggle for life.* John Murray.

Darwin, C. (1871). *The descent of man, and selection in relation to sex.* John Murray.

Gould, S. J., & Eldredge, N. (1972). Punctuated equilibria: An alternative to phyletic gradualism. In *Models in Paleobiology* (pp. 82–115).

Hall, E. T., & Hall, M. R. (1990). *Understanding cultural differences: Germans, French and Americans.* Intercultural Press.

Hamilton, W. D. (1964). The genetical evolution of social behaviour I and II. *Journal of Theoretical Biology, 7*(1), 1–52.

Hofstede, G. (1983). The cultural relativity of organizational practices and theories. *Journal of International Business Studies, 14*(2), 75–89. https://doi.org/10.1057/palgrave.jibs.8490867

Hofstede, G. (2001). *Culture's consequences: Comparing values, behaviors, institutions, and organizations across nations* (2nd ed.). Sage.

Ijzerman, H., Lindenberg, S., Dalğar, İ., Weissgerber, S. S. C., Vergara, R. C., Cairo, A. H., Zickfeld, J. H., et al. (2018). The human penguin project: Climate, social integration, and core body temperature. *Collabra: Psychology, 4*(1), 37. https://doi.org/10.1525/collabra.165

Kimura, M. (1968). Evolutionary rate at the molecular level. *Nature, 217*(5129), 624–626.

Kimura, M. (1983). *The neutral theory of molecular evolution.* Cambridge University Press.

Lamarck, J.-B. (1809). *Philosophie zoologique* [Zoological philosophy]. Dentu.

Leydesdorff, L., Van den Besselaar, P., & Heimeriks, G. (1994). *Evolutionary economics and chaos theory: New directions in technology studies.* Pinter.

Lipsey, R. G. (2018). *A reconsideration of the theory of non-linear scale effects: The sources of varying returns to, and economies of, scale.* Cambridge University Press.

Lyell, C. (1830–1833). *Principles of geology* (Vols. 1–3). John Murray.

Marshall, A. (1920). *Principles of economics* (8th ed.). Macmillan.

Mayr, E. (1942). *Systematics and the origin of species from the viewpoint of a zoologist.* Columbia University Press.

Mintzberg, H. (1994). The rise and fall of strategic planning. *Harvard Business Review, 72*(1), 107–114.

Nelson, R. R., Dosi, G., Helfat, C., Pyka, A., Saviotti, P., Lee, K., ... & Malerba, F. (2018). *Modern evolutionary economics: An overview.* Cambridge University Press.

Rugman, A. M., & Verbeke, A. (2004). A perspective on regional and global strategies of multinational enterprises. *Journal of International Business Studies, 35*(1), 3–18. https://doi.org/10.1057/palgrave.jibs.8400073

Schluter, D. (2000). *The ecology of adaptive radiation.* Oxford University Press.

Schumpeter, J. A. (1959). *The theory of economic development: An inquiry into profits, capital, credit, interest, and the business cycle* (Redvers Opie, Trans.). Harvard University Press. (Original work published 1911)

Shenkar, O. (2004). One more time: International business in a global economy. *Journal of International Business Studies, 35*(3), 161–171.

Söilen, K. S. (2012). *Geoeconomics.* Bookboon.

Søilen, K. S. (2012b). The fallacy of the service economy: A materialist perspective. *European Business Review, 24*(3), 206–223.

Stewart, E. C., & Bennett, M. J. (1991). *American cultural patterns: A cross-cultural perspective* (Rev. ed.). Intercultural Press.

Trompenaars, F., & Hampden-Turner, C. (1997). *Riding the waves of culture: Understanding diversity in global business* (2nd ed.). Nicholas Brealey Publishing.

Van de Vliert, E. (2013). *Climate, affluence, and culture.* Cambridge University Press.

Veblen, T. (1898). Why is economics not an evolutionary science? *The Quarterly Journal of Economics, 12*(4), 373–397.

Witt, U. (2008). What is specific about evolutionary economics? *Journal of Evolutionary Economics, 18*(5), 547–575.

Wright, S. (1931). Evolution in Mendelian populations. *Genetics, 16*(2), 97–159.

Further Reading

Audretsch, D. B., & Feldman, M. P. (1996). R&D spillovers and the geography of innovation and production. *American Economic Review, 86*(3), 630–640.

Boschma, R. A., & Frenken, K. (2006). Why is economic geography not an evolutionary science? *Journal of Economic Geography, 6*(3), 273–302.

Cantner, U., & Pyka, A. (1998). Technological evolution: An analysis within the knowledge-based approach. *Structural Change and Economic Dynamics, 9*(1), 85–107.

Dosi, G. (1988). Sources, procedures, and microeconomic effects of innovation. *Journal of Economic Literature, 26*(3), 1120–1171.

Frenken, K. (2006). *Innovation, evolution and complexity theory.* Edward Elgar.

Georgescu-Roegen, N. (1966). *Analytical economics: Issues and problems.* Harvard University Press.

Hodgson, G. M., & Knudsen, T. (2010). *Darwin's conjecture: The search for general principles of social and economic evolution.* University of Chicago Press.

Kluckhohn, F. R., & Strodtbeck, F. L. (1961). *Variations in value orientations.* Row, Peterson and Company

Metcalfe, J. S. (1994). Evolutionary economics and technology policy. *Economic Journal, 104*(425), 931–944.

Nelson, R. R., & Winter, S. G. (1982). *An evolutionary theory of economic change.* Harvard University Press.

Penrose, E. T. (1959). *The theory of the growth of the firm*. Oxford University Press.

Pyka, A., & Fagiolo, G. (2007). *Agent-based modelling: A methodology for neo-Schumpeterian economics*. Edward Elgar.

Schumpeter, J. A. (1934). *The theory of economic development*. Harvard University Press.

Aligning Evolutionary Principles with Market Dynamics

Abstract

This chapter argues that economics is fundamentally evolutionary in nature and should not be treated as a discipline requiring external evolutionary theory to make sense. Instead, evolutionary principles—such as adaptation, variation, selection, niche formation, and coevolution—offer the most scientifically grounded framework for understanding complex market dynamics. By mapping these biological concepts directly onto economic behavior, the chapter challenges the longstanding dominance of physics-based models in economics, which have failed to explain crises like the 2008 financial collapse or the climate transition. Drawing on key thinkers such as Schumpeter, Nelson and Winter, and Kauffman, the chapter explores how firms and markets adapt over time, specialize, and coevolve with policy and technological environments. Core theoretical insights are supported by real-world analogies and summarized in conceptual tables. The chapter concludes by framing markets as dynamic systems subject to the same selection and survival pressures as biological organisms—thus setting the stage for later chapters that illustrate these processes historically and in applied policy contexts.

Keywords

Evolutionary economics · Adaptation · Variation · Natural selection · Niche formation · Coevolution · Fitness landscapes · Complexity · Market dynamics · Institutional change · Nelson and Winter · Schumpeter · Systems theory

Let's continue by asking what the core principles of evolutionary economics are.

But first, by using the term "evolutionary economics," the discipline implies that economics, in its most scientific essence, is *not* inherently evolutionary or rooted in

© The Author(s), under exclusive license to Springer Nature Switzerland AG 2025
K. Solberg Söilen, *Applied Evolutionary Economics*, Management for Professionals, https://doi.org/10.1007/978-3-032-03683-4_3

evolutionary theory but instead requires such a perspective to be *imposed* upon it as an addition. This framing creates a false impression. Evolutionary economics is, as we will argue, not an external or "heterodox" perspective, but rather the approach that provides the most robust scientific foundation for understanding complex economic systems, aligning them more closely with the empirical rigor and dynamic models of the natural sciences, based, like the study of all living organisms, on biology. In other words, economics is and must be evolutionary economics, as there are no better theories for the study of economics, at least not at present, than evolutionary theory.

This reorientation is not merely academic. It helps policymakers, firms, and institutions better anticipate market shifts, design resilient strategies, and respond to crises. For instance, using evolutionary principles, governments can better understand why certain sectors collapse during shocks while others adapt or thrive—allowing for more targeted interventions.

For decades, physics has been treated as a template for economics, but half a century of attempts to adapt its principles for real-world decision-making have shown that this path is mainly ineffective. The assumptions underpinning these efforts have been so detached from reality that they obscure rather than illuminate the complexities they seek to explain. This issue has been particularly evident in the neoclassical project, which, while initially a valid scientific direction, has revealed its limitations to both economists and non-economists alike, and for decades.[1]

For example, the 2008 global financial crisis exposed the fragility of models built on equilibrium assumptions. Likewise, the failure of *climate economics* to fully account for systemic feedbacks—both those that amplify warming and those that might, over much longer timescales, induce cooling—has hindered our ability to anticipate and manage transitions effectively. By ignoring the complex interplay between anthropogenic emissions, ecological tipping points, and natural cycles such as orbital variations, much of the field has underestimated both the urgency and the unpredictability of climate-related change. These failures underscore the need for a theory grounded in complexity and adaptation.

To operationalize evolutionary thinking in economics, we begin with its core principles and show how they map onto real-world market behavior.

3.1 Core Principles of Evolutionary Theory Applied to Economics

Evolutionary economics is not simply one approach among many; it represents a natural and necessary development of the discipline—one that reflects the adaptive, path-dependent, and complex nature of real-world economic systems. By grounding our understanding in the principles of variation, selection, and cumulative change, we gain tools better suited to explain economic behavior as it actually unfolds.

---

[1] Hodgson (2001), Keen (2011), Mirowski (1989), Sen (1977), Lawson (1997), and Daly and Cobb (1989).

Theoretical Foundation: We begin by outlining the core principles of evolutionary theory and show how these align with fundamental economic processes.

In Table 3.1 illustrates how foundational concepts from evolutionary theory map directly onto economic behavior and institutional change. By drawing parallels between biological and economic systems, we can better understand how markets evolve, how firms adapt, and how innovation spreads over time.

Table 3.1 Aligning core principles of evolutionary theory with economic phenomena

Core principle	Evolutionary context	Economic analogy	Key authors	Example
Adaptation	Organisms change to survive in changing environments	Firms adjust strategies to remain competitive in dynamic markets	Nelson and Winter (1982), Dosi (1988)	Firms modifying production processes to meet new environmental regulations (e.g., emissions standards)
Variation	Genetic mutations create diversity within populations	Innovation and diversification generate new products, services, and business models	Schumpeter (1934), Metcalfe (1994)	Development of smartphones transforming global communication
Selection	Traits enhancing survival are favored over time	Market forces favor efficient and desirable firms or products	Witt (1999), Hodgson and Knudsen (2010)	Electric vehicles gaining dominance due to cost-efficiency and consumer/ environmental preferences
Competition	Organisms compete for limited resources	Firms compete for customers, capital, and labor	Penrose (1959), Cantner and Pyka (1998)	Price competition between Amazon and Walmart to capture market share
Niche formation	Species evolve to specialize within ecological niches	Firms focus on specialized markets or customer segments	Boschma and Frenken (2006), Audretsch and Feldman (1996)	Niche cafés offering artisanal coffee to local high-end consumers
Coevolution	Species evolve in response to changes in other species	Firms and institutions evolve in tandem with technology, culture, or regulation	Nelson (1994), Pyka and Fagiolo (2007)	Renewable energy firms evolving alongside government green policies and carbon pricing
Fitness landscapes	Organisms adapt based on changing environmental constraints	Firms seek optimal strategies in fluctuating market environments	Frenken (2006), Kauffman (1993)	Firms restructuring supply chains in response to global shocks like the COVID-19 pandemic

While the principles listed in the table represent the core elements of evolutionary theory, they do not capture the entire framework. Additional principles that are often crucial for understanding economic and social dynamics include *inheritance, replication, mutation, path dependence, emergence, nonlinearity, self-organization, feedback loops, multilevel selection, drift, punctuated equilibrium, historical contingency,* and *resilience*. Each of these contributes to a more nuanced understanding of how systems evolve over time—sometimes gradually, sometimes through sudden shifts—shaped by both internal mechanisms and external pressures.

Summary: Real-World Applications of Evolutionary Principles in Economics
- *Adaptation*: Helps firms and policymakers anticipate and navigate regulation and innovation shifts.
- *Variation*: Encourages product diversification, driving consumer choice and market dynamism.
- *Selection*: Improves understanding of market exit and survival—why some firms fail and others thrive.
- *Niche formation*: Enables specialization and entrepreneurial targeting of underserved markets.
- *Coevolution*: Clarifies how industries shape and are shaped by policy, tech, and culture.
- *Fitness landscapes*: Useful in modeling crises (e.g., COVID-19), guiding strategic flexibility.

Taken together, these applications demonstrate that evolutionary thinking is not only theoretically robust but also practically relevant.

3.2 Markets as Evolving Systems: Variation, Adaptation, and Selection

The conceptual parallels laid out above are more than metaphorical—they reflect real patterns observed in market behavior. Let's now examine these principles in action:

From the examples above, we see that the principles of evolutionary theory provide a compelling framework for understanding economic phenomena. *Adaptation*, a core concept in evolution, parallels how economic agents adjust strategies to thrive under changing market conditions, as highlighted by Nelson and Winter (1982). For instance, firms adopt sustainable technologies in response to stricter environmental policies. Similarly, *variation* in evolution, such as genetic mutations, finds an economic counterpart in innovation, where new products and technologies reshape industries, as discussed by Schumpeter (1934) and Metcalfe (1994).

Natural selection, a hallmark of evolutionary theory, mirrors market competition, where consumer demand drives the survival of certain firms or products, such as the growing preference for electric vehicles over traditional ones. *Competition* itself aligns with the struggle for resources in biology, exemplified economically by price wars among major retailers like Amazon and Walmart, a concept explored by Penrose (1959) and Cantner and Pyka (1998).

Niche formation in evolution, where species specialize to survive, has analogs in economic specialization, such as boutique coffee shops targeting specific consumer preferences, an idea explored by Boschma and Frenken (2006). *Coevolution* further connects the two fields, with industries and institutions evolving in tandem, as renewable energy sectors adapt alongside supportive government policies, a phenomenon analyzed by Nelson (1994) and Pyka and Fagiolo (2007).

Lastly, *fitness landscapes* in biology, which describe how species optimize traits in challenging environments, align with firms navigating economic constraints, such as adjusting supply chains during global disruptions like the COVID-19 pandemic.

Beyond biology, the concept of fitness landscapes has become a powerful metaphor in *strategic management*, especially in the fields of foresight and scenario planning. Much like species must navigate uneven terrains of survival potential, firms must orient themselves within complex, uncertain environments shaped by trade-offs, feedback loops, and path dependencies. Strategic foresight tools—such as scenario analysis, backcasting, and horizon scanning, widely used in intelligence studies—function as navigational instruments in this terrain. They allow organizations to visualize possible futures, test adaptive pathways, and position themselves with resilience amid volatility and ambiguity. The aim is not to identify a single "optimal" strategy, but to explore adjacent possibilities, experiment with new directions, and avoid getting locked into maladaptive trajectories.

This strategic logic reflects a core insight of evolutionary theory: success does not lie in reaching equilibrium but in continuously adapting to dynamic, uncertain environments. Scholars like Frenken (2006) and Kauffman (1993) have shown how the metaphor of fitness landscapes helps explain processes of economic innovation, competition, and coevolution—favoring adaptation over static optimization.

With these conceptual foundations in place, we can now turn to a historical analysis of economic systems themselves, tracing how evolutionary mechanisms—variation, selection, coevolution—have operated at the macro level, shaping economic eras and their responses to systemic crises.

References

Audretsch, D. B., & Feldman, M. P. (1996). R&D spillovers and the geography of innovation and production. *The American Economic Review, 86*(3), 630–640.

Boschma, R., & Frenken, K. (2006). Applications of evolutionary economic geography. *Papers in Evolutionary Economic Geography, 6*(2), 1–34.

Cantner, U., & Pyka, A. (1998). Technological evolution—An analysis within the knowledge-based approach. *Structural Change and Economic Dynamics, 9*(1), 85–107.

Daly, H. E., & Cobb, J. B. (1989). *For the common good: Redirecting the economy toward community, the environment, and a sustainable future.* Beacon Press.

Dosi, G. (1988). Sources, procedures, and microeconomic effects of innovation. *Journal of Economic Literature, 26*(3), 1120–1171.

Frenken, K. (2006). *Innovation, evolution, and complexity theory*. Edward Elgar.

Hodgson, G. M. (2001). *How economics forgot history: The problem of historical specificity in social science*. Routledge.

Hodgson, G. M., & Knudsen, T. (2010). *Darwin's conjecture: The search for general principles of social and economic evolution*. University of Chicago Press.

Kauffman, S. A. (1993). *The origins of order: Self-organization and selection in evolution*. Oxford University Press.

Keen, S. (2011). *Debunking economics: The naked emperor dethroned?* Zed Books.

Lawson, T. (1997). *Economics and reality*. Routledge.

Metcalfe, J. S. (1994). Evolutionary economics and technology policy. *The Economic Journal, 104*(425), 931–944.

Mirowski, P. (1989). *More heat than light: Economics as social physics, physics as nature's economics*. Cambridge University Press.

Nelson, R. R. (1994). Co-evolution of industry structure, technology and supporting institutions, and the making of comparative advantage. *International Journal of the Economics of Business, 1*(2), 171–184.

Nelson, R. R., & Winter, S. G. (1982). *An evolutionary theory of economic change*. Belknap Press of Harvard University Press.

Penrose, E. T. (1959). *The theory of the growth of the firm*. Wiley.

Pyka, A., & Fagiolo, G. (2007). Agent-based modelling: A methodology for neo-Schumpeterian economics. In *Elgar companion to neo-Schumpeterian economics* (pp. 467–487).

Schumpeter, J. A. (1934). *The theory of economic development: An inquiry into profits, capital, credit, interest, and the business cycle*. Harvard University Press.

Sen, A. K. (1977). Rational fools: A critique of the behavioral foundations of economic theory. *Philosophy & Public Affairs, 6*(4), 317–344.

Witt, U. (1999). Bioeconomics as economics from a Darwinian perspective. *Journal of Evolutionary Economics, 9*(4), 443–463.

Further Reading

Cantner, U., & Pyka, A. (2001). Classifying technology policy from an evolutionary perspective. *Research Policy, 30*(5), 759–775. https://doi.org/10.1016/S0048-7333(00)00120-5

Economic Systems in Evolution: Historical Transformations and Adaptive Patterns

Abstract

This chapter explores the evolution of economic systems through an explicitly evolutionary lens, emphasizing how societies adapt to systemic shocks via institutional, cultural, and technological coevolution. From prehistoric communities to today's digital economies, we trace historical patterns of variation, selection, and adaptation that have defined economic transformation across eras. Drawing on concepts such as punctuated equilibrium, niche formation, and coevolution, the chapter argues that dynamic change—not equilibrium—is the norm in economic history. It also revisits intellectual traditions from Roscher to Schumpeter, showing how early economic thinkers approached change as an organic and developmental process, in contrast to the static, physics-inspired models dominant after the Second World War. We highlight how political shocks—not just scientific developments—shaped the trajectory of economic thought, sidelining evolutionary ideas for decades. Ultimately, evolutionary economics emerges not only as a descriptive tool for past transformations but also as a vital strategic framework for navigating future uncertainty.

Keywords

Evolutionary economics · Economic systems · Historical evolution · Institutional change · Cultural evolution · Technological adaptation · External shocks · Coevolution · Niche formation · Punctuated equilibrium · Schumpeter · Roscher · Georgescu-Roegen · Frisch · Complexity theory · Circular economy · Digital economy · AI systems · Fitness landscapes · Scenario planning

© The Author(s), under exclusive license to Springer Nature   63
Switzerland AG 2025
K. Solberg Söilen, *Applied Evolutionary Economics*, Management for
Professionals, https://doi.org/10.1007/978-3-032-03683-4_4

To understand how economies adapt and evolve, we must look at their historical trajectories. Rather than treating economic systems as fixed structures, we approach them as dynamic organisms—shaped over time by the coevolution of institutions, cultures, and technologies. These forces interact not in isolation but in response to external shocks such as environmental collapse, war, pandemics, or disruptive innovations. What follows is a condensed historical overview of how economic systems emerged, transformed, and responded to such pressures, setting the stage for the adaptive models discussed later in the book.

4.1   Institutional and Cultural Evolution in Historical Perspective

Economic systems have historically evolved through a dynamic interplay of institutional frameworks, cultural shifts, and technological innovations, enabling societies to adapt to a wide range of shocks, from environmental crises to economic disruptions. This progression highlights how each system developed unique mechanisms to address challenges and leverage opportunities specific to its era (Table 4.1).

These are just a handful of examples. There are, of course, many more. To explore these transformations further, readers may consult foundational works on the coevolution of institutions, technologies, and cultures.[1] These studies examine how economic systems adapt to shocks over time and how human societies evolve in response to both internal and external pressures.[2] Together, they provide a multidisciplinary lens for understanding the layered processes underlying systemic change.[3] Particularly useful are historical syntheses,[4] institutional analyses,[5] and evolutionary economic frameworks.[6]

4.2   Coevolution of Institutions, Technology, and Culture in Response to Shocks

To better understand how coevolution unfolds in practice, we can turn to historical examples. These cases illustrate how institutions, technologies, and cultural norms have not only responded to external shocks but also often evolved together in a mutually reinforcing process. Each transformation reflects the dynamics of variation, selection, and adaptation that define evolutionary change—and helps reveal the structural patterns underlying economic resilience across time.

---

[1] Arthur (2009).

[2] Diamond (2005).

[3] Hodgson (1993).

[4] Graeber and Wengrow (2021).

[5] North (1990).

[6] Lipsey et al. (2005).

Table 4.1 Evolution of economic systems and their adaptation to shocks

Time period	Economic system	Institutional characteristics	Cultural context	Technological changes	Adaptation to major shocks
Prehistoric	*Hunter-gatherer societies*	Tribal organization, communal resource sharing	Kinship ties, oral traditions, animism	Stone tools, fire, basic weapons	Adapted to climatic shifts (e.g., Ice Age) via tool-making and migratory strategies
~10,000 BCE	Agricultural societies	Property rights, early governance, surplus management	Settled communities, early religion	Plows, irrigation, domesticated crops and animals	Survived droughts and floods by inventing irrigation and food storage methods
~3000 BCE	*Early civilizations*	Centralized administration, codified laws, taxation	Stratified societies, written religious and legal systems	Writing systems, bronze tools, construction techniques	Responded to invasion and scarcity through fortifications and long-distance trade
500 BCE	*Classical antiquity*	Market systems, legal codes, land ownership, slavery	Rise of civic identity, philosophy, citizenship	Aqueducts, roads, metallurgy, logistics	Mobilized resources during wars through taxation and efficient military logistics
800–1400 CE	*Feudalism*	Decentralized rule, manorial systems, serfdom	Dominance of religion in life and law	Windmills, water mills, horse collars	Adjusted to invasions and plagues by redistributing land and labor; early peasant mobility

(continued)

Table 4.1 (continued)

Time period	Economic system	Institutional characteristics	Cultural context	Technological changes	Adaptation to major shocks
1400–1700 CE	Mercantilism	National control of trade, chartered monopolies, bullionism	Rising nationalism, colonial expansion	Printing press, navigation tools, early machines	Survived trade wars via monopolies and tariffs; expanded empire networks to access resources
1700–1800 CE	Early capitalism	Emergence of markets, legal institutions, and banking systems	Enlightenment, secularism, liberal thought	Steam engines, mechanized looms, metallurgy	Recovered from Napoleonic Wars and industrialized rapidly through urban migration and finance
1800–1900 CE	Industrial capitalism	Factory labor, wage systems, urban infrastructure	Labor movements, rise of working-class identity	Railroads, telegraphs, mechanized production	Withstood economic depressions through tariffs and monetary reforms; expanded global trade
1900–1945 CE	Managed capitalism	State intervention, Keynesian economics, welfare programs	Growth of welfare state, rise of ideological regimes	Electricity, mass production, early computing	Recovered from the Great Depression and war mobilization through public investment and rationing
1945–1970 CE	Post-war mixed economies	Bretton Woods institutions, welfare states, public–private balance	Middle-class expansion, consumerism, Cold War values	Telecommunications, space race tech, mass housing	Rebuilt war-torn economies with international aid (e.g., Marshall plan) and state-led growth

1970–2000 CE	Neoliberalism	Deregulation, privatization, global financial integration	Rise of digital culture, individualism, consumer choice	Internet, biotechnology, personal computing	Adapted to oil shocks and inflation via energy diversification and globalized production
2000–present	Globalized digital economy	Platform economies, gig work, algorithmic management	Emphasis on sustainability, diversity, ESG frameworks	AI, blockchain, renewable energy, cloud computing	Adjusted to the 2008 crisis with QE and regulation; pivoted to remote work during COVID-19
Future projected	Circular economy and AI systems	Decentralized production, zero-waste systems, automation in governance	Focus on *ethical consumption* and *post-growth values*	Advanced robotics, quantum tech, regenerative energy solutions	Designed to harmonize technological innovation with ecological integrity and resource efficiency

4.2.1 Historical Examples of Economic Adaptation

Looking at history, we learn that economic systems have evolved significantly over time, shaped by institutional, cultural, and technological advancements.

To make the evolutionary framework more explicit, we highlight three core insights: (1) shocks act as selection mechanisms, eliminating fragile systems or accelerating transitions, (2) institutions coevolve with cultural and technological environments, and (3) economic resilience depends on adaptability, not equilibrium. These principles will serve as touchstones for later chapters focused on strategy, policy, and applied modeling.

Early hunter-gatherer societies relied on communal sharing and primitive tools, adapting to environmental changes like the Ice Age through migratory patterns and basic innovation. The advent of agriculture introduced property rights and settled communities, enabling societies to adapt to droughts and floods through irrigation and food storage systems. In ancient civilizations, centralized administration and trade networks helped mitigate the impacts of invasions and resource scarcity.

The classical period saw the rise of market-based economies and infrastructure advancements, enabling societies to efficiently mobilize resources during wars. Feudalism followed, characterized by decentralized power and agrarian economies, which gradually evolved after events like the Black Death disrupted labor and social structures. This shift, in evolutionary terms, can be seen as niche reorganization—where the collapse of old structures enabled new institutional forms to emerge. Mercantilism in the early modern period emphasized state-controlled trade and colonial expansion, with technological breakthroughs like the printing press enhancing navigation and global commerce.

Industrial capitalism emerged with the rise of factories and urbanization, adapting to shocks like trade depressions through state policies and legal frameworks. This transition was not gradual—it illustrates punctuated equilibrium, where innovations like the steam engine rapidly restructured entire economies. The twentieth century witnessed managed capitalism and mixed economies, where state intervention addressed crises like the Great Depression and World Wars, spurring advancements in manufacturing and logistics. The neoliberal era embraced deregulation and globalization, responding to challenges like the 1970s oil shocks and the 2008 financial crisis with innovation in supply chains and energy strategies.

Today's globalized digital economy integrates technologies like AI, robots, and blockchain, focusing on sustainability and resilience, as exemplified during the COVID-19 pandemic. These transformations represent a new level of coevolution between firms and digital infrastructures—AI, for instance, shapes economic behavior even as it evolves in response to market demands. Innovation networks evolve as adaptive systems. Cantner and Graf (2011) discuss how similar networks develop and respond to environmental changes.[7]

---

[7] Cantner and Graf (2011).

4.2.2 Evolutionary Patterns and Takeaways

Key Takeaways: Evolutionary Patterns Across Economic History
- Variation: New ideas, institutions, and technologies introduce diversity.
- Selection: Crises and shocks act as filters, amplifying successful adaptations.
- Adaptation: Systems restructure to meet environmental and social pressures.
- Niche formation: Specialization arises as different systems evolve to meet distinct needs.
- Coevolution: Institutions, technology, and culture evolve in tandem.
- Punctuated equilibrium: Major shifts often follow long periods of relative stability.

These patterns reveal that economic history is far from linear—it unfolds through cycles of disruption and adjustment, where innovation, crisis, and institutional change drive long-term transformation. A recent example, as I write this, is how the United States has imposed steep customs tariffs in an effort to protect—and hopefully rebuild—its industrial base, signaling a return to a mercantilist or, perhaps more accurately, neo-mercantilist policy orientation. The change this represents is monumental, reshaping global alliances practically overnight—sometimes literally over a phone call. Whether this strategy will succeed remains uncertain; it may prove effective, or it may come too late to reverse decades of offshoring and industrial decline. Rebuilding a manufacturing base once lost is no small task. Understanding these dynamics allows us to see economies not as static systems, but as evolving organisms shaped by their environments.

Before we conclude this chapter, it is useful to recall the intellectual traditions that first framed economics as an evolutionary science. These early ideas, particularly from nineteenth-century German and Austrian thinkers, form a conceptual backbone for understanding how economists have interpreted change, stages of development, and dynamic systems.

4.3 Intellectual Roots of Economic Evolutionism

In the mid-1800s, economics was being developed as an evolutionary science, particularly in Germany by thinkers like Wilhelm Roscher in Leipzig and later by the Austrian Joseph Schumpeter.

Schumpeter addressed evolutionary theory as it applies to the social sciences under the concept of "evolutionism" in his *History of Economic Analysis* (pp. 435–446). While social scientists were, of course, aware of societal changes, many did not adopt an evolutionary approach in the sense of relying on evolution to explain events, as seen, for instance, with J.S. Mill. Schumpeter notes that evolutionism in this context emerged in the eighteenth century and reached its high-water mark in the nineteenth century (p. 436). During the eighteenth century, the prevailing idea was that reason would naturally lead to societal progress, and the task was simply to follow this rational path. Hegel exemplified this philosophical stance by defining mechanisms of change in society as part of a broader model of transformation.[8] His work borrowed from earlier notions by Auguste Comte[9] and Condorcet,[10] whose ideas of evolutionism focused on societal advancement through stages of reason.[11]

Marx's materialistic interpretation of history can be seen as a continuation of Hegel's framework, applying it to economic and class structures.[12] In what Schumpeter describes as the "historian's evolutionism," figures like Friedrich List introduced the idea of societal development through stages such as "hunting, agriculture, agriculture plus manufacture, agriculture and manufacture plus commerce."[13] Similarly, Bruno Hildebrand conceptualized stages of "exchange economy, money economy, and credit economy," though the processes of evolution in these models remained imprecisely defined.[14]

Roscher was not simply one voice among many—he was the dominant authority in his time. His *Grundriss der allgemeinen Volkswirtschaftslehre*[15] served as the leading economics textbook of the nineteenth century, much as Paul Samuelson's *Economics*[16] shaped the discipline from the 1940s through the early twenty-first century. Roscher's influence extended well beyond Germany, defining how economics was taught across generations and continents.

He was also the first to formalize a developmental view of economic systems, outlining a progression through "youth, manhood, and old age." His notion of "laws of economic history" offered a distinctive alternative to Gustav von Schmoller's more structural and geographical staging.[17] While Roscher emphasized temporal development through stages of civilizational maturity, Schmoller, in contrast, described stages like "village economy, town economy, territorial economy, and national economy," offering a framework based on geographical and structural development (Schumpeter, p. 442).[18] Though less remembered today, Roscher's

---

[8] Hegel (1837).

[9] Comte (1830–1842).

[10] Condorcet (1795).

[11] For anyone wanting to delve deeper into the history of the social sciences, see Söilen (2025), which corresponds to another course I am fortunate to teach in Advanced Scientific Methods.

[12] Marx (1867).

[13] List (1841).

[14] Hildebrand (1848).

[15] Roscher (1843).

[16] Samuelson (1948).

[17] Schmoller (1900).

[18] Schumpeter (1954).

legacy profoundly shaped both German and American economic thoughts—impacting figures like Thorstein Veblen, who drew deeply from the German Historical School before developing his own evolutionary framework.

Schumpeter, who belonged to a generation of economists who had spent time reading all these books, as was common in those days, discusses the "intellectualist evolutionism" of Condorcet and Comte, which emphasizes mankind's use of reason to overcome physical challenges, thereby improving living conditions. Comte advanced these ideas by developing a scientific system for realizing them, which later evolved into the discipline we now recognize as sociology. However, this intellectualist evolutionism did not delve into the biological processes of evolution. In contrast, *Darwinian evolutionism*, which emerged later, introduced a biological perspective that fundamentally differed from the intellectualist approach. Darwin's ideas influenced the social sciences indirectly, with figures like Herbert Spencer integrating evolutionary principles into sociology.[19] Both Comte's intellectualist evolutionism and Darwinian evolutionism also left a mark on the emerging field of psychology. Darwin, notably inspired by Malthus's principles of population, acknowledges in the introduction to his *Historical Sketch* that "more individuals of each species are born than can possibly survive."[20] However, Darwin himself refrains from extending these biological ideas explicitly into the social sciences, leaving their application to others.

After the Second World War, the rise of the United States as a global superpower influenced the development of economics along lines resembling physics, emphasizing mathematical formalism.

This shift influenced generations of economists and policymakers to favor calculability over adaptability—often designing economic systems that respond poorly to crises, innovation, or changing societal needs. Notably, when confronted with their inability to predict or comprehend stock market crashes, some economists revisited the Kiel School's business cycle theories, which incorporated elements of evolutionary thinking. The *Kiel School*, active during the interwar period, emphasized dynamic, non-equilibrium processes in economic analysis, aligning with evolutionary perspectives. For instance, Fritz Burchardt, a prominent figure of the Kiel School, contributed significantly to the understanding of cyclical growth processes in modern industrial economies, challenging static models and highlighting the importance of adaptability in economic systems.[21]

The general idea of the Americans was not far-fetched. The Allied forces—and indeed the world—sought to prevent a resurgence of fascism and promote the spread of democracy. Clinging to the historical method, or worse to notions of states as expanding organisms, was seen not only as outdated but also as a potentially dangerous ideology. To steer away from such frameworks, the social sciences were thought to require a more rigorous and progressive role model. Physics, which had demonstrated extraordinary advances in the early twentieth century—epitomized by

---

[19] Spencer (1876).
[20] Malthus (1798).
[21] Burchardt (1942).

the groundbreaking work of Albert Einstein[22] and Niels Bohr[23]—was held up as an ideal model of scientific progress.

This shift also aligned economics more closely with the study of static, idealized systems, moving it away from the dynamic, evolving, and adaptive nature of real-world entities. In doing so, it overlooked the inherent complexity and adaptability that lie at the heart of economic systems—systems fundamentally intertwined with the principles of evolution.

Scholars such as Auyang (1999) and Aoyama et al. (2020) have emphasized that understanding economic systems requires embracing methods from *complex systems theory* and *statistical physics*, which are better suited to capturing the heterogeneity, feedback loops, and emergent patterns that characterize real economies. These approaches reintroduce dynamics into the core of economic thinking, offering tools to model economies as living, evolving systems rather than mechanistic or equilibrium-bound abstractions.

These intellectual traditions, spanning from Roscher and Schmoller to Schumpeter and Frisch, laid an early conceptual foundation for understanding economic systems as dynamic and evolving. Their efforts—though at times eclipsed by more static and formalist schools—offer a valuable interpretive lens for analyzing how economic systems respond to disruption, shift over time, and adapt under pressure.

To fully appreciate the relevance of these ideas, we must place them in historical perspective. Evolutionary theory, formalized by Darwin and Wallace in the mid-nineteenth century, quickly revolutionized the natural sciences. Its application in biology, geology, and ecology was transformative. But its reception in the social sciences—particularly economics—was far more conflicted.

In the early twentieth century, some German thinkers began applying organic analogies to state and society. Oswald Spengler's *The Decline of the West* (1918) famously described civilizations as living organisms, passing through predictable cycles of birth, growth, and decline.[24] Rudolf Kjellén[25] and Karl Haushofer[26] also drew on biological and geographic concepts to describe state power and development. Though their work predated National Socialism and neither were party members, aspects of their thinking—particularly around geopolitics and territorial expansion—were later appropriated and distorted by Nazi ideology.

The consequences were far-reaching. After the Second World War, evolutionary frameworks in the social sciences fell into disrepute by association. Even figures like Herbert Spencer and Thomas Malthus were swept aside, despite their

---

[22] Einstein (1905).

[23] Bohr (1913).

[24] Spengler (1926).

[25] Kjellén is known as a conservative nationalist who laid intellectual foundations for Sweden's modern welfare state—advocating strong state organization and public welfare long before such ideas were mainstream in Europe. His thinking became an important source of inspiration for the Swedish Social Democratic Party. See Kjellén (1916).

[26] Haushofer (1934).

foundational—if controversial—roles in earlier discourse. In Germany especially, decades of scholarship were discredited or simply forgotten. Evolutionary thinking in economics vanished from serious academic debate for nearly half a century. While biology embraced evolution as its foundation, the social sciences retreated into more abstract, mechanistic models—distancing themselves from anything resembling biological or historical realism.

Only recently has evolutionary economics begun to regain legitimacy. Pioneers like Hodgson (1993) have helped revive interest in economic systems as adaptive and historically embedded, shaped by institutions, culture, and long-term path dependencies.[27] What was once marginalized has since reemerged—not as dogma, but as a flexible, interdisciplinary framework for understanding real-world economic change.

What this transition reveals is how fragile ideas—and indeed reason itself—can be in the face of major political upheaval. Intellectual frameworks once seen as promising were sidelined not by debate, but by association. While this is troubling from a normative standpoint, it fits squarely within an evolutionary perspective: the development of the social sciences, like any adaptive system, is shaped not only by scientific logic but also by historical contingencies and selection pressures.

With this broader historical perspective in place, we are now prepared to examine specific episodes in economic history where evolutionary mechanisms can be observed in action—demonstrating how institutions, cultures, and technologies coevolve in response to systemic shocks.

4.4 Concluding Reflections: What History Teaches Us About Evolutionary Economics

What becomes clear from this historical sweep is that economic systems evolve through processes that mirror biological and ecological change: variation, selection, and adaptation. At each stage—whether feudalism, mercantilism, or industrial capitalism—we see societies responding to shocks not by returning to equilibrium, but by transforming their institutional and technological landscapes. These transformations are not random. They follow patterns of coevolution, where changes in one domain (e.g., technology or the result of wars) create selective pressures on others (e.g., institutions or cultural norms).

This chapter has also shown that shocks, such as wars, pandemics, or climate disruptions, rarely cause collapse in isolation. Instead, they act as filters, revealing which systems are resilient and which must give way. Economies that survive and thrive are those capable of reorganizing under pressure—those that evolve.

---

[27] Hodgson (1993).

Box: The Dodo and the Danger of Unchallenged Adaptation

The dodo (*Raphus cucullatus*) evolved in isolation on the island of Mauritius without natural predators. Over generations, it lost its ability to fly and its instinct for self-defense—traits that had become unnecessary in its stable, threat-free environment. But this specialization, once adaptive, became fatal when new pressures arrived. With the arrival of humans and invasive species in the seventeenth century, the dodo was quickly driven to extinction.

This story offers more than a cautionary tale in natural history. It is a powerful metaphor for civilizations that grow accustomed to stability and lose their adaptive edge. For decades, much of the Western world operated in a post-Cold War context with limited strategic competition. But just as the dodo had no answer to new predators, Western economies now face renewed pressure—from rising powers like China, shifting global alliances, and internal structural imbalances.

Evolution does not reward complacency. Survival depends not so much on past success as on the capacity to adapt to new threats. In economic competition—whether between companies or nations—there is no ceasefire. After the Cold War, much of the Western world adopted policies that in retrospect appear overly optimistic. Many countries opened their borders, reduced military spending, and downsized strategic industries—convinced that liberal democracy had triumphed for good. This was accompanied by a wave of triumphalism, best captured in declarations like Fukuyama's *The End of History*, which suggested that Western institutions and values would inevitably become universal.

That assumption, however, underestimated how economic interests unfold in practice. For many emerging powers, what proved attractive was not the Western political model itself, but the material prosperity associated with it—a standard of living they aimed to emulate. Instead, they positioned themselves as fierce competitors, leveraging strategic planning, industrial policy, and long-term investment to challenge the very system they once looked to for benchmarks.

Perhaps most importantly, we learn that history is not linear. Long periods of stability are frequently punctuated by sudden change. The evolutionary concept of *punctuated equilibrium* helps explain why economic development often proceeds through abrupt leaps rather than smooth trajectories. We also observe that successful systems are rarely static. They are adaptive organisms shaped by cultural values, institutional legacies, and technological opportunities.

This historical understanding challenges the static, mechanistic models that still dominate much of mainstream economics. It underscores that economies are not equilibrium machines but living, evolving systems shaped by history, institutions, and human behavior. More than just a technical limitation, the persistence of *static worldviews* in the social sciences may be dangerous. By training generations to think in terms of fixed models and optimal states, we risk encouraging rigidity in both policy and mindset—at precisely the moment when adaptability is most needed. A static science teaches *static thinking*, and static thinking is ill-equipped for a world defined by complexity, feedback, and constant change. Evolutionary theory, in contrast, offers not only a robust framework for understanding the past but also a more honest and useful lens for navigating the future. It prepares us to think in motion—something our institutions, strategies, and education systems can no longer afford to ignore. Besides, it builds on a really strong theory.

The lesson of the dodo is stark: adaptation is not optional. In a changing environment, past success offers no immunity. The same principle applies to economies—those that grow complacent risk obsolescence. Evolutionary thinking, then, is more than a theory; it's a *strategic mindset*, one that values anticipation over inertia. It urges responsiveness, flexibility, and the foresight to adjust before disruption becomes collapse. In this way, evolutionary economics does more than explain history—it helps us prepare for what's next. Static models, by contrast, lull us into a false sense of stability, blinding us to the very changes we need to confront.

The next chapter picks up this thread by exploring how evolutionary thinking can be translated into concrete methods of modeling change—particularly through tools that simulate dynamic systems, scenario building, and agent-based design. Having explored where we have been, we now turn to how we might understand—and shape—where we are going.

References

Aoyama, H., Aruka, Y., & Yoshikawa, H. (2020). *Complexity, heterogeneity, and the methods of statistical physics in economics*. Springer. https://doi.org/10.1007/978-981-15-3632-3

Arthur, W. B. (2009). *The nature of technology: What it is and how it evolves*. Free Press.

Auyang, S. Y. (1999). Foundations of complex-system theories: In *Economics, evolutionary biology, and statistical physics*. Cambridge University Press.

Bohr, N. (1913). On the constitution of atoms and molecules. *Philosophical Magazine, 26*(151), 1–25. https://doi.org/10.1080/14786441308634955

Burchardt, F. (1942). *Economic cycles in modern industrial economies*. Kiel Institute for the World Economy.

Cantner, U., & Graf, H. (2011). Innovation networks: Formation, performance, and dynamics. In *Handbook on the economic complexity of technological change* (pp. 366–394).

Comte, A. (1830–1842). *Cours de philosophie positive* [The course of positive philosophy] (Vols. 1–6). Bachelier.

Condorcet, M. J. A. N. C. (1795). *Esquisse d'un tableau historique des progrès de l'esprit humain* [Sketch for a historical picture of the progress of the human Spirit]. Agasse.

Diamond, J. (2005). *Collapse: How societies choose to fail or succeed*. Viking.

Einstein, A. (1905). Zur Elektrodynamik bewegter Körper. *Annalen der Physik, 17*(10), 891–921. https://doi.org/10.1002/andp.19053221004

Graeber, D., & Wengrow, D. (2021). *The dawn of everything: A new history of humanity*. Farrar.

Haushofer, K. (1934). *Geopolitik des Pazifischen Ozeans* [Geopolitics of the Pacific Ocean]. Kurt Vowinckel Verlag.

Hegel, G. W. F. (1837). *The philosophy of history* (J. Sibree, Trans.). Dover (1956). (Original work published 1837)

Hildebrand, B. (1848). *Die Nationalökonomie der Gegenwart und Zukunft* [The National Economy of the present and future]. Frankfurt am Main: Heinrich Hoff.

Hodgson, G. M. (1993). *Economics and evolution: Bringing life back into economics*. University of Michigan Press.

Kjellén, R. (1916). *Staten som livsform* [The state as a form of life]. Hugo Gebers Förlag.

Lipsey, R. G., Carlaw, K. I., & Bekar, C. T. (2005). *Economic transformations: General purpose technologies and long-term economic growth*. Oxford University Press.

List, F. (1841). *Das nationale system der politischen Ökonomie* [The National System of political economy]. J. G. Cotta'scher Verlag.

Malthus, T. R. (1798). *An essay on the principle of population*. J. Johnson.

Marx, K. (1867). *Capital: A critique of political economy*. Volume I. Penguin (1990). (Original work published 1867)

North, D. C. (1990). *Institutions, institutional change and economic performance*. Cambridge University Press.

Roscher, W. (1843). *Grundriss zu Vorlesungen über die Staatswirtschaft nach geschichtlicher Methode* [Outline for lectures on political economy according to the historical method]. J.G. Cotta.

Samuelson, P. A. (1948). *Economics: An introductory analysis* (1st ed.). McGraw-Hill.

Schmoller, G. (1900). *Grundriss der Allgemeinen Volkswirtschaftslehre*. Duncker & Humblot.

Schumpeter, J. A. (1954). History of economic analysis. Oxford University Press.

Söilen, K. S. (2025). *The researcher's journey: A guide to methodology and academia in social sciences*. Springer.

Spencer, H. (1876). *The principles of sociology*. Williams and Norgate.

Spengler, O. (1926). *The decline of the west* (C. F. Atkinson, Trans.). Alfred A. Knopf. (Original work published 1918–1922).

Further Reading

Frisch, R. (1933). Propagation problems and impulse problems in dynamic economics. In *Economic Essays in Honour of Gustav Cassel* (pp. 171–205). George Allen & Unwin.

Veblen, T. (1899). *The theory of the leisure class: An economic study in the evolution of institutions*. Macmillan.

Integrating Methodologies: Tools for Studying Economic Evolution

5

Abstract

This chapter introduces the methodological foundation for studying economic systems as dynamic, evolving entities. It critiques the limitations of static, equilibrium-based approaches and presents a flexible, interdisciplinary toolkit suited for the complexity of real-world economies. The chapter showcases how evolutionary economics benefits from methodological pluralism—combining qualitative depth, quantitative precision, simulation modeling, and historical insight. With the addition of a new section on prediction, it further explores how scenario-based modeling, probabilistic reasoning, and artificial intelligence can be integrated into evolutionary thinking. Rather than forecasting fixed outcomes, this approach emphasizes adaptive foresight—mapping possibilities, testing resilience, and modeling nonlinear system behavior. Throughout, readers are shown how methodological choices must align with the nature of the phenomena being studied, echoing the evolutionary principle that adaptation, not perfection, ensures survival. The chapter prepares the ground for concrete applications in innovation, policy, and institutional design explored in later chapters.

Keywords

Evolutionary economics · Methodology · Prediction · Adaptive foresight · Agent-based modeling · Scenario planning · Evolutionary game theory · Network analysis · Historical institutionalism · Complexity economics · Artificial intelligence · Brier score · Critical thinking · Interdisciplinary research · Methodological pluralism · Simulation · Dynamic systems

Having laid the conceptual foundation, we now turn to methodology: how can we effectively study economies as evolving systems? Traditional economic models—grounded in static assumptions and equilibrium thinking—often fail to capture the feedback loops, adaptation, and historical path dependencies that characterize real-world dynamics. Evolutionary economics requires a methodological framework that embraces this complexity. It must draw from multiple disciplines and combine qualitative depth with quantitative rigor. This chapter introduces such a framework—not as a fixed formula, but as a flexible, problem-driven approach grounded in methodological diversity.

5.1   Bridging History and Simulation: Mixed Methods in Evolutionary Economics

Qualitative methods, such as historical and comparative analysis, provide depth and context, allowing us to trace patterns of change over time and across societies.

Case in a Box: The "Tears of Malmö"—A Historical Method Case of Industrial Adaptation

The 2002 transfer of Malmö's Kockums Crane to Hyundai Heavy Industries in Ulsan, South Korea, offers a striking example of how historical method in evolutionary economics helps us make sense of economic transformation—not only through facts but also through competing narratives.

To South Koreans, the crane—dismantled, shipped, and reassembled halfway around the world—became known as the "Tears of Malmö." It symbolized Sweden's industrial decline and Korea's rise as a global shipbuilding power. The transfer marked not just a physical move, but a shift in economic and geopolitical positioning.

In Malmö, the same event was interpreted very differently. Local leaders framed it as a necessary step in transitioning from heavy industry to a *knowledge economy*. The former shipyard site became home to Malmö University—a physical and symbolic sign of reinvention, of moving from "low-tech" to "high-tech," from manual labor to sustainability and innovation.

These two views—decline versus progress—coexisted at the time. And like many historical moments, it was difficult for observers to know which framing was closer to the long-term truth.

But with time, consequences clarify narratives. A February 2025 Economist article highlights how South Korea's shipbuilding industry, anchored by Hyundai in Ulsan, has become a central force in global naval production. The same crane now symbolizes not just technical capability but geopolitical leverage. Meanwhile, Sweden's service- and university-driven economy struggles with productivity stagnation in its former industrial hubs.

The historical method brings into focus not just the chain of events, but how different actors frame and respond to them—and how those frames are later judged in light of evolving realities. In evolutionary economics, this matters. Institutional change, adaptation, and long-term success or failure are shaped by stories we tell ourselves, but ultimately revealed through time-bound results.

But it also raises a methodological question: what kind of reasoning guided Malmö's policymakers in choosing this transition? Clearly, there was hope—hope that the shift would go well. But more than that, their decision reflected dominant economic theories at the time: the belief that *production economies* could be replaced by *service economies*; that investment in higher education—regardless of subject—would naturally benefit the economy more than vocational training in fields like welding; and that the more people who go to university, the better for society.

All of these assumptions were not merely practical—they were methodological choices, rooted in theoretical models. And all must now be critically examined. The Malmö case shows how methodological commitments—whether explicit or implicit—can shape economic pathways, often with consequences that only become clear over decades.

This kind of historical case analysis highlights how path dependence, cultural framing, and institutional learning shape long-term economic trajectories. Yet to complement such deep contextual understanding, evolutionary economics also relies on formal tools that allow us to simulate and test adaptive processes across systems.

On the other hand, quantitative tools like evolutionary game theory, agent-based modeling, and network analysis enable the simulation of adaptive behaviors and interactions within systems, offering insights into how change emerges and evolves over time. These methods have been applied in practical scenarios such as modeling market entry and exit in competitive industries, or simulating consumer adaptation to green technologies.

By combining these approaches, we can develop a more comprehensive and nuanced understanding of social dynamics, one that reflects both the richness of human experience and the precision of formal models. This integration of methods is crucial for bridging gaps between theory and practice, fostering a deeper understanding of the mechanisms driving societal and economic evolution (Table 5.1).

These methodological families provide tools to model adaptation, identify patterns, trace institutional shifts, and simulate system behavior—each contributing uniquely to evolutionary inquiry.

This list is far from exhaustive—these are only selected examples—but it provides a clear sense of the diverse directions that research in evolutionary economics can pursue. Much of my motivation in writing *The Researcher's Journey: A Guide to Methodology and Academia in Social Sciences* was to show not only why and

Table 5.1 Methodological approaches for evolutionary economics

Methodological approach	Key features	Tools/methods	Purpose	Examples in economics	Key authors/references
Qualitative methods	In-depth understanding of historical, social, and institutional contexts	Historical analysis, comparative analysis	To explore long-term adaptation, institutional change, and cultural evolution	Studying the progression of industrial revolutions and their social impacts	North (1990), Mokyr (1990)
Quantitative methods	Uses statistical tools to identify patterns and forecast economic outcomes	Regression analysis, econometrics, time-series analysis	To test hypotheses and model economic dynamics using numerical data	Analyzing GDP growth trends across countries and decades	Granger (1969), Wooldridge (2010)
Evolutionary game theory	Models adaptive strategies in competitive or cooperative contexts	Replicator dynamics, Nash equilibria	To simulate strategic interactions and predict equilibrium behavior	Modeling firm behavior in oligopolistic markets	Weibull (1995), Nowak and Sigmund (2004)
Agent-based modeling	Simulates individual agent behavior and interactions to observe system-level patterns	NetLogo, AnyLogic, python	To study how micro-level actions lead to macro-level dynamics	Simulating how firms compete for market share under changing rules	Tesfatsion and Judd (2006), Epstein (1996)
Network analysis	Examines structural relationships between agents or institutions	Social network analysis, graph theory, centrality measures	To identify key actors, measure connectivity, and map innovation diffusion	Mapping global supply chains to detect systemic vulnerabilities	Granovetter (1973), Watts (1999)
Comparative analysis	Contrasts systems or institutions across time or place	Cross-national studies, comparative historical analysis	To uncover best practices and pathways of economic adaptation	Comparing pandemic responses in different healthcare systems	Ragin (1987), Collier and Mahoney (1996)

Method	Description	Techniques	Purpose	Application	References
Mixed methods	Integrates qualitative and quantitative research for broader insight	Sequential explanatory design, triangulation	To validate findings and understand complex adaptive systems holistically	Combining ethnography with statistical sales data to track market adaptation	Creswell and Clark (2017), Tashakkori and Teddlie (1998)
Dynamic systems modeling	Models economic systems as adaptive, feedback-driven processes over time	System dynamics, differential equations, chaos theory	To analyze resilience and nonlinear adaptation to shocks	Modeling how industries restructure after global economic crises	Forrester (1961), Sterman (2000)
Scenario analysis	Explores future pathways under uncertainty and evaluates potential outcomes	Scenario planning, Monte Carlo simulations	To assess the robustness of strategies across alternative futures	Projecting trade responses to climate policy interventions	Schoemaker (1995), Schwartz (1991)
Historical institutional analysis	Studies the evolution of institutions and their long-term economic effects	Archival research, institutional mapping	To understand how past institutional developments shape current economic performance	Tracing the impact of land tenure systems on national productivity	Acemoglu and Robinson (2012), North (1990)
Big data analytics	Leverages massive, real-time data to detect emerging economic patterns	Machine learning, sentiment analysis, NLP	To forecast behavior and identify shifts in economic systems from unstructured data	Analyzing real-time consumer sentiment via social media and its impact on stock trends	Varian (2014), Brynjolfsson and McAfee (2014)

how the social sciences should be interdisciplinary but also to argue for a pragmatic approach to research methodology.[1] That means letting the problem dictate the method—whether quantitative, qualitative, or mixed—rather than defaulting to the researcher's academic background or personal preference.

One of the most common critiques leveled against evolutionary economics is its perceived inability to offer predictive models on par with those of the neoclassical tradition. Yet this critique reveals more about our assumptions regarding prediction than about the limits of evolutionary thinking itself.

While the preceding section emphasized the value of combining historical insight with simulation models, we now turn to one of the most debated areas of methodology in evolutionary economics: *prediction*. Can we anticipate future economic transformations without falling back on equilibrium-based simplifications? How do we use models not just to explain the past, but to map possible futures? Section 5.2 explores how evolutionary theory, enriched by artificial intelligence and probability-based reasoning, offers a more realistic and adaptive approach to prediction.

5.2   Prediction in Evolutionary Economics

One of the enduring claims of neoclassical economics is its purported ability to make predictions—a built-in temptation and a subtle, often unspoken promise that runs through much of the social sciences. These forecasts typically rely on equilibrium models built under highly simplified ceteris paribus assumptions—holding all else constant. While such models can yield elegant mathematical solutions, they often collapse under the weight of real-world complexity. The number of assumptions required to sustain their internal logic tends to undermine their external relevance. When the models fail—as they often do during crises, shocks, or systemic changes—they offer little practical guidance.

By contrast, evolutionary economics does not promise precision in the narrow, deterministic sense. It sees economies as adaptive systems—historically contingent, path-dependent, and shaped by feedback, coevolution, and trial-and-error learning. From this view, the future is not a singular path waiting to be discovered but a branching, *probabilistic* terrain influenced by past adaptations, emergent structures, and competing alternatives.

That does not mean evolutionary economics shies away from foresight. Quite the opposite. It offers a more realistic toolkit for dealing with uncertainty: agent-based modeling, network simulation, and scenario planning help us explore how systems evolve under varying pressures. While we may not be able to forecast exact outcomes, we can simulate *plausible trajectories* and identify the conditions under which they become more or less likely.

The rise of artificial intelligence has expanded these possibilities dramatically. We are no longer limited to simplified models with a handful of variables. AI enables us to model large-scale systems with dozens—or hundreds—of interacting dimensions.

[1] Söilen (2025).

This shift allows for deeper and more adaptive scenario-building, moving beyond intuition or expert opinion alone. We still won't achieve 100% predictive accuracy—no social science can—but we will outperform unaided human judgment, particularly in mapping structural patterns, early signals, and nonlinear feedbacks.

In *Intelligence Studies in Business*, I introduced a collective forecasting method rooted in critical thinking and evolutionary reasoning.[2] The approach begins with individual probability assessments of *future events* (FEs), which are then revised downward based on counterarguments. These rounds are followed by group calibration—without sharing actual scores—to prevent anchoring or groupthink. The final probabilities are averaged and weighted, and results are evaluated using the *Brier score*. The method mimics evolutionary logic: beliefs are selected, challenged, and adapted over time based on evidence and feedback (Fig. 5.1).

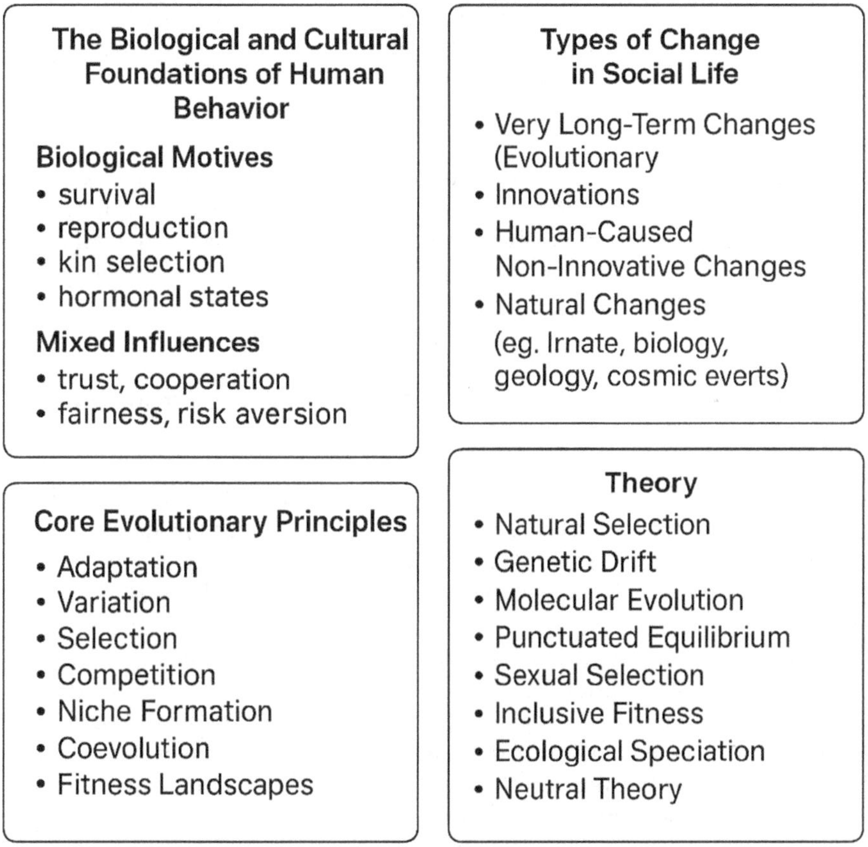

The Biological and Cultural Foundations of Human Behavior

Biological Motives
- survival
- reproduction
- kin selection
- hormonal states

Mixed Influences
- trust, cooperation
- fairness, risk aversion

Types of Change in Social Life
- Very Long-Term Changes (Evolutionary
- Innovations
- Human-Caused Non-Innovative Changes
- Natural Changes (eg. Irnate, biology, geology, cosmic everts)

Core Evolutionary Principles
- Adaptation
- Variation
- Selection
- Competition
- Niche Formation
- Coevolution
- Fitness Landscapes

Theory
- Natural Selection
- Genetic Drift
- Molecular Evolution
- Punctuated Equilibrium
- Sexual Selection
- Inclusive Fitness
- Ecological Speciation
- Neutral Theory

Fig. 5.1 Categorizing dimensions of evolutionary economic prediction

---

[2] Söilen (2024).

The figure summarizes the multiple dimensions that evolutionary economics uses to ground its predictive reasoning—from biological and cultural motives, to types of social change, to core principles like adaptation and niche formation, and to theoretical anchors drawn from modern evolutionary science. Rather than building forecasts on layers of speculative assumptions, we model outcomes based on these well-defined, empirically grounded processes.

Importantly, evolutionary economics also draws heavily on historical reasoning and dialectical processes, as discussed in Chap. 4. We do not treat the future as a linear extension of the present but as something shaped by competing logics, institutional memory, and systemic constraints. History does not repeat itself, but it does narrow the range of viable futures. Knowing how systems have responded to shocks in the past improves our ability to anticipate how they might adapt—or fail to adapt—in the face of future disruptions.

What evolutionary economics offers, then, is not false certainty, but *adaptive foresight*. It trades prediction for preparedness, equilibrium for resilience, and idealization for realism. By integrating short-term forecasting tools with long-term evolutionary models, the field helps us bridge the gap between theory and practice, between strategy and structure, and between today's questions and tomorrow's realities.

By rethinking prediction as a matter of adaptive foresight—rather than deterministic forecasting—evolutionary economics equips researchers with a more robust and honest approach to complexity. In the following section, we build on this foundation by showing how multiple methods can be integrated to capture the interplay of innovation, feedback, and institutional evolution.

5.3   Methodological Synergies in Evolutionary Economics

Methodological integration in evolutionary economics reflects more than analytical versatility—it signals a commitment to complexity. Understanding economic systems as adaptive, path-dependent, and historically contingent requires us to go beyond single-method reasoning. No single technique can fully capture emergent dynamics; it is in the combination of perspectives that the system becomes intelligible.

Using both qualitative and quantitative approaches for the same research problem—such as pairing historical case analysis with agent-based modeling—can yield richer, more nuanced insights. This is not *methodological redundancy*, but rather a form of *methodological triangulation* or *methodological pluralism* that strengthens findings by approaching the same phenomenon from multiple angles.

Yet in much of academia today, researchers often feel pressured to choose one methodological "camp," treating it as the sole legitimate path. This not only narrows inquiry but also reinforces disciplinary silos. In contrast, evolutionary economics encourages researchers to match tools to problems, not ideologies or "traditions"— to embrace a pluralism that reflects the real-world complexity they seek to understand.

Example Box: A Simple Illustration of Methodological Pluralism
Students often ask whether surveys should be based on open-ended questions, structured numerical scales like a Likert scale, or some combination of both. Each design reflects a different methodological orientation. Open-ended questions yield depth but are harder to generalize. Numerical scales generate data that are easy to analyze statistically but can miss context and intention.

A useful compromise is to pair a *Likert scale* with optional comment fields. This way, we retain the ability to test hypotheses with quantitative data, while also gaining insight into *why* respondents answered as they did. For example, a "2" on a workplace satisfaction scale might seem straightforward—until the respondent adds that the rating reflects a temporary conflict with a supervisor rather than overall dissatisfaction. Now we have a pattern *and* a reason.

This small example doesn't aim to represent the full methodological tool-kit of evolutionary economics. Instead, it illustrates a broader principle: that mixing quantitative and qualitative approaches often leads to richer understanding. When studying complex systems, numbers alone or narratives alone are rarely enough. It's the combination—the ability to see both structure and nuance—that allows us to make better sense of the world.

Qualitative tools like *historical institutionalism* provide deep insight into long-term transformation, while quantitative techniques—ranging from econometrics to evolutionary game theory—help identify recurring patterns and test probabilistic relationships. Simulation-based approaches, such as agent-based modeling and *dynamic systems analysis*, model interaction effects and feedback loops that drive change over time. Scenario analysis and big data analytics then allow us to explore future pathways and stress-test strategies across possible worlds.[3]

Recent advances in artificial intelligence have dramatically extended the reach of these tools. We are no longer limited to simplified models or narrow datasets. AI allows us to simulate systems with dozens or even hundreds of variables—capturing nonlinearity, coevolution, and emergent behavior with far greater fidelity. These tools make possible new forms of scenario-building and probabilistic forecasting that align closely with evolutionary logic: not forecasting as a claim to certainty, but as a means to prepare for a range of *plausible futures*.

This is especially important when applied to decision-making. Adaptive forecasting methods—combining individual estimates, counterfactual reasoning, and Brier score calibration—help reduce bias, improve judgment, and enhance

---

[3] Stress-testing refers to the practice of evaluating how systems or strategies perform under extreme or unexpected conditions. In scenario analysis, this often involves posing "what-if" questions—such as, "What if a key resource fails?" or "What if demand drops by 50%?"—to assess vulnerabilities and adaptive capacity. It is widely used in fields such as finance, policy planning, and engineering, and increasingly in economics to test the resilience of strategies under different future scenarios.

group-level foresight. Such tools do not eliminate uncertainty, but they structure it, making us better equipped to navigate surprise and ambiguity.

Evolutionary economics, then, is not simply a theoretical lens—it is also a methodological approach grounded in realism. It equips researchers and practitioners with the tools to model transformation, assess resilience, and anticipate long-term shifts. This flexibility mirrors the logic of evolution itself: success lies not in a single blueprint, but in recombination, variation, and adaptation.

In the next section, we move from method to application, examining how innovation, competition, and institutional emergence unfold in real economic landscapes.

5.4   From Method to Mechanism: Linking Tools to Economic Evolution

As we have seen, evolutionary economics draws strength from its methodological diversity—from historical and comparative analysis to dynamic systems modeling and agent-based simulation. Yet these methods do not exist in a vacuum. They are rooted in deep principles of biological and cultural evolution and are deployed to investigate the mechanisms through which economic systems change: innovation, competition, cooperation, market emergence, and more.

To clarify how these layers relate, we can visualize the structure of evolutionary economic reasoning as a three-tiered model (Fig. 5.2):

Explanation of the figure:

- Layer 1: Evolutionary Foundations
    - Biological and cultural drivers of human behavior
    - Core principles like adaptation, selection, and coevolution
    - Evolutionary theories from biology (e.g., natural selection, punctuated equilibrium)
- Layer 2: Modeling and methods
    - Historical and institutional analysis
    - Agent-based and game-theoretic simulations
    - Scenario analysis, network theory, and statistical learning
- Layer 3: Economic mechanisms and outcomes
    - Concepts like innovation, competition, cooperation, and path dependence
    - Emergent institutions and niche specialization
    - Technological change, cultural evolution, and market transformation

This layered approach underscores how evolutionary economics operates: grounded in theory, powered by method, and applied to real-world dynamics. It clarifies how and why evolutionary economists work differently from their peers. Instead of modeling abstract equilibrium outcomes, we focus on tracing adaptive trajectories over time and across contexts—applying multiple methods in parallel, each chosen to fit the problem at hand.

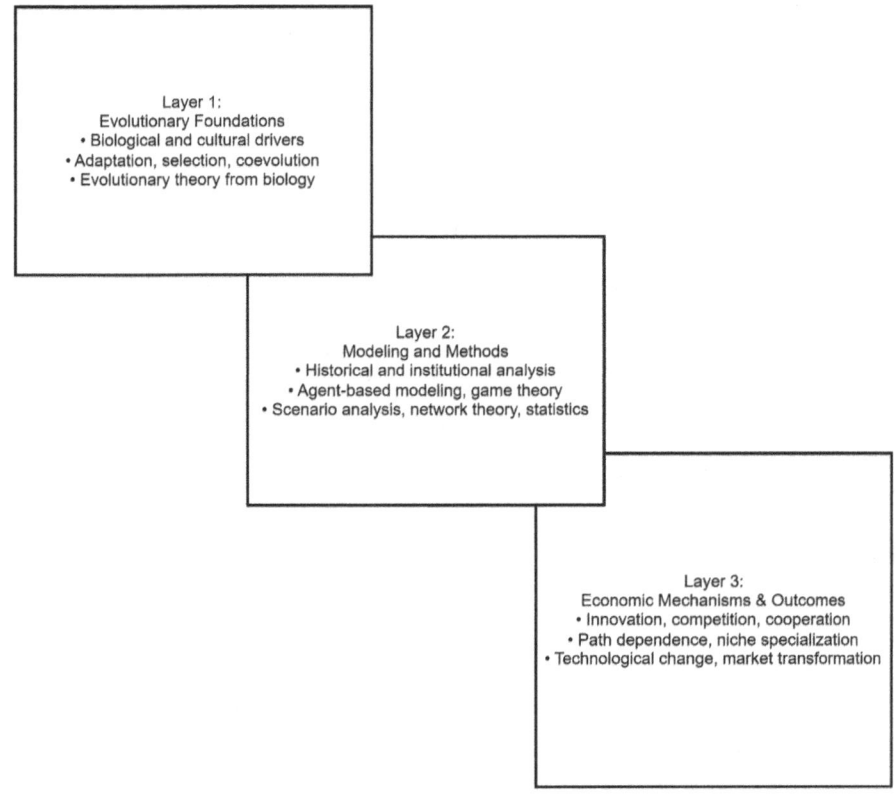

Fig. 5.2 The evolutionary economics framework—from foundations to mechanisms

The next chapter now turns to Layer 3, introducing the core concepts and mechanisms through which economic systems evolve—illustrated by concrete examples from markets, technologies, and policy. With the methodological scaffolding in place, we can explore how these dynamic forces play out across domains.

References

Acemoglu, D., & Robinson, J. A. (2012). *Why nations fail: The origins of power, prosperity, and poverty*. Crown Publishers.

Brynjolfsson, E., & McAfee, A. (2014). *The second machine age: Work, progress, and prosperity in a time of brilliant technologies*. W. W. Norton & Company.

Collier, D., & Mahoney, J. (1996). Insights and pitfalls: Selection bias in qualitative research. *World Politics, 49*(1), 56–91.

Creswell, J. W., & Plano Clark, V. L. (2017). *Designing and conducting mixed methods research* (3rd ed.). Sage.

Economist, The. (2025, February 20). *Only Asia can help America counter China's shipbuilding prowess.* https://www.economist.com/asia/2025/02/20/only-asia-can-help-america-counter-chinas-shipbuilding-prowess

Epstein, J. M. (1996). *Growing artificial societies: Social science from the bottom up.* MIT Press.

Forrester, J. W. (1961). *Industrial dynamics.* MIT Press.

Granovetter, M. (1973). The strength of weak ties. *American Journal of Sociology, 78*(6), 1360–1380.

Granger, C. W. J. (1969). Investigating causal relations by econometric models and cross-spectral methods. *Econometrica, 37*(3), 424–438.

Mokyr, J. (1990). *The lever of riches: Technological creativity and economic progress.* Oxford University Press.

North, D. C. (1990). *Institutions, institutional change and economic performance.* Cambridge University Press.

Nowak, M. A., & Sigmund, K. (2004). Evolutionary dynamics of biological games. *Science, 303*(5659), 793–799.

Ragin, C. C. (1987). *The comparative method: Moving beyond qualitative and quantitative strategies.* University of California Press.

Schoemaker, P. J. H. (1995). Scenario planning: A tool for strategic thinking. *MIT Sloan Management Review, 36*(2), 25–40.

Schwartz, P. (1991). *The art of the long view: Planning for the future in an uncertain world.* Doubleday.

Sterman, J. D. (2000). *Business dynamics: Systems thinking and modeling for a complex world.* McGraw-Hill.

Söilen, K. S. (2025). *The researcher's journey: A guide to methodology and academia in social sciences* (1st ed.). Springer Cham.

Tashakkori, A., & Teddlie, C. (1998). *Mixed methodology: Combining qualitative and quantitative approaches.* Sage.

Tesfatsion, L., & Judd, K. L. (2006). *Handbook of computational economics: Agent-based computational economics.* Elsevier.

Varian, H. R. (2014). Big data: New tricks for econometrics. *Journal of Economic Perspectives, 28*(2), 3–28.

Watts, D. J. (1999). *Small worlds: The dynamics of networks between order and randomness.* Princeton University Press.

Weibull, J. W. (1995). *Evolutionary game theory.* MIT Press.

Wooldridge, J. M. (2010). *Econometric analysis of cross section and panel data* (2nd ed.). MIT Press.

Further Reading

Cantner, U., & Krüger, J. J. (2007). Empirical tools for the analysis of technological change and productivity growth. In H. Hanusch & A. Pyka (Eds.), *Elgar companion to neo-Schumpeterian economics* (pp. 739–749). Edward Elgar.

Core Concepts and Mechanisms in Evolutionary Economics

6

Abstract

This chapter introduces the core concepts and mechanisms that emerge in the third layer of evolutionary economic analysis—observable patterns of economic transformation such as innovation, competition, cooperation, and market emergence. Building on the foundational theories of human behavior and evolutionary dynamics (Layer 1) and the methodological tools used to study adaptive systems (Layer 2), this chapter explores how these forces manifest in real-world outcomes. Through examples ranging from the rise of digital platforms to the evolution of regulatory institutions, we show how economic systems coevolve with technological, cultural, and institutional environments. These mechanisms—shaped by deeper feedback loops, selection pressures, and historical contingencies—help explain how economies adapt, specialize, and transform over time.

Keywords

Adaptation · Innovation · Competition · Cooperation · Path dependence · Technological change · Market emergence · Cultural evolution · Emergent institutions · Niche specialization · Fitness landscapes · Evolutionary economics · Coevolution · Complexity · Economic transformation

Having outlined the foundational theories and methodological tools that define evolutionary economics, we now turn to its most visible expressions: the economic mechanisms and outcomes that emerge from these deeper dynamics. This third layer of analysis focuses on how evolutionary processes manifest as patterns of innovation, competition, cooperation, and institutional transformation. These are not isolated phenomena—they are the surface effects of continuous feedback between human behavior, environmental change, and systemic adaptation. In what follows, we unpack these concepts and examine how they help explain the dynamic evolution of economic systems.

6.1   Core Mechanisms of Economic Evolution

This section explores the key concepts that characterize evolutionary economic behavior in practice. Mechanisms such as market emergence, niche specialization, and technological disruption reflect the cumulative effects of variation, selection, and coevolution. Drawing on insights from earlier chapters, we show how these mechanisms interact to produce shifting economic landscapes across industries, institutions, and societies (Table 6.1).

The examples in the table demonstrate how foundational evolutionary mechanisms manifest in tangible economic outcomes, summarizing their application to processes like adaptation, competition, and cooperation. Each concept is linked to empirical cases, emphasizing how evolutionary dynamics enrich our understanding of economic systems. Technological advances, for instance, often act as *primary catalysts* for change—steam engines sparked the Industrial Revolution, while AI and blockchain now redefine finance, manufacturing, and service delivery. Cantner and Pyka (2001) argue that principles like variation, selection, and adaptation can inform technology policies, fostering innovation "within economic frameworks."

Adaptation mirrors biological responses to environmental shifts, with firms adjusting strategies—like supermarkets adopting self-checkout systems—or pivoting to delivery models during COVID-19 to meet market demands. Competition, akin to natural selection, favors efficient and innovative firms, as seen in Amazon's outpacing of retailers like Sears. Innovation drives progress through new products, such as smartphones transforming communication, while path dependence explains the persistence of legacy systems like the QWERTY keyboard despite superior alternatives.

While many of the clearest examples of evolutionary dynamics come from technology and firm behavior, institutions and public policies also evolve through similar mechanisms. For instance, the development of universal healthcare systems in various countries emerged in response to sociopolitical pressures and wartime medical mobilization. Public sector evolution often involves slower, path-dependent change, shaped by social pressures, political negotiation, and cultural norms. Processes like coevolution and institutional emergence dominate here. *Historical-comparative analysis* and *qualitative case studies* remain essential for capturing these dynamics, though *agent-based simulations* can also illustrate how policy diffusion or reform spreads through interconnected governance systems.

These systems gradually adapted through feedback loops between population health needs, professional norms, and administrative reforms. Similarly, financial oversight bodies like central banks or anti-monopoly commissions evolved to

Table 6.1 Key concepts in economics driven by evolutionary dynamics

Concept	Explanation	Economic dynamics	Key references	Example
Innovation	Introduces new products, services, or processes, driving growth and change	Firms innovate to survive technological shifts and evolving demand	Schumpeter (1934), Dosi (1988)	The rise of electric vehicles (e.g., Tesla) transforming the auto industry
Competition	Firms compete for limited resources, mirroring natural selection	Less efficient firms are displaced; market leaders adapt faster	Nelson and Winter (1982), Hodgson (1993)	Amazon overtaking Borders through logistics and tech innovation
Cooperation	Economic agents collaborate for mutual benefit and system efficiency	Cooperation enhances resilience, especially in supply chains and innovation networks	Ostrom (1990), Axelrod (1984)	Open-source platforms like Linux thrive through collective development
Market emergence	New markets evolve in response to socio-technological shifts	Evolutionary pressures lead to new industries and business models	Audretsch and Feldman (1996), Metcalfe (1995)	Gig economy platforms like Uber and Airbnb emerging from digital and cultural trends
Adaptation	Agents change behavior in response to environmental and economic pressures	Firms adjust pricing, products, or strategies to maintain relevance	Nelson and Winter (1982), Frenken (2006)	Supermarkets implementing self-checkouts to meet demand for speed
Path dependence	Present outcomes are shaped by historical choices and institutional legacies	Early decisions constrain future options, reinforcing existing trajectories	Arthur (1989), North (1990, 2010)	Continued dominance of the QWERTY keyboard despite alternatives
Technological change	Technological advancement drives industry reconfiguration	Innovation cycles disrupt market structures and competitive hierarchies	Freeman and Perez (1988), Mokyr (1990)	Streaming platforms like Spotify displacing physical music formats

(continued)

Table 6.1 (continued)

Concept	Explanation	Economic dynamics	Key references	Example
Emergent institutions	Institutions evolve in response to economic complexity and coordination needs	New rules and structures form to stabilize interactions in changing markets	Hodgson (2001), Young (1998)	Emergence of central banks to regulate modern financial systems
Niche specialization	Firms specialize to serve specific market segments, reducing direct competition	Niche markets offer survival advantages in crowded economic landscapes	Boschma and Frenken (2006), Pyka (2002)	Local craft breweries differentiating from global beer brands
Cultural evolution	Economic behavior evolves alongside shifting cultural norms and preferences	Cultural change shapes demand patterns and business models	Rogers (1962), Henrich (2004)	Global rise in plant-based diets driving demand for meat alternatives like Beyond Meat

stabilize increasingly complex markets, often following economic crises or shifts in political consensus. These examples highlight that *institutional evolution* is not merely reactive but often anticipatory, driven by both necessity and strategic vision.

6.2   Mechanisms at Work: How Economies Evolve Over Time

Having introduced the central concepts of evolutionary economics, we now examine how these forces interact in practice—driving institutional change, market formation, and strategic behavior across time. This section highlights how evolutionary mechanisms operate in real economic systems, generating new structures and patterns in response to shifting environments.

Technological change frequently acts as a *catalyst*, disrupting existing markets and enabling new ones to form. The replacement of physical music media with streaming services like Spotify is one such transformation. At the institutional level, we see emergent systems such as carbon credit markets or central banks evolve to address new coordination problems. Cultural shifts, meanwhile, shape demand and influence firm behavior—for example, the rise of plant-based diets has created entirely new supply chains in alternative proteins.

Mechanisms like cooperation and *niche specialization* are essential to understanding how resilience emerges. Firms that collaborate across networks, as seen in open-source ecosystems, often outpace more siloed competitors. Similarly, businesses that target specific consumer segments—like craft breweries or local fintech apps—can thrive by avoiding direct competition and creating differentiated value.

These mechanisms unfold through coevolution: firms, institutions, and technologies adapt in tandem with one another. Renewable energy markets illustrate this well, evolving alongside green regulations, technological breakthroughs, and shifting consumer norms. Fitness landscapes help model how firms adjust their strategies under changing constraints, such as supply chain bottlenecks or inflation shocks. Regional innovation systems—like Shenzhen's high-tech cluster—show how co-adaptation between firms, governments, and knowledge institutions drives localized evolutionary success.

What emerges is not a single mechanism, but an interdependent set of processes that link micro-level actions to macro-level transformations. These visible economic shifts—new markets, fading technologies, reorganized industries—are surface expressions of deeper adaptive dynamics, rooted in the principles introduced in Chaps. 4 and 5. They are, in essence, the observable outcomes of Layer 3 in our evolutionary framework.

Understanding these mechanisms helps us see beyond linear cause-effect models and into the complex, path-dependent world of real economic change. This layered perspective brings coherence to otherwise fragmented developments, revealing how individual behavior, institutional history, and environmental feedback converge in shaping economic evolution.

The next chapter applies this lens through a series of case studies. From the rapid growth of fintech to the obsolescence of physical media, these examples illustrate how evolutionary dynamics play out in different contexts—bringing the theory to life and offering practical insights into the transformation of economic systems.

References

Arthur, W. B. (1989). Competing technologies, increasing returns, and lock-in by historical events. *The Economic Journal, 99*(394), 116–131.

Audretsch, D. B., & Feldman, M. P. (1996). R&D spillovers and the geography of innovation and production. *American Economic Review, 86*(3), 630–640.

Axelrod, R. (1984). *The evolution of cooperation*. Basic Books.

Boschma, R., & Frenken, K. (2006). Why is economic geography not an evolutionary science? Towards an evolutionary economic geography. *Journal of Economic Geography, 6*(3), 273–302.

Cantner, U., & Pyka, A. (2001). Classifying technology policy from an evolutionary perspective. *Research Policy, 30*(5), 759–775. https://doi.org/10.1016/S0048-7333(00)00120-5

Dosi, G. (1988). The nature of the innovative process. In G. Dosi et al. (Eds.), *Technical change and economic theory* (pp. 221–238). Pinter.

Frenken, K. (2006). *Innovation, evolution and complexity theory*. Edward Elgar.

Freeman, C., & Perez, C. (1988). Structural crises of adjustment: Business cycles and investment behaviour. In G. Dosi et al. (Eds.), *Technical change and economic theory* (pp. 38–66). Pinter.

Henrich, J. (2004). Demography and cultural evolution: Why adaptive cultural processes produced maladaptive losses in Tasmania. *American Antiquity, 69*(2), 197–214.

Hodgson, G. M. (1993). *Economics and evolution: Bringing life back into economics*. Polity Press.

Hodgson, G. M. (2001). *How economics forgot history: The problem of historical specificity in social science*. Routledge.

Metcalfe, J. S. (1995). The economic foundations of technology policy: Equilibrium and evolutionary perspectives. In P. Stoneman (Ed.), *Handbook of the economics of innovation and technological change* (pp. 409–512). Blackwell.

Mokyr, J. (1990). *The lever of riches: Technological creativity and economic progress*. Oxford University Press.

Nelson, R. R., & Winter, S. G. (1982). *An evolutionary theory of economic change*. Belknap Press.

North, D. C. (1990). *Institutions, institutional change, and economic performance*. Cambridge University Press.

Ostrom, E. (1990). *Governing the commons: The evolution of institutions for collective action*. Cambridge University Press.

Pyka, A. (2002). Innovation networks in economics: From the incentive-based to the knowledge-based approaches. *European Journal of Innovation Management, 5*(3), 152–163. https://doi.org/10.1108/14601060210436736

Rogers, E. M. (1962). *Diffusion of innovations*. Free Press.

Schumpeter, J. A. (1934). *The theory of economic development: An inquiry into profits, capital, credit, interest, and the business cycle* (R. Opie, Trans.). Harvard University Press. (Original work published 1911)

Young, H. P. (1998). *Individual strategy and social structure: An evolutionary theory of institutions*. Princeton University Press.

Further Reading

Cantner, U., & Meder, A. (2010). Technological proximity and the choice of cooperation partner. *Journal of Economic Interaction and Coordination, 5*(3), 271–291. https://doi.org/10.1007/s11403-010-0076-5

Evolution in Practice: Case Studies of Economic Adaptation

7

Abstract

This chapter presents real-world case studies that illustrate how evolutionary principles—adaptation, variation, selection, and coevolution—operate across industries, technologies, and institutions. From the rise of electric vehicles and fintech to the fall of Kodak and the growth of microfinance, these examples show how firms and systems evolve in response to external pressures and internal dynamics. The cases provide practical insights into how evolutionary thinking helps explain market transformation and organizational change, laying the groundwork for evaluating the strengths and limitations of this approach in the next chapter.

Keywords

Evolutionary economics · Case studies · Adaptation · Selection · Coevolution · Innovation · Institutional change · Market transformation · Technological disruption · Economic resilience

To move from theory to practice, this chapter offers a set of illustrative *case studies*. Each example has been selected not only to demonstrate core evolutionary mechanisms—such as adaptation, selection, innovation, and coevolution—but also to reflect how these dynamics play out across sectors. The goal is not to be exhaustive but to show the diverse ways in which evolutionary thinking helps us make sense of real-world change. The following section introduces the business and institutional cases, structured to highlight how economic actors evolve in response to shifting environments.

Taken together, these cases reflect the methodological pluralism discussed in Chap. 5. Whether through modeling individual agent behavior, tracing institutional legacies, or mapping interfirm dynamics, evolutionary economics calls for toolkits

K. Solberg Söilen, *Applied Evolutionary Economics*, Management for Professionals, https://doi.org/10.1007/978-3-032-03683-4_7

that match the layered complexity of economic life. The cases here serve not just as illustrations of theory, but as invitations to refine our methods for capturing real-world change.

Before diving into the full set of cases, we begin with a brief example that illustrates how evolutionary dynamics—especially timing, institutional coevolution, and niche formation—can determine which innovations succeed and which fail.

Case in a Box: Why Spotify Succeeded Where Others Failed
In Chap. 6, we wrote that technological change reshapes market structures—citing Spotify as a key example of how new technologies transform consumption patterns. But the full story of Spotify illustrates a more complex evolutionary narrative. The technology for streaming music existed years earlier: Kazaa and Napster had already developed peer-to-peer systems and challenged the music industry head-on. Yet both failed—because they emerged at a time when institutions were not ready to adapt, and because their *antagonistic strategies* triggered resistance from entrenched actors.

Spotify succeeded primarily not because it invented new technology, but because it adapted to an evolving environment. By the late 2000s, after years of digital piracy and crumbling CD sales, record labels were finally willing to experiment. Spotify offered a model that balanced user demand with institutional compensation. It survived through institutional coevolution, timing, and niche adaptation, demonstrating that in evolutionary economics, success is often about fit—not force.

This chapter builds on that logic. Here, we move from abstract theory to concrete illustration. The following case studies show how evolutionary principles—variation, adaptation, selection, and coevolution—operate across different domains. We examine firms, technologies, and institutions as evolving systems, shaped by feedback loops, path dependencies, and selective environments.

The goal is not comprehensiveness, but clarity: to show how evolutionary thinking helps explain real-world change. Whether it's the rise of electric vehicles, the fall of Kodak, or the transformation of global supply chains, these cases underscore a central insight of this book: economic systems evolve. And if we want to understand the future, we must first learn to see the patterns in their evolution.

7.1　Illustrating Evolutionary Mechanisms Through Business Cases

Each case has been selected not only for its illustrative value but also for its relevance in demonstrating how evolutionary principles apply to both firm-level and systemic transformations.

In Table 7.1 aligns each case with specific evolutionary mechanisms, offering a structured way to analyze how adaptation, variation, and competition manifest in diverse economic sectors.

Table 7.1 Cases that illustrate the evolutionary process in business

Case	Industry	Evolutionary process	Description	Outcome	References
Rise of electric vehicles	Automotive	Adaptation and competition	Firms shifted from internal combustion to electric vehicles in response to regulation and demand	Tesla led EV adoption; legacy firms like Ford and GM adapted to electrification	Bohnsack et al. (2014). *Technovation*
Fall of Kodak	Photography	Technological disruption and selection	Kodak failed to transition from film to digital photography	Filed for bankruptcy in 2012; digital and smartphone firms dominated	Lucas and Goh (2009). *Business Case Journal*
Streaming vs. DVDs	Entertainment	Niche formation and technological revolution	Netflix shifted to streaming, anticipating digital demand	Blockbuster collapsed; Netflix became a global streaming leader	Sundararajan (2013). *MIS Quarterly*
Renewable energy growth	Energy	Coevolution of industries and policies	Green energy industries grew with tech advances and policy support	Solar and wind adoption surged globally; firms like Siemens and Vestas led	Jacobsson and Bergek (2004). *Research Policy*
E-commerce revolution	Retail	Adaptation and competition	E-commerce firms disrupted traditional retail through logistics and digital innovation	Traditional stores declined; Amazon and Alibaba dominated global retail	Brynjolfsson and McAfee (2014). *The Second Machine Age*
Fintech disruption	Banking and finance	Technological revolution and competition	Fintech firms offered digital finance alternatives, challenging traditional banks	PayPal, Square, and Robinhood gained share; banks digitized services	Philippon (2016). *AER Papers and Proceedings*
COVID-19 supply chains	Global supply chains	Fitness landscape adaptation	Firms restructured supply chains to manage pandemic disruptions	Increased flexibility, resilience, and localization of sourcing	Ivanov and Das (2020). *Intl. J. of Logistics Mgmt*

(continued)

Table 7.1 (continued)

Case	Industry	Evolutionary process	Description	Outcome	References
Open-source software	Technology and IT	Cooperation and inclusive fitness	Developers collaborated to build platforms like Linux for collective benefit	Open-source became industry standard; firms like Red Hat profited from services	Raymond (1999). *The Cathedral and the Bazaar*
Luxury goods adaptation	Fashion and retail	Sexual selection and niche formation	Luxury brands used design and exclusivity to attract high-value customers	Continued profitability and cultural prestige during downturns	Kapferer and Bastien (2012). *The Luxury Strategy*
Microfinance institutions	Financial services	Adaptation and niche formation	Microfinance emerged to serve underserved communities with small loans	Greater financial inclusion; Grameen Bank became a global model	Yunus (1999). *Banker to the Poor*
Agricultural mechanization	Agriculture	Technological change and selection	Farmers adopted machinery and precision agriculture to boost productivity	Higher yields and efficiency; rural labor displacement	Ruttan (2002). *J. of Economic Perspectives*
Gig economy rise	Labor and employment	Adaptation and competition	Platforms like Uber and Airbnb created flexible work and service models	Rapid growth; sparked debate on labor rights and long-term stability	Sundararajan (2016). *The Sharing Economy*
Telecommunications evolution	Telecommunications	Coevolution of technology and policy	Industry shifted from landlines to mobile and internet communication	Firms like Nokia and Huawei rose; others declined with tech transitions	Rogers (2003). *Diffusion of Innovations*
Cryptocurrency emergence	Finance and technology	Technological revolution and variation	Cryptocurrencies introduced decentralized digital alternatives to fiat	Blockchain adoption spread; debates on regulation and the future of money	Nakamoto (2008). *Bitcoin: A Peer-to-Peer Electronic Cash System*

Together, these cases illustrate how evolutionary principles—adaptation, variation, selection, and coevolution—play out in real-world business dynamics, shaping the rise and fall of firms, industries, and technologies.

Tesla Motors exemplifies how technological innovation and first-mover advantages disrupt traditional industries, reshaping the automotive sector with electric vehicles as a competitive norm. In contrast, Kodak's downfall reveals the cost of failing to adapt to technological revolutions, as its reluctance to embrace digital photography ceded dominance to competitors. The entertainment industry showcases adaptation through Netflix's shift from DVD rentals to streaming, redefining consumer habits and industry standards. Similarly, renewable energy markets demonstrate how policy shifts and technological advancements drive rapid growth, altering the global energy landscape.

The fintech revolution illustrates innovation disrupting traditional banking, fostering a dynamic, accessible financial system. The COVID-19 pandemic—frequently cited for its broad impact—underscores resilience and rapid adaptation, as firms restructured supply chains to address disruptions. Open-source software, like Linux, highlights collaborative evolution through decentralized innovation. Meanwhile, the luxury goods market thrives on differentiation, with brands like Gucci leveraging exclusivity to maintain loyalty amid economic shifts.

Microfinance, pioneered by Grameen Bank, addresses systemic challenges by empowering marginalized groups through adaptive financial models—examples of institutional evolution aligned with broader economic development goals (North, 2010). Agricultural mechanization reflects long-term adaptation to resource constraints, boosting productivity via technological innovation. These trends are part of a larger transformation in financial systems that can be understood through the lens of *evolutionary financial macroeconomics*, which explores how financial institutions and behaviors adapt over time to uncertainty and structural shifts (Argitis, 2019).

Institutional Case 1: Universal Healthcare Systems and the Path-Dependent Evolution of Public Health

In the aftermath of the Second World War, several European countries, notably the United Kingdom and the Nordic states, implemented universal healthcare systems as responses to wartime devastation and shifting political values. These systems did not emerge fully formed but evolved through iterative reforms shaped by institutional legacies and public demand. The United Kingdom's NHS, for instance, built on preexisting regional services and trade union pressure, while Nordic models emphasized decentralization and equity. These examples reflect how path dependence and cultural evolution shaped institutional design in response to societal stress and reconstruction needs.

References: Hacker (2002) and Rothstein (1998)

Institutional Case 2: Digital Education Infrastructure and the Coevolution of the Education Sector
The rise of digital learning platforms in public education systems, particularly since the 2010s, illustrates state-led adaptation to technological and demographic change. Estonia's national digital learning strategy, initiated well before COVID-19, reflects anticipatory policy aligned with infrastructure development, digital literacy, and teacher training. During the pandemic, countries with stronger pre-existing digital infrastructures, like South Korea and Finland, adapted more rapidly to school closures. This case highlights how institutional foresight and coevolution with technological ecosystems influence resilience and inclusion in public education.
References: European Commission (2019) and Sahlberg (2011)

In parallel, the *adaptive markets hypothesis*, developed by Lo and Zhang (2024), reframes financial rationality as an evolutionary process where market efficiency fluctuates depending on environmental conditions and participant learning. This evolution is increasingly modeled through computational simulations and *agent-based models*, such as those developed by Mizuta and Yagi (2025), which provide insight into how decentralized strategies interact under conditions of limited information. The gig economy, led by platforms like Uber, exemplifies such decentralized adaptation, revolutionizing labor and services through digital networks. Telecommunications, too, evolve under co-influence from technology and policy, as seen in the global shift from landlines to mobile communication and Internet-based systems.

Cryptocurrency, with Bitcoin at the forefront, redefines economic systems by introducing decentralized digital currencies, sparking debates about regulation, monetary policy, and the broader institutional evolution of money. As Berg et al. (2019) argue, blockchain-based systems represent a shift toward *institutional cryptoeconomics*, challenging traditional centralized structures of financial governance. Schlaile (2020) extends this view through a memetic lens, suggesting that the spread of cryptocurrency technologies can be understood as a cultural-evolutionary process, shaped by the replication and adaptation of digital norms and behaviors. The financial sector case studies reflect processes of coevolution and institutional emergence. As new financial tools like fintech or cryptocurrencies evolve, they reshape and are shaped by regulatory frameworks and user behaviors. These cases are well-suited to *hybrid modeling strategies*, combining historical institutional analysis with simulation-based tools to explore systemic adaptation over time.

The *static mind* tends to see these firms and industries as fixed structures, but in reality, they are constantly transforming—quietly evolving into something else. Most companies we recognize today will no longer exist in their current form within a generation. The average lifespan of a company listed on the S&P 500 has dropped from around 60 years in the 1950s to under 20 years today, and it continues to shrink. Off the stock exchange, the average life expectancy of a small- or medium-sized enterprise (SME) is often less than 10 years.

If we could fully internalize this transitional perspective, we would not only be better prepared for work in these environments—but for the uncertainties of life itself.

7.2 Concluding Reflections on Evolution in Practice

These cases not only demonstrate the explanatory power of evolutionary theory but also offer practical insights for policy design, investment strategy, and innovation management. For instance, Cantner and Graf (2006) explore innovation networks, showing evolutionary principles at work in regional contexts.

By viewing market dynamics through this lens, scholars and practitioners can better anticipate disruptions and design *adaptive institutions*. Adaptation reflects how firms respond to shifting environments—like supermarkets adopting self-checkout systems or restaurants pivoting to delivery during the COVID-19 pandemic. Competition operates like natural selection, favoring efficient innovators, such as Amazon surpassing Sears. Innovation propels economic transformation, from the rise of smartphones to the dominance of streaming platforms, while coevolution captures how industries and policies evolve in tandem—as seen in the renewable energy sector. Together, these examples highlight how economic systems evolve through patterns of variation, selection, and adaptation across firms, sectors, and entire economies.

Yet, evolutionary economics is not without limitations. Its inherent complexity can sometimes obscure causal mechanisms, and there's a risk that broad generalizations reduce analytical precision. To strengthen its contribution, future work must address these challenges—clarifying its assumptions and testing its claims against competing theories. The next chapter turns to these critiques, offering a balanced assessment of the strengths and weaknesses of applying evolutionary theory to economic life.

References

Argitis, G. (2019). *Evolutionary financial macroeconomics*. Routledge.

Berg, C., Davidson, S., et al. (2019). *Understanding the blockchain economy: An introduction to institutional cryptoeconomics*. Edward Elgar Publishing.

Bohnsack, R., Pinkse, J., & Kolk, A. (2014). Tesla motors: Disrupting the auto industry. *Technovation, 34*(2), 99–100.

Brynjolfsson, E., & McAfee, A. (2014). *The second machine age: Work, progress, and prosperity in a time of brilliant technologies*. W.W. Norton & Company.

Cantner, U., & Graf, H. (2006). The network of innovators in Jena: An application of social network analysis. *Research Policy, 35*(4), 463–480.

European Commission. (2019). *2nd survey of schools: ICT in education*. Publications Office of the European Union. https://doi.org/10.2759/23401

Hacker, J. S. (2002). *The divided welfare state: The battle over public and private social benefits in the United States*. Cambridge University Press.

Ivanov, D., & Das, A. (2020). Coronavirus (COVID-19/SARS-CoV-2) and supply chain resilience: A research note. *International Journal of Logistics Management, 31*(2), 337–340.

Jacobsson, S., & Bergek, A. (2004). Transforming the energy sector: The evolution of renewable energy. *Research Policy, 33*(5), 755–768.

Kapferer, J. N., & Bastien, V. (2012). *The luxury strategy: Break the rules of marketing to build luxury brands*. Kogan Page.

Lo, A. W., & Zhang, R. (2024). *The adaptive markets hypothesis: An evolutionary approach to understanding financial system dynamics*. Oxford University Press.

Lucas, H. C., & Goh, J. M. (2009). Kodak and the digital revolution. *Business Case Journal, 16*(2), 1–22.

Mizuta, T., & Yagi, I. (2025). *Financial market design by an agent-based model*. Springer.

Nakamoto, S. (2008). *Bitcoin: A peer-to-peer electronic cash system*. Retrieved from https://bitcoin.org/bitcoin.pdf

North, D. C. (2010). *Understanding the process of economic change*. Princeton University Press.

Philippon, T. (2016). The fintech revolution. American Economic Review Papers and Proceedings, 106(5), 141–145.

Raymond, E. S. (1999). *The cathedral and the bazaar: Musings on Linux and open source by an accidental revolutionary*. O'Reilly Media.

Rogers, E. M. (2003). *Diffusion of innovations* (5th ed.). Free Press.

Rothstein, B. (1998). *Just institutions matter: The moral and political logic of the universal welfare state*. Cambridge University Press.

Ruttan, V. W. (2002). Productivity growth in world agriculture: Sources and constraints. *Journal of Economic Perspectives, 16*(4), 161–184.

Sahlberg, P. (2011). *Finnish lessons: What can the world learn from educational change in Finland?* Teachers College Press.

Schlaile, M. P. (2020). *Memetics and evolutionary economics: To boldly go where no meme has gone before*. Springer.

Sundararajan, A. (2013). The Netflix effect: Streaming wars in entertainment. *MIS Quarterly, 37*(4), 777–792.

Sundararajan, A. (2016). *The sharing economy: The end of employment and the rise of crowd-based capitalism*. MIT Press.

Yunus, M. (1999). *Banker to the poor: Micro-lending and the battle against world poverty*. Public Affairs.

Critique and Renewal: Evolutionary Economics in Dialogue with the Mainstream

8

Abstract

This chapter critically assesses the current position of evolutionary economics, identifying both its potential and its persistent challenges. While the field offers powerful tools for understanding economic transformation, it faces critique on grounds of causal ambiguity, inconsistent terminology, and limited empirical formalization. We suggest that many of these issues can be addressed through a layered research architecture—integrating foundational theory, modeling methods, and observed outcomes. This *three-layer approach*, introduced earlier in the book, provides a coherent framework for clarifying definitions, improving methodological rigor, and aligning research across disciplines. Through methodological integration, interdisciplinary dialogue, and advances in simulation and data science, evolutionary economics can move from a marginal position to a central role in guiding adaptive policy, innovation, and institutional design.

Keywords

Evolutionary economics · Critique · Mainstream economics · Complexity · Agent-based modeling · Causal inference · Empirical testing · Policy translation · Interdisciplinary research · Institutional inertia · Paradigm shift

Before we turn to the actual critique of *neoclassical economics*, it's important to clarify a common misunderstanding: evolutionary economics is not a marginalized approach because its ideas are weak or its arguments unconvincing. On the contrary, many of its insights—about innovation, adaptation, coevolution, and institutional change—have proven deeply relevant. The reasons for its limited influence lie elsewhere.

© The Author(s), under exclusive license to Springer Nature   103
Switzerland AG 2025
K. Solberg Söilen, *Applied Evolutionary Economics*, Management for
Professionals, https://doi.org/10.1007/978-3-032-03683-4_8

To understand where evolutionary economics stands today, we must situate it not only in relation to mainstream models but also within its own trajectory of development. This chapter explores the critiques often raised against it—not to dismiss the approach, but to identify areas of growth and renewal. Many of the challenges stem from its divergence from equilibrium-centered traditions and its resistance to simplification. But these challenges must be viewed in context.

Arguably the most significant reason for its marginalization, as we demonstrated in Chap. 4, lies in its historical context. After the Second World War, Anglo-Saxon—particularly American—academic and institutional leadership reshaped economics to resemble the hard sciences, especially physics. The aim was to develop a universal, deductive system that could model economic behavior with clarity and mathematical precision. This made sense at the time: by concentrating intellectual effort around a shared paradigm, it became easier to build consensus, develop policy tools, and establish *authoritative institutions*. Global bodies like the IMF, the World Bank, and later the Nobel Prize in Economics all benefited from this coherence—and, in turn, helped reinforce the neoclassical model as the dominant global standard.

There was nothing inherently misguided in this logic. Coordinating around a strong framework has obvious advantages for any scientific discipline. The challenge only emerges when the framework, despite its internal elegance, fails to deliver real-world insight.[1] Over the past several decades, neoclassical economics has struggled to account for some of the most pressing economic phenomena—financial instability, technological disruption, inequality, and environmental collapse. Yet because so much institutional and intellectual capital has been invested in the neoclassical model, serious alternatives like evolutionary economics often remain sidelined—not due to weak reasoning, but because they rely on different assumptions, methods, and objectives. They are also unjustly linked to a different, less developed, and at times slightly discredited tradition.

One of the consequences of this historical sidelining is that research in evolutionary economics tends to appear scattered and under-organized. But this is not a reflection of conceptual weakness. In fact, the work already produced could be coherently structured in multiple ways: by theoretical roots (Chap. 2), evolutionary principles (Chap. 3), historical periods (Chap. 4), methods (Chap. 5), key concepts (Chap. 6), or applied case studies (Chap. 7). Better still, combinations of these approaches could yield layered insights into economic systems.

Fortunately, the rise of artificial intelligence opens new possibilities for synthesis and structure. Tools like semantic clustering, citation mapping, and probabilistic

---

[1] This limitation first became clear to me during my master's studies in 1993, while doing a short thesis project at the Milan Stock Exchange as an exchange student from HEC to SDA Bocconi. Together with a colleague, I examined several models used to price options and found that they lacked predictive power in real market conditions. Some of these models even drew on analogies from physics—such as equations describing the flow of energy in a tungsten filament—which seemed strikingly out of place in financial contexts. Years later, the collapse of Long-Term Capital Management (LTCM), co-founded by Nobel laureates Robert Merton and Myron Scholes, seemed to confirm these doubts. LTCM's heavy reliance on such models and extreme leverage ultimately led to a near-systemic crisis in 1998, requiring intervention by the Federal Reserve.

modeling can help reveal connections across the field—making its insights more accessible, comparable, and practically useful.

To support this process, this book has proposed a three-layer framework to help organize evolutionary economics. Rather than treating theory, method, and outcome in isolation, the layered model links (1) foundational biological and cultural dynamics, (2) integrative modeling and methodological tools, and (3) emergent economic mechanisms and outcomes. This structure is not only a way to clarify terminology—it helps strengthen empirical testing and improves dialogue between theory and practice.

This point bears repeating because it is crucial to keep in mind as we enter the critique of evolutionary economics: the main obstacles it faces are not rooted primarily in the strength of its arguments, but in the dominant paradigm into which those arguments are introduced. It is the existing paradigm—deeply embedded in our current world order—that sets the boundaries for what counts as legitimate knowledge. Any approach that challenges these boundaries, no matter how insightful or rigorous, risks being sidelined. Evolutionary economics has struggled not because it lacks substance, but because it operates outside the frame that has come to define economic thought over the past 70 years.

8.1   Key Critiques of Evolutionary Economics

We now turn to the internal critiques and challenges facing evolutionary economics as a field of study. While the approach offers a powerful lens for understanding economic change, it is not without limitations.

In Table 8.1 summarizes some of the most frequently raised concerns—from difficulties in isolating causal factors to challenges in empirical validation and policy translation.

Several of these critiques stem from the very strength of evolutionary economics: its commitment to complexity. For example, the difficulty in isolating causal factors reflects the fact that real-world systems are dynamic and interconnected. Rather than seeing this as a flaw, evolutionary economists have responded by developing tools such as agent-based modeling and simulation techniques that allow for the exploration of multi-causal, feedback-driven processes.

Other critiques highlight risks of overgeneralization. Concepts like "selection" or "fitness" can become vague if applied too broadly or without attention to context. The solution here lies in tighter grounding—drawing directly from institutional theory, history, and empirical specificity to ensure that metaphors don't float free from substance.

The field has also faced questions about quantitative rigor. Unlike neoclassical economics, which privileges *mathematical formalism*, evolutionary approaches have sometimes been seen as lacking structure. This has spurred efforts to integrate formal tools such as evolutionary game theory, system dynamics, and econometrics—bringing precision without sacrificing relevance.

Table 8.1 Challenges and critiques of the evolutionary approach to economics

Challenge	Explanation	Contrast with mainstream economics	Proposed solutions	Three-layer model solution	Key references
Isolating causal factors	Evolutionary models involve complex, dynamic interactions that obscure causality	Mainstream simplifies with ceteris paribus and static frameworks	Use agent-based models and simulations to explore multi-causal scenarios	Use Layer 2 tools (agent-based modeling, scenario analysis) to trace causal links from Layer 1 to Layer 3	Nelson and Winter (1982), Dosi (1997)
Risk of overgeneralization	Broad metaphors like "selection" can miss institutional or cultural specifics	Mainstream uses narrow assumptions but often lacks realism	Ground models in history and institutional theory	Tie Layer 3 outcomes (e.g., competition, institutions) to context-specific Layer 1 foundations	Hodgson (1993), Witt (2003)
Lack of quantitative rigor	Some work lacks formalization, lowering analytical precision	Neoclassical relies on mathematics, sometimes at the cost of relevance	Integrate with game theory, econometrics, and statistical learning	Combine Layer 2 formal tools (e.g., evolutionary game theory, data science) with Layer 3 case analysis	Pyka and Fagiolo (2007), Metcalfe (1994)
Ambiguity in definitions	Terms like "adaptation" and "selection" used inconsistently	Mainstream benefits from standardized definitions	Develop clear glossaries and conceptual frameworks	Use Layer 1 principles (e.g., adaptation, fitness) as definitional anchors across studies and scales	Nelson (1995), Hodgson and Knudsen (2010)
Policy translation difficulty	Complexity makes direct policy application harder	Mainstream is more linear and easily translated to policy	Use adaptive tools, scenario planning, and resilience frameworks	Ground policy tools in Layer 2, with feedback loops in Layer 3 reflecting real-world conditions	Dosi and Nelson (2010), Frenken (2006)

Critique	Issue	Mainstream position	Response	Three-Layer Model application	References
Incomplete method integration	Evolutionary work is scattered across traditions	Mainstream models dominate methods, curricula, and funding	Build interdisciplinary bridges, embed evolutionary thinking into teaching	Use the Three-Layer Model to align diverse approaches under a coherent framework	Schumpeter (1934), Witt (1999)
Focus on long-term dynamics	Long-term focus may neglect short-term behaviors and tools	Mainstream emphasizes equilibrium and short-term predictions	Combine long-run insights with near-term forecasting	Use Layer 2 tools for short-term forecasting, linked to Layer 1 structures and Layer 3 behaviors	Cantner and Pyka (2001), Boschma and Frenken (2006)
Limited empirical testing	Evolutionary claims often lack strong empirical validation	Mainstream uses abundant data and testable models	Leverage big data, machine learning, and new metrics	Use Layer 2 methods (machine learning, natural language processing) to test Layer 3 patterns grounded in Layer 1 and 2 dynamics	Pyka (2017), Nelson and Winter (1982)
Institutional resistance	Challenges dominant paradigms and is perceived as marginal	Neoclassical enjoys institutional and educational hegemony	Demonstrate real-world success and build policy applications	Highlight successful Layer 3 outcomes and connect them back to Layer 1 theory and Layer 2 design	Hodgson (2001), Nelson (1994)
Micro-macro disconnect	Difficult to connect micro behaviors to macro patterns	Mainstream models favor macro-level aggregates over emergence	Develop multilevel simulation and modeling frameworks	Use Layer 2 models (multi-agent systems, system dynamics) to link Layer 1 motives with Layer 3 institutional structures	Dosi (1988), Metcalfe (1994)

Definitional ambiguity is another recurring issue. Terms like "adaptation" or "innovation" may mean different things across different studies. Recent work has emphasized the need for conceptual clarity through shared glossaries, definitional anchors, and typologies that cut across disciplines.

When it comes to policy, critics argue that evolutionary models are too complex or indirect to be useful. In response, many researchers now focus on adaptive policy design—using techniques like scenario analysis and resilience thinking to guide action in uncertain environments. These approaches don't offer optimal solutions in the traditional sense, but they do provide strategic orientation and robustness.

Fragmentation remains a deeper structural challenge. Because evolutionary work spans economics, sociology, innovation studies, and organizational theory, it often lacks a unified academic home. This has prompted calls for greater methodological integration and educational reform—embedding evolutionary thinking into curricula and building stronger interdisciplinary institutions.

There are also concerns about the field's long-term orientation. Critics argue that an emphasis on historical path dependence and macro-evolutionary change leaves little room for understanding short-term dynamics. Yet here too, the field has begun to evolve—combining long-run perspectives with near-term forecasting tools such as behavioral simulation and real-time data analytics.

A related challenge is the limited empirical testing of many evolutionary claims. This reflects both the difficulty of modeling open-ended, non-equilibrium systems and the relative youth of the field. But advances in big data, machine learning, and automated text analysis now make it possible to empirically track patterns of adaptation and diffusion across large-scale systems.

Finally, institutional resistance continues to limit the field's growth. Evolutionary economics challenges not just the assumptions of mainstream economics, but its formal logic and research culture. The most effective strategy here is not confrontation but contribution—demonstrating value through practical applications, case-based successes, and tools that help navigate uncertainty in ways neoclassical models often can't.

There are other examples too. For example, the critiques of evolutionary economics, including its treatment of heterogeneity and systemic adaptation, are discussed by Cantner and Hanusch (2001).[2]

By working through these challenges directly, evolutionary economics can move from a promising alternative to a mature and credible field. Addressing these critiques—methodologically, empirically, and conceptually—is less about defending a paradigm and more about refining a dynamic, evolving approach to understanding economic life.

---

[2] Cantner and Hanusch (2001).

8.2 Enhancing the Framework: Toward a Stronger Evolutionary Model

The critiques discussed in this chapter point less to any failure of evolutionary economics and more to its developmental stage—rich with potential but still maturing. As demonstrated throughout this book, the evolutionary perspective offers robust tools for understanding economic complexity. Its limited mainstream traction stems not from conceptual weakness but from the lingering dominance of an older scientific paradigm—one rooted in equilibrium logic and the aesthetics of mathematical elegance. Progress will depend not only on better arguments or richer data but also on a fundamental shift in how we imagine economies: not as clockwork machines, but as adaptive, historically grounded, and coevolving systems.

Evolutionary economics provides this vision. Yet like all emerging paradigms, it must refine its vocabulary, sharpen its methods, and demonstrate practical relevance. One way forward is through the *three-layer framework* articulated in this book. Beginning with foundational drivers of human behavior and cultural evolution (Layer 1), incorporating dynamic methodologies (Layer 2), and culminating in concrete mechanisms and outcomes like innovation, cooperation, and institutional change (Layer 3), this layered structure helps clarify causality, compare findings across studies, and bridge the micro-macro divide.

Importantly, it offers a common reference point to integrate diverse tools—from case-based reasoning and historical analysis to simulation and machine learning—within a unified theoretical system.

Fortunately, many of the field's challenges are already being met by promising developments:

- Causal inference is improving through the use of agent-based modeling and scenario simulations, which allow for the exploration of counterfactuals and dynamic feedback loops without reducing systems to linear relationships.
- To avoid overgeneralization, scholars are rooting evolutionary models in historical specificity and institutional analysis—often drawing on anthropology, sociology, and economic history to ground broad mechanisms in real-world variation.
- The push for quantitative rigor is gaining ground via hybrid approaches that combine evolutionary insights with econometrics, game theory, and data science. Recent advances in big data analytics, machine learning, and natural language processing make it possible to validate complex, adaptive models empirically.
- Conceptual ambiguity is being tackled through the development of clearer definitions and more coherent frameworks. Core terms such as adaptation, selection, and fitness need to be standardized across levels of analysis—ideally through shared glossaries, collaborative handbooks, and interdisciplinary research networks.

- Turning theory into policy means embracing adaptive governance—designing institutions that learn, experiment, and evolve over time. This requires scenario planning, built-in feedback mechanisms, and a tolerance for uncertainty, rather than the pursuit of static "optimal" solutions.
- Institutional resistance from within the mainstream remains, but this is best overcome not by debate alone, but by demonstration: real-world applications, case studies, and policy tools that outperform traditional approaches can shift perceptions more effectively than critique. Embedding evolutionary economics in graduate curricula, interdisciplinary journals, and academic societies can further accelerate this transition.
- The micro-macro divide remains a persistent challenge, yet it is one evolutionary economics is uniquely suited to overcome. Tools such as multi-agent modeling, coevolutionary mapping, and system dynamics modeling enable researchers to trace how individual behaviors scale into institutional structures and systemic patterns.

These responses signal a shift: evolutionary economics is not only responding to criticism—it is improving. It is no longer just an alternative to orthodoxy, but a framework capable of guiding meaningful inquiry and informing real-world decisions in complex, uncertain environments.

To consolidate these insights, the following figure presents a visual synthesis of the key critiques discussed in this chapter alongside targeted strategies drawn from the three-layer framework. This illustration is not exhaustive, but it captures the major paths through which the field can evolve without losing its epistemological richness or practical utility. It also marks a transition—from inward reflection to outward application—as we prepare to examine how evolutionary economics can inform next-generation policy design.

In Fig. 8.1 summarizes how evolutionary economics is addressing its core challenges—not by simplifying complexity, but by developing tools and strategies suited to it. Each response reinforces the field's capacity to model dynamic change, translate theory into practice, and offer meaningful alternatives to static, equilibrium-based thinking. As these efforts continue to mature, evolutionary economics is well-positioned to become not only a critique of the mainstream but also a foundational pillar in the economics of the future.

But building a stronger framework is only part of the task—the field must also build the *institutional foundations* that can support its long-term development.

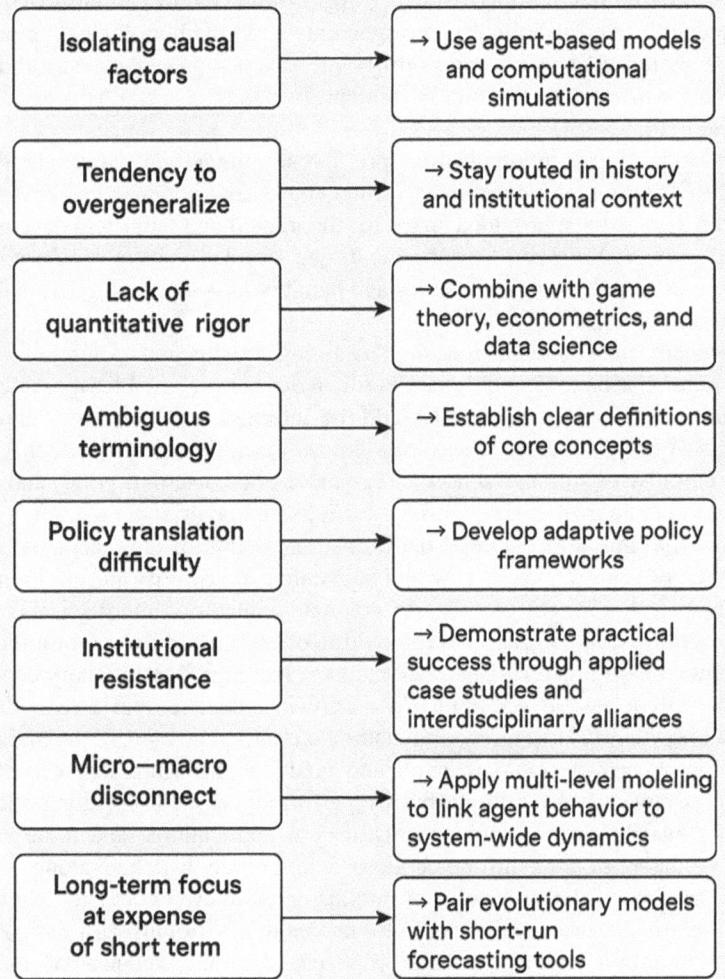

Fig. 8.1 Pathways to strengthen the evolutionary economics research program

8.3   Building the Field: Institutions, Dialogue, and Future Directions

If evolutionary economics is to mature into a widely used and policy-relevant framework, it must continue not only to improve its methods and conceptual clarity but also to strengthen its institutional infrastructure. That means cultivating shared standards, building research communities, and fostering platforms for visibility and dialogue.

Cantner (2016) has outlined some of these future pathways, emphasizing the importance of interdisciplinary engagement and methodological pluralism.[3] Creating a shared vocabulary across different branches of evolutionary thought—whether focused on innovation, development, or behavior—can help bring coherence to the field.

Efforts toward institutionalization are already underway. Journals like the *Journal of Evolutionary Economics* (Springer) and *Evolutionary and Institutional Economics Review* have provided space for theoretical and empirical development. Publishers such as Springer, Edward Elgar, and Routledge have supported evolutionary scholarship through book series and handbooks—often long before the field gained broader traction.

Conferences play a vital role in sustaining intellectual communities. The European Association for Evolutionary Political Economy (EAEPE), the Association for Evolutionary Economics (AFEE), and the International Joseph A. Schumpeter Society (ISS) bring together researchers across disciplines and continents. These venues—along with summer schools, regional workshops, and policy labs—help foster a vibrant and evolving network of scholars and practitioners.

At the same time, more unified platforms, larger interdisciplinary conferences, and coordinated research agendas would help enhance visibility and strengthen collective identity. A stronger presence in graduate education, interdisciplinary journals, and digital research infrastructure would also deepen the field's institutional base.

Of course, institutional resistance remains a challenge. Evolutionary economics differs from neoclassical economics not only in substance but also in logic: it embraces uncertainty, adaptation, and historical contingency where the mainstream has traditionally prized formal precision and general equilibrium. But resistance can be overcome not only by critique but by performance. Demonstrating success—through real-world policy tools, successful case applications, and more accurate forecasts—can do more to shift perceptions than theoretical debate alone.

By continuing to develop both its intellectual framework and its institutional footing, evolutionary economics can fulfill its potential—not just as a critique of the dominant paradigm, but as a fully realized, dynamic science of economic transformation.

In the next chapter, we explore what this means for policy. If economies are better understood as evolving ecosystems than as stable machines, what kinds of institutions do we need? How should we design for innovation, resilience, and sustainability in systems that are always in flux?

---

[3] Cantner (2016).

References

Boschma, R., & Frenken, K. (2006). Applications of evolutionary economic geography. *Economic Geography, 82*(3), 273–287.

Cantner, U. (2016). Foundations of economic change—An extended Schumpeterian approach. *Journal of Evolutionary Economics, 26*(4), 701–736.

Cantner, U., & Hanusch, H. (2001). Heterogeneity and evolutionary change: Empirical conception, findings, and unresolved issues. In *Frontiers of evolutionary economics* (pp. 228–267).

Cantner, U., & Pyka, A. (2001). Classifying technology policy from an evolutionary perspective. *Research Policy, 30*(5), 759–775.

Dosi, G. (1997). Opportunities, incentives and the collective patterns of technological change. *The Economic Journal, 107*(444), 1530–1547. https://doi.org/10.1111/j.1468-0297.1997.tb00070.x

Dosi, G. (1988). Sources, procedures, and microeconomic effects of innovation. *Journal of Economic Literature, 26*(3), 1120–1171.

Dosi, G., & Nelson, R. R. (2010). Technical change and industrial dynamics as evolutionary processes. *Handbook of the Economics of Innovation, 1*, 51–127.

Frenken, K. (2006). Innovation, evolution, and complexity theory. *Journal of Evolutionary Economics, 16*(5), 559–576.

Hodgson, G. M. (1993). *Economics and evolution: Bringing life back into economics*. University of Michigan Press.

Hodgson, G. M. (2001). *How economics forgot history: The problem of historical specificity in social science*. Routledge.

Hodgson, G. M., & Knudsen, T. (2010). *Darwin's conjecture: The search for general principles of social and economic evolution*. University of Chicago Press.

Metcalfe, J. S. (1994). Evolutionary economics and technology policy. *The Economic Journal, 104*(425), 931–944.

Nelson, R. R. (1994). The co-evolution of technology, industrial structure, and supporting institutions. *Industrial and Corporate Change, 3*(1), 47–63.

Nelson, R. R. (1995). Recent evolutionary theorizing about economic change. *Journal of Economic Literature, 33*(1), 48–90.

Nelson, R. R., & Winter, S. G. (1982). *An evolutionary theory of economic change*. Harvard University Press.

Pyka, A. (2017). Der kooperative Unternehmer: Eine evolutorische Perspektive. In M. Held, G. Kubon-Gilke, & R. Sturn (Eds.), *Jahrbuch Normative und institutionelle Grundfragen der Ökonomik* (Vol. 16, pp. 103–127). Metropolis.

Pyka, A., & Fagiolo, G. (2007). Agent-based modelling: A methodology for neo-Schumpeterian economics. In H. Hanusch & A. Pyka (Eds.), *Elgar companion to neo-Schumpeterian economics* (pp. 467–487). Edward Elgar Publishing.

Schumpeter, J. A. (1934). *The theory of economic development: An inquiry into profits, capital, credit, interest, and the business cycle*. Harvard University Press.

Witt, U. (1999). Bioeconomics as economics from a Darwinian perspective. *Journal of Evolutionary Economics, 9*(4), 443–463.

Witt, U. (2003). *The evolving economy: Essays on the evolutionary approach to economics*. Edward Elgar.

Further Reading

Söilen, K. S. (2024). *Intelligence studies in business: Foundations and applications*. Spring. https://doi.org/10.1007/978-3-031-51924-6

Policy Evolution: Adaptive Strategies for Economic Resilience

9

Abstract

This chapter shows how evolutionary economics reframes public policy as a process of continuous adaptation, experimentation, and institutional learning. It contrasts traditional models—focused on static optimization and short-term control—with a dynamic framework rooted in complexity, diversity, and coevolution. Drawing on the book's three-layer approach, it demonstrates how policy design can integrate behavioral realism, methodological pluralism, and systemic responsiveness. Case examples from innovation, finance, health, labor, and trade illustrate how evolutionary strategies such as variation, selection, and feedback can guide more resilient and forward-looking governance in uncertain environments.

Keywords

Adaptive policy · Evolutionary economics · Institutional resilience · Public governance · Complexity economics · Coevolution · Long-term strategy · Policy innovation · Agent-based modeling · Policy feedback · Systemic adaptation

To understand how evolutionary economics can inform public policy, we must first recognize that policies, like economies themselves, must adapt to preserve the viability of the systems they serve. The goal of policy is not just to manage short-term outcomes, but to sustain the long-term capacity of a society to function, thrive, and remain competitive.

In nature, most adaptations are aimed at survival. Yet some evolutionary paths can lead to fragility. The peacock's extravagant tail, for instance, though attractive, comes at a high cost—it makes the bird more vulnerable to predators. Likewise, certain traits or behaviors in other species may evolve in ways that reduce long-term

K. Solberg Söilen, *Applied Evolutionary Economics*, Management for Professionals, https://doi.org/10.1007/978-3-032-03683-4_9

fitness, particularly if environments shift too quickly or unpredictably. The analogy applies to societies as well: policy strategies rooted in fixed ideologies or outdated assumptions may once have been adaptive, but they can become liabilities. These are evolutionary mismatches—not failures of logic, but failures to align with new conditions.

In this light, policy itself must be understood as an adaptive system. But here lies a deeper challenge: the fatal flaw in many current policymaking processes is not just short-termism. It is a structural inability to think in terms of dynamic change, long-term adaptation, and the actual time it takes to prepare for and respond to new realities. The inertia is built in. When new problems arise, the response is typically to launch lengthy investigations followed by extended efforts to build political consensus across fragmented party lines. In the meantime, circumstances continue to evolve, and damage accumulates. It is often said that such inertia serves a purpose—that it prevents hasty or poorly thought-out decisions. And this may hold true when society is broadly on the right track. But when it is not, when the system is already misaligned with reality, the same inertia becomes even more dangerous. Delay doesn't just slow progress—it deepens dysfunction.

Unlike private firms, which can often pivot within days or weeks, the public sector is frequently bound to timelines of years. This delay in *institutional response time* is itself a form of maladaptation—a costly one. Evolutionary economics provides a way to think through these limitations. It does not offer quick fixes, but it encourages experimentation, learning loops, and institutional setups better suited to a world in flux.

This chapter begins by contrasting mainstream policy approaches with evolutionary ones, highlighting how the latter prioritize long-term adaptation, systemic feedback, and the coevolution of institutions and behaviors. We then examine key domains—such as innovation, crisis response, inequality, and trade—where adaptive strategies grounded in evolutionary thinking are already in play.

These examples are not endorsements, but illustrations of how an evolutionary lens offers alternative tools and assumptions for designing policy in a volatile and complex world (Table 9.1).

These are examples of ongoing debates. As of today, Europe and much of the world are navigating a volatile geopolitical landscape marked by escalating trade and security tensions. The United States has begun raising tariffs on select imports, signaling a renewed era of *protectionism*. In response, the European Union and other major economies are debating how best to respond—whether to mirror these measures in a tit-for-tat fashion or to de-escalate, mindful of the fact that EU tariffs on many US goods are already comparatively high.

Simultaneously, a wave of military rearmament is unfolding globally, triggered by the Russian invasion of Ukraine. Governments are now grappling with the challenge of developing coherent defense strategies—deciding where to source or localize production and, perhaps most urgently, how to finance these efforts in an already debt-laden global economy. These developments illustrate in real time how adaptive policy frameworks, grounded in evolutionary principles, are not only useful but also necessary.

Table 9.1 Policy implications of evolutionary economics

Policy domain	Policy implication	Explanation	Adaptive strategies	Example	Key references
Fostering innovation	Promote diversity in funding and experimentation	Variation is essential for innovation; systems evolve by generating diverse options	Fund diverse R&D programs, support startups, protect intellectual property	Green energy innovation supported through public R&D funding	Nelson and Winter (1982), Dosi (1988)
Managing crises	Build resilience through diversification and decentralization	Evolutionary systems survive shocks by adapting and spreading risk	Redundancy in supply chains, scenario planning, decentralized response units	Stockpiling medical supplies and localizing supply during pandemics	Frenken (2006), Pyka and Fagiolo (2007)
Addressing inequality	Design inclusive systems that support diverse capabilities	Evolutionary models highlight the need for enabling environments for all actors	Invest in education, digital access, and inclusive institutions	Universal access to online learning platforms for low-income communities	Hodgson (1993), Metcalfe (1994)
Sustainable development	Guide markets toward adaptive ecological alignment	Systems must evolve within environmental constraints to survive	Carbon taxes, circular economy incentives, renewable subsidies	Carbon trading schemes to reduce emissions while promoting market flexibility	Boschma and Frenken (2006), Nelson (1994)
Industrial policy	Enable flexible industrial transitions	Industries evolve unevenly; policy must support dynamic sectors and ease transitions	Invest in emerging sectors, create safety nets for declining ones, public-private co-innovation	EV infrastructure to assist transition from fossil fuel-based auto industries	Schumpeter (1934), Hodgson and Knudsen (2010)
Workforce development	Foster lifelong learning and adaptive skill systems	Adaptive economies require adaptive workers	Expand vocational education, support upskilling, promote digital literacy	National retraining initiatives for displaced workers due to automation	Dosi and Nelson (2010), Pyka and Fagiolo (2007)

(continued)

Table 9.1 (continued)

Policy domain	Policy implication	Explanation	Adaptive strategies	Example	Key references
Urban planning	Develop cities that evolve with social and technological trends	Urban systems coevolve with infrastructure, demographics, and tech	Mixed-use zoning, smart city integration, flexible transit systems	Zoning reform to accommodate hybrid work and decentralized offices	Audretsch and Feldman (1996), Cantner and Pyka (2001)
Healthcare policy	Create adaptive health systems for evolving threats	Public health must respond to biological, demographic, and behavioral evolution	Global data-sharing, flexible funding models, rapid response platforms	COVID-19 vaccine pipelines coordinated across nations and institutions	Nelson and Winter (1982), Frenken (2006)
Financial regulation	Design resilient financial systems that evolve with market dynamics	Evolutionary models emphasize systemic risk and adaptation under complexity	Macroprudential tools, systemic risk monitoring, financial innovation with regulatory oversight	Basel III implementation after the 2008 crisis to increase systemic resilience	Hodgson (2001), Schumpeter (1934)
Technology policy	Align technological development with ethical and social goals	Technologies coevolve with society and institutions	AI governance frameworks, ethical review boards, equitable digital access	National AI ethics frameworks for autonomous vehicles and facial recognition	Metcalfe (1994), Witt (1999)
Trade and globalization	Build flexible trade regimes responsive to shocks and interdependence	Global networks evolve rapidly; policies must adapt to disruptions	Resilient supply chains, regional diversification, adaptive agreements	Flexible trade policies during COVID-19 supply chain breakdowns	Nelson (1994), Frenken (2006)

To better appreciate how these evolutionary approaches differ from conventional policy models, the next table outlines the key distinctions between traditional and evolutionary policy thinking (Table 9.2).

This comparison clarifies how evolutionary economics offers not just an alternative set of tools, but a fundamentally different approach to policymaking—one grounded in realism, adaptability, and long-term systemic insight. With this foundation in place, we now turn to concrete examples of how these principles can be applied across key policy domains.

One reason our societies measure the wrong things is that both our political and economic systems are structured around short-term incentives. Just as many corporations are driven by quarterly results, political actors are locked into cycles of re-election, media soundbites, and party discipline. In many countries, party leaders demand total loyalty, and a single misstep can end a political career. This fosters extreme *risk aversion* and discourages long-term thinking.

Table 9.2 How evolutionary policy differs from traditional economic policy

Dimension	Traditional economic policy	Evolutionary economic policy
Time horizon	Short-term focus (e.g., quarterly results, electoral cycles)	Long-term orientation; systemic resilience and historical awareness are prioritized
Policy design	Top-down, based on optimizing fixed variables and models	Iterative, experimental, and responsive to feedback and real-world learning
Metrics of success	Efficiency, GDP growth, quarterly results, interest rates, inflation, unemployment, balanced budgets, price stability	Innovation capacity, adaptability, institutional learning, and social robustness: Measured via *Shanghai Ranking* (research excellence) and *ASPI Tech Tracker* (industry leadership)
Role of failure	Seen as breakdowns to be avoided or corrected	Considered essential for learning, experimentation, and adaptation
Intervention logic	Fixing market failures using predesigned models	Shaping enabling environments and selection conditions that evolve over time
Institutional view	Institutions as stable constraints or top-down enforcers	Institutions as evolving systems, co-adapting with technology, behavior, and norms
Response to shocks	Reactive stabilization (e.g., stimulus packages, bailouts)	Proactive resilience-building, redundancy, and decentralization to absorb unpredictable change
Knowledge assumptions	Assumes rational agents and predictable outcomes	Accepts uncertainty, bounded rationality, and emergent system dynamics
Disciplinary culture	Specialized silos, technical jargon, and academic turf wars	Emphasis on generalist thinking, practical common sense, cross-disciplinary collaboration
Professional standards	Credentials and affiliations often prioritized over output or insight	Focus on merit, practical wisdom, explanatory power, and long-term contribution to public value
Political orientation	Vulnerable to ideological capture, buzzwords, and identity politics	Values institutional neutrality, realism, and policy grounded in adaptive performance

Labor policies, too, are often manipulated to generate the appearance of success—creating temporary jobs to boost monthly statistics rather than investing in meaningful, future-oriented employment. In contrast, several East Asian countries emphasize deeply rooted work ethics and personal responsibility.[1]

In this light, *evolutionary policy* must aim deeper. It must look beyond short-term efficiency metrics and instead cultivate long-term resilience, institutional learning, and social robustness—not just through governance, but through culture itself.

9.1   From Principle to Practice: Policy Applications of Evolutionary Thinking

Evolutionary economics provides a valuable framework for public policy by recognizing that both economies and policies must adapt to survive. Adaptation means responding to change, managing complexity, and sometimes making difficult decisions about what to preserve and what to let go. Not everything should be saved; not every intervention improves a system's adaptability. The key is knowing when to intervene—and when not to.

At the core of this question lies a distinction: should we support the survival of systems (like businesses or institutions) or individuals? Evolutionary thinking suggests the following balance:

- Firms and institutions should generally be allowed to fail unless they serve a strategic purpose—such as national security, essential infrastructure, or systemic stability. Even then, any intervention must be temporary, transparent, and carefully scrutinized to prevent fraud, rent-seeking, and the distortion of market signals.
- Individuals, by contrast, should be protected from the worst outcomes of systemic failure. A society should not tolerate starvation or destitution. However, support must be designed so that it does not remove incentives for productive effort. There is a risk when benefits are structured in such a way that they disincentivize job-seeking or entrepreneurial risk. This creates a dependency loop that is maladaptive—just as in nature, where overprotection can weaken an organism's fitness over time.

This logic applies across domains of policy.

---

[1] During a brief period living in Chengdu, I was struck by how the day began early—people were at work by 6:00 AM—and how energy remained high until dinner late in the evening. These were not the results of policy nudges but of *cultural norms*—expectations that one should not live at the expense of others. As I sometimes say in lectures: Europe may have 450 million people, but it often feels like only half of the adult population get up in the morning to do some serious work. Without a strong cultural ethic of contribution, societies overcompensate by layering policy on top of policy—many of which attempt to fix symptoms rather than causes.

Innovation policy, for example, should encourage variation and experimentation, not protect incumbents or prematurely pick winners. Governments have a role in supporting early-stage technologies—like green energy or digital infrastructure—but they must resist the temptation to lock in one path at the expense of others. Over-subsidizing a particular solution, like electric vehicles, may crowd out alternatives (e.g., hydrogen, public transport innovation) and reduce overall system adaptability. Subsidies, to be truly evolutionary, must enable variation, stimulate experimentation, and leave room for failure.

Crisis response benefits from adaptive thinking. Localized management, diversified supply chains, and decentralized decision-making create resilient systems. During pandemics, for example, stockpiles and modular response protocols reflect this approach.

Inequality policy presents a more delicate case. Evolutionary logic suggests designing environments where all actors can participate meaningfully in adaptation. This might include universal access to education, digital tools, or retraining programs. However, blanket transfers that create dependency or reduce the motivation to contribute productively can have unintended, system-wide effects—such as labor shortages, reduced innovation, and lower competitiveness.

This raises a critical evolutionary tension: support should reduce harm but not eliminate struggle entirely, because struggle—managed properly—is a driver of adaptation and innovation. In a society, just as in an ecosystem, selective pressure spurs change.

Case Box: Are Subsidies Evolutionary? The Transition to Electric Vehicles

The global shift toward electric vehicles (EVs) is often cited as an example of policy-led adaptation to environmental pressures. Governments have mobilized subsidies, tax breaks, and infrastructure investments to accelerate the transition. At first glance, this appears to align with evolutionary logic: external stress (climate change) prompts systemic adaptation (low-emission transport).

But the evolutionary lens complicates this picture. The central question is not whether change is occurring, but *how* that change is being steered—and with what consequences for long-term adaptability.

In evolutionary systems, variation and selection occur through distributed experimentation. Not all mutations succeed; failure is part of the process. Yet subsidies can pre-empt this selection dynamic by steering resources toward specific technologies or firms before their relative fitness is clear. This can suppress diversity and reduce space for alternatives—like hydrogen fuel, advanced public transport, or yet-to-emerge mobility models.

The risk is *premature convergence*: when policy locks in one path before others have been tested. This not only reduces variation but also can entrench inefficiencies if the favored solution turns out to be suboptimal in the long run. Evolutionary economics warns against narrowing the space of possibilities too early.

At the same time, markets do not operate in a vacuum. High initial costs, infrastructure requirements, and incumbent resistance often stall transitions that might otherwise be desirable. In this sense, policy can play a *catalytic role*—not by choosing winners, but by creating conditions for experimentation and entry. If subsidies lower the threshold for competition and encourage parallel pathways, they may enhance, rather than distort, evolutionary dynamics.

The key distinction is between *supporting adaptation* and *managing outcomes*. Evolutionary policy should avoid protecting incumbents or forcing singular solutions. Instead, it should aim to expand the opportunity space—stimulating diverse responses to shared challenges.

The EV transition thus highlights a broader tension in policy design: how to intervene without overriding the self-organizing capacities of markets and institutions. From an evolutionary standpoint, the question is not whether to intervene, but how to structure interventions to preserve variation, promote learning, and avoid rigidity.

The broader point is that intervention must be strategic, limited, and aimed at *enhancing adaptability*—not freezing systems in place. Evolution does not reward *stasis*; it rewards variation, learning, and resilience. Governments, as part of the broader system, can act as *catalysts*—but only when they avoid the trap of over-control. The challenge is not choosing between markets and states, but ensuring that policy interventions act in harmony with evolutionary dynamics—supporting failure when necessary, and designing safety nets that preserve dignity without distorting incentives.

9.2   Designing Policy Through the Three-Layer Evolutionary Framework

To understand how evolutionary policies can be designed, tested, and refined, it is useful to revisit the integrated framework presented throughout this book. The three-layer model—consisting of foundational drivers (Layer 1), methodological tools (Layer 2), and observable mechanisms (Layer 3)—offers a coherent structure for aligning policy design with the realities of complex, adaptive systems.

Layer 1: Foundational Principles. Policies should begin from an understanding of the deep drivers of human behavior—biological, cognitive, and cultural. Concepts like bounded rationality, social learning, moral heuristics, and institutional memory help explain why actors respond differently to similar incentives. These insights support the design of policies that are behaviorally realistic and culturally grounded.

Layer 2: Methodological Tools. A range of methodological instruments can be deployed to simulate and evaluate adaptive policy dynamics. These tools allow for experimentation, counterfactual testing, and real-time responsiveness:

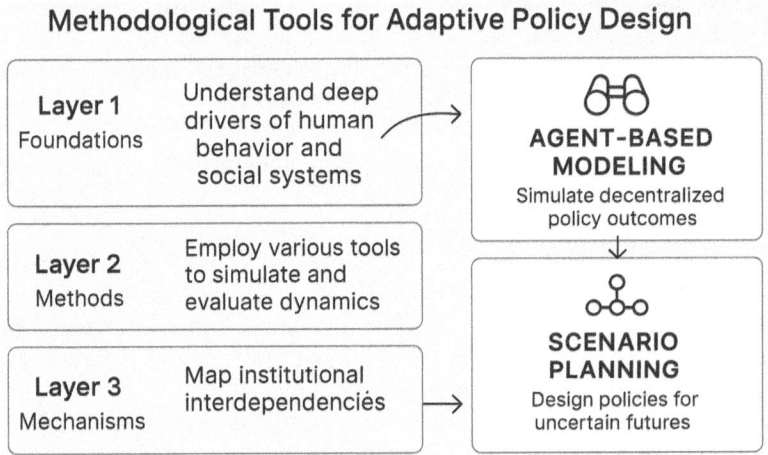

Fig. 9.1 Methodological tools for adaptive policy design

- Agent-based modeling explores how decentralized decisions produce emergent outcomes—useful for labor markets, innovation policy, or regulatory design.
- Network analysis maps interdependencies, tracing how shocks travel and where resilience can be reinforced (e.g., in supply chains or institutional linkages).
- Scenario planning provides structured ways to evaluate policy robustness under uncertain future conditions, such as geopolitical shocks or technological disruption.

Together, these methods enable policymakers to anticipate complexity rather than react to it, offering a testing ground where strategies can fail safely before being implemented (Fig. 9.1).

Layer 3: Observable Mechanisms. What ultimately matters is how these policies perform in practice. Observable mechanisms—such as adaptation, cooperation, competition, and institutional change—provide feedback on whether interventions align with evolutionary dynamics or generate unintended consequences. By linking foundational principles with practical outcomes, the three-layer model closes the loop between theory and application. So the transition runs smoothly.

- Workforce development: Prioritizing lifelong learning and modular reskilling to prepare for automation and AI transitions
- Urban planning: Enabling responsive, decentralized infrastructures that evolve with demographic and technological shifts
- Healthcare systems: Designing flexible platforms (e.g., COVID-19 vaccine strategies) with embedded feedback loops for future correction

- Financial regulation: Moving beyond rigid capital rules to dynamic risk-sensitive frameworks, such as Basel III
- Technology and trade: Coevolving governance to meet ethical, infrastructural, and geopolitical demands through agile frameworks.

By linking Layers 1, 2, and 3, evolutionary policymaking becomes a process—not a single act—characterized by feedback, experimentation, and institutional learning.

Studies like Cantner and Kösters (2012) show how R&D subsidies not only stimulate firm-level innovation but also shape the selection environment of entire sectors. Such tools can be iteratively refined using feedback loops that track spillover effects, systemic resilience, and long-term knowledge diffusion—an ideal example of policy acting across all three layers.

This layered approach reinforces a central claim of the book: public policy must be understood as a continuous process of experimentation, feedback, and co-adaptation. Rather than simply correcting market failures through top-down optimization, evolutionary policymaking emphasizes:

- Generating variation.
- Selecting through evidence.
- Coevolving institutions alongside technological, social, and environmental change.

Figure 9.2 translates these abstract strategies into concrete functions. *Variation* supports inclusive design, *selection* informs pilot testing, *adaptation* ensures iterative correction, and *coevolution* encourages stakeholder learning. *Resilience*, *path dependence*, and *emergence* add depth, guiding policy toward redundancy, historical grounding, and system-level awareness.

Methodological tools like agent-based modeling, network analysis, and scenario planning operationalize these ideas—allowing policymakers to test alternatives, anticipate system-level consequences, and adapt as feedback unfolds.

Based on this, we can outline some examples of implications across policy domains:

- *Workforce*: Promoting anticipatory training and resilient careers in light of automation
- *Cities*: Using smart infrastructure and adaptive zoning to respond to change
- *Healthcare*: Building real-time learning into public health infrastructure
- *Finance*: Embracing risk-sensitive and flexible regulatory models
- *Technology and ethics*: Aligning technological governance with evolving public values
- *Trade*: Designing resilient, decentralized global supply strategies.

Evolutionary frameworks move beyond critique. They offer a blueprint for designing flexible, resilient, and socially grounded policy systems—capable of learning and evolving in sync with society itself.

Fig. 9.2 Mapping evolutionary strategies to policy functions

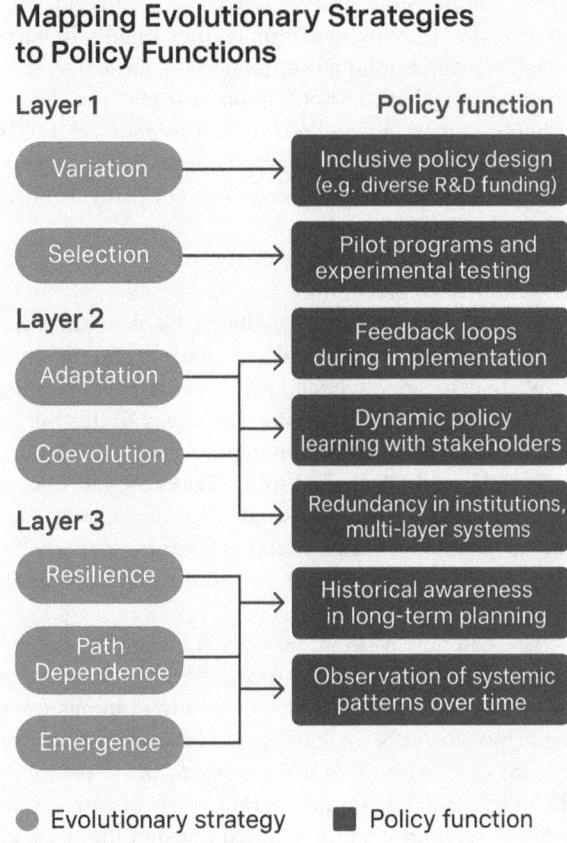

9.3 Concluding Thoughts: Toward Broader Adaptive Understanding

The adaptive strategies emphasized in evolutionary economics underscore the need for policy frameworks that are not only responsive but also structured to learn, adjust, and coevolve over time. Rather than seeking to optimize for narrow or static objectives, evolutionary thinking challenges us to design for uncertainty—building systems that are robust, redundant, and capable of continuous improvement.

One of the central contributions of this perspective is its long-term orientation. In contrast to the short-termism that characterizes much of today's economic and political decision-making—especially in Western democracies—evolutionary economics asks us to take a generational view, as Georgescu-Roegen advocated. Quarterly earnings, polling cycles, and media soundbites often dominate the agenda, crowding out more strategic considerations. Political incentives are frequently misaligned with systemic resilience, as parties enforce loyalty and punish dissent, while economic policies are too often designed to manufacture temporary job boosts or fiscal impressions without long-term institutional grounding.

By comparison, countries that have embedded long-range planning into their governance structures—China is often cited—illustrate how national strategies can be built around adaptation, technological learning, and structural transformation. These approaches are not without critique, but they demonstrate how evolutionary thinking can be embedded in *institutional DNA*. The evolutionary lens reframes strategy as a long game: one that emphasizes ecosystem shaping, not just firm-level optimization; institutional learning, not just rule enforcement; and adaptive capacity, not just efficiency.

This broader framing also reconnects us to neglected traditions of economic thought that valued complexity, temporality, and systemic resilience. Evolutionary economics revives those traditions by providing the conceptual scaffolding and methodological tools needed to study economies not as machines, but as ecosystems: diverse, adaptive, and subject to irreversible historical change.

The three-layer framework developed in this book illustrates how we can operationalize these insights—linking deep behavioral and cultural foundations (Layer 1) to flexible methodological tools (Layer 2) and to concrete policy mechanisms and outcomes (Layer 3). It shows us that the capacity for institutional renewal, technological adaptation, and social robustness cannot be achieved through top-down planning alone. It must emerge through iteration, feedback, and coevolution between state, market, and society.

This can now be more feasibly achieved than ever before. The widespread use of digital platforms and social media has trained a new generation of citizens to engage frequently with public issues—sharing opinions, reviewing services, and demanding responsiveness. In such an environment, there are increasingly few compelling reasons to resist more *participatory forms of democracy*, at least on selected political questions. Direct democratic mechanisms—once limited by logistical constraints—can now be reimagined through the twenty-first-century technology. The Swiss model of *referenda* and *citizen-led initiatives* offers a historical precedent, but digital infrastructure allows for more fluid, scalable, and frequent input.

Politicians often frame direct democracy as a threat, when in reality, it strengthens democracy itself. What it threatens is the dominance of existing party structures. When traditional political parties face pressure from new entrants or citizen-led movements, they often dismiss this as "populism"—a term that, at its core, simply refers to increased democratic participation and listening to the concerns of the population. The problem is not populism per se, but the lack of filters for informed decision-making on complex issues.

One way forward could be to combine more participatory mechanisms with *competency thresholds* for voting on strategic national matters. For instance, major questions on monetary policy (e.g., central bank independence), technological infrastructure (e.g., nuclear power, AI governance), or defense and neutrality (e.g., military alliances or data sovereignty) might require voters to first pass basic civic or issue-specific literacy modules. This would preserve democratic legitimacy while raising the level of informed engagement. It would also shift the focus from party loyalty to public reasoning—a core ideal of *democratic evolution*.

Ultimately, evolutionary economics does not promise control—it offers orientation. It provides a logic of governance suited to systems in motion: a form of policy design and strategic thinking that accepts volatility not as failure, but as the price of learning. This shift in mindset is critical if we are to build institutions capable of facing the twenty-first-century challenges—environmental degradation, technological disruption, demographic transition, and geopolitical realignment.

The next chapter builds on this foundation by exploring how insights from fields such as evolutionary biology, anthropology, systems theory, and philosophy of science can deepen our understanding of economies as evolving cultural and ecological systems. In doing so, it expands the scope of evolutionary economics and lays the groundwork for a transdisciplinary research agenda that goes beyond economics as we know it.

References

Audretsch, D. B., & Feldman, M. P. (1996). R&D spillovers and the geography of innovation and production. *American Economic Review, 86*(3), 630–640.

Boschma, R., & Frenken, K. (2006). Why is economic geography not an evolutionary science? Towards an evolutionary economic geography. *Journal of Economic Geography, 6*(3), 273–302. https://doi.org/10.1093/jeg/lbi022

Cantner, U., & Pyka, A. (2001). Classifying technology policy from an evolutionary perspective. *Research Policy, 30*(5), 759–775. https://doi.org/10.1016/S0048-7333(00)00120-5

Cantner, U., & Kösters, S. (2012). Picking the winner? Empirical evidence on the targeting of R&D subsidies to start-ups. *Small Business Economics, 39*(4), 921–936.

Dosi, G. (1988). Sources, procedures, and microeconomic effects of innovation. *Journal of Economic Literature, 26*(3), 1120–1171.

Dosi, G., & Nelson, R. R. (2010). Technical change and industrial dynamics as evolutionary processes. In B. H. Hall & N. Rosenberg (Eds.), *Handbook of the economics of innovation* (Vol. 1, pp. 51–127). Elsevier. https://doi.org/10.1016/S0169-7218(10)01003-8

Frenken, K. (2006). *Innovation, evolution, and complexity theory*. Edward Elgar Publishing.

Hodgson, G. M. (1993). *Economics and evolution: Bringing life back into economics*. Polity Press.

Hodgson, G. M. (2001). *How economics forgot history: The problem of historical specificity in social science*. Routledge.

Hodgson, G. M., & Knudsen, T. (2010). *Darwin's conjecture: The search for general principles of social and economic evolution*. University of Chicago Press.

Metcalfe, J. S. (1994). Evolutionary economics and technology policy. *The Economic Journal, 104*(425), 931–944. https://doi.org/10.2307/2234988

Nelson, R. R. (1994). The co-evolution of technology, industrial structure, and supporting institutions. *Industrial and Corporate Change, 3*(1), 47–63. https://doi.org/10.1093/icc/3.1.47

Nelson, R. R., & Winter, S. G. (1982). *An evolutionary theory of economic change*. Belknap Press of Harvard University Press.

Pyka, A., & Fagiolo, G. (2007). Agent-based modelling: A methodology for neo-Schumpeterian economics. In H. Hanusch & A. Pyka (Eds.), *Elgar companion to neo-Schumpeterian economics* (pp. 467–487). Edward Elgar.

Schumpeter, J. A. (1934). *The theory of economic development: An inquiry into profits, capital, credit, interest, and the business cycle*. Harvard University Press.

Witt, U. (1999). Bioeconomics as economics from a Darwinian perspective. *Journal of Evolutionary Economics, 9*(4), 443–463. https://doi.org/10.1007/s001910050089

Further Reading

Acemoglu, D., & Robinson, J. A. (2012). *Why nations fail: The origins of power, prosperity, and poverty.* Crown.

Metcalfe, J. S. (1995). The economic foundations of technology policy: Equilibrium and evolutionary perspectives. In P. Stoneman (Ed.), *Handbook of the economics of innovation and technological change* (pp. 409–512). Blackwell.

Perez, C. (2002). *Technological revolutions and financial capital: The dynamics of bubbles and golden ages.* Edward Elgar.

Pyka, A., & Andersen, E. S. (2013). Introduction: Long term economic development—Demand, finance, organization, policy and innovation in a Schumpeterian perspective. *Journal of Evolutionary Economics, 23*(5), 767–777. https://doi.org/10.1007/s00191-013-0327-0

Rodrik, D. (2011). *The globalization paradox: Democracy and the future of the world economy.* W. W. Norton.

Schot, J., & Steinmueller, W. E. (2018). Three frames for innovation policy: R&D, systems of innovation and transformative change. *Research Policy, 47*(9), 1554–1567. https://doi.org/10.1016/j.respol.2018.08.011

Smil, V. (2017). *Energy and civilization: A history.* MIT Press.

Stiglitz, J. E. (2012). *The price of inequality: How today's divided society endangers our future.* W. W. Norton.

Tainter, J. A. (1988). *The collapse of complex societies.* Cambridge University Press.

Zysman, J. (1994). How institutions create historically rooted trajectories of growth. *Industrial and Corporate Change, 3*(1), 243–283. https://doi.org/10.1093/icc/3.1.243

Evolutionary Economics as the Core of the Evolutionary Social Sciences

10

Abstract

This chapter argues that evolutionary economics is best understood not as a niche subfield, but as the conceptual and methodological foundation for a broader paradigm: the *Evolutionary Social Sciences*. It highlights how core research principles—adaptation, variation, selection, and feedback—are shared across disciplines such as sociology, psychology, political science, anthropology, and economics, despite surface-level differences in language and method. The chapter critiques the increasing specialization and fragmentation of the social sciences, tracing it to a misplaced imitation of the natural sciences. It warns that this trend not only undermines explanatory power but also risks making the disciplines socially irrelevant. Using the three-layer framework introduced earlier in the book, the chapter shows how shared behavioral assumptions (Layer 1), integrative methods (Layer 2), and common mechanisms of change (Layer 3) can reconnect disciplines around a scientifically grounded understanding of real-world dynamics. It calls for a reinvention of social science on evolutionary terms—interdisciplinary, empirical, and fit for the complexity of the twenty-first-century challenges.

Keywords

Evolutionary social sciences · Adaptation · Coevolution · Research methodology · Institutional change · Behavioral foundations · Interdisciplinarity · Complexity · Systems thinking · Academic silos

It is a curious inconsistency in the history of ideas that while biology has long been understood in evolutionary terms, the same logic has not been consistently applied across the social sciences. Evolutionary economics is often treated as a niche or heterodox subfield, while neighboring disciplines—sociology, psychology, anthropology, and political science—remain largely unintegrated under a common evolutionary framework.

Yet this separation is not intellectually defensible. All these fields, whether constructivist or empiricist in orientation, are fundamentally concerned with the same core question: how humans and their institutions adapt over time. The logic of studying change through variation, selection, and contextual feedback applies no less to social systems than it does to biological ones. To apply evolutionary reasoning only to economics, while excluding it from other human-centered disciplines, is not only inconsistent—it is scientifically flawed.

Despite disciplinary boundaries, the underlying structure of reasoning across the social sciences is surprisingly unified. Whether the focus is on markets, rituals, norms, cognitive biases, or political behavior, researchers seek to understand how complex systems evolve—how ideas spread, institutions stabilize or collapse, and behaviors shift in response to changing environments.

Such a shift is not about replacing existing theories, but about aligning them with a more consistent and dynamic view of human systems—one that reflects how change actually unfolds.

10.1   A Framework for the Evolutionary Social Sciences

The *Evolutionary Social Sciences* refer to a coherent yet flexible paradigm in which all human-centered disciplines—economics, sociology, anthropology, political science, psychology, and others—contribute to a unified understanding of how social systems evolve.[1] This is not a call for homogenization, nor a superficial interdisciplinarity. Rather, it reflects a deeper logic already embedded across serious work in the social sciences: the effort to understand how human behavior, institutions, and norms change over time in response to internal dynamics and external pressures.

What links these disciplines is not their subject matter, but their scientific structure. All are concerned with systems that adapt through variation, interaction, selection, and feedback. What differs are the scale, the context, and the methods of observation.

The three-layer framework developed in this book applies not only to economics but also to all social sciences because it reflects this universal logic of system evolution. Every serious social science inquiry, at its core, deals with:

---

[1] The book *Evolutionary Social Sciences: A Tour* by Hammerl, Schwarz, and Willführ (Eds) (2025) introduces the argument for a unified evolutionary framework across the social sciences. It presents an interdisciplinary overview of fields such as psychology, sociology, demography, behavioral genetics, and archaeology, illustrating how Darwinian concepts have increasingly informed research agendas and led to the development of new subfields.

- *Foundational dynamics* of human behavior—whether cognitive biases, cultural transmission, or institutional memory.
- *Methodological strategies* for tracing change over time—through modeling, historical analysis, ethnography, or statistical inference.
- *Emergent patterns*—such as the rise of new norms, innovations, belief systems, power structures, or cooperation strategies.

These three layers are not disciplinary silos; they are analytic necessities. Any attempt to study human systems that ignores behavioral foundations, methodological tools, or real-world mechanisms is incomplete.

The point of proposing an evolutionary social science is not to invent a new discipline, but to recognize the scientific consistency that already unites serious scholarship across fields. The fragmentation we see today is institutional, not intellectual. The principles of evolution—variation, selection, adaptation, and coevolution—are not the property of any one field. They are simply the most realistic way we have to understand how complex social life unfolds over time.

By adopting a shared framework rooted in these dynamics, we gain a common language that connects disciplines without reducing them. It enables collaboration without forcing uniformity. And most importantly, it brings social science closer to the kind of integrative, adaptive, and empirically grounded knowledge needed to navigate the challenges of the twenty-first century.

Box 10.1: Core Principles of the Evolutionary Social Sciences

Unlike traditional interdisciplinarity, which often blends tools without deep integration, the Evolutionary Social Sciences are unified by several core principles:

- *Change Over Time:* Societies, norms, and institutions are seen as dynamic, historically shaped systems.
- *Feedback Loops:* Social processes are governed by mutual influence across levels—individual, institutional, and systemic.
- *Coevolution*: Behavior, culture, technology, and policy develop together, not in isolation.
- *Adaptive Systems Thinking*: Human systems are nonlinear, path-dependent, and shaped by both variation and selection.
- *Pluralistic Methodology*: Multiple forms of evidence and reasoning are used—qualitative, quantitative, historical, and computational.

This approach offers a common language for researchers and practitioners to study real-world complexity, grounded in empirical processes rather than disciplinary silos.

As shown in Box 10.1, the transition in higher education exemplifies how coevolution, institutional inertia, and adaptive policy interact across layers of the model.

This approach echoes what many prominent researchers have long emphasized: that social life must be understood as part of a larger *systemic ecology*. As discussed in my earlier doctoral work, begun some three decades ago,[2] Niklas Luhmann, in *Soziale Systeme*, argued that society is composed of interdependent, self-organizing subsystems that communicate recursively and evolve over time.[3] Similarly, Kenneth Boulding—drawing from both economics and *systems theory*—stressed the need for a general evolutionary framework to understand how economic, ecological, and social systems co-develop.[4] Both thinkers recognized that the boundaries between disciplines are artificial when what we are studying—human behavior, institutions, innovation, adaptation—is deeply interconnected.

However, the major difference is that while their systems thinking is compatible with evolutionary logic, it was not firmly rooted in biological or Darwinian evolutionary theory. Luhmann's focus was on the *autopoiesis* and differentiation of communication systems, not on variation and selection mechanisms. Boulding came closer, especially in *Ecodynamics*, but often treated evolution more metaphorically than as a structured explanatory framework.[5]

By contrast, the Evolutionary Social Sciences take the evolutionary process—variation, selection, retention, and coevolution—as the central organizing mechanism for understanding social and institutional change. In this sense, they extend and deepen the systemic vision offered by Luhmann and Boulding, grounding it more directly in contemporary evolutionary theory.

10.2   The Problem of Specialization: Reclaiming Social Science Through Evolutionary Thinking

Understanding economic systems as evolutionary requires more than new models—it demands a reconsideration of how the social sciences are structured and practiced. Historically, economics, political theory, moral philosophy, and sociology were not sharply separated. Thinkers like Adam Smith and David Ricardo worked across domains, seeking to understand how human behavior, institutions, and society evolved as interconnected systems.

But over the past century, academic disciplines have fractured. As fields professionalized, they also narrowed. Economics distanced itself from ethics and politics. Sociology developed its own internal debates, separate from economics or psychology. Political science became increasingly formalized. Anthropology, psychology, and history fragmented further. The result was *hyper-specialization*: a division of labor that may have increased technical output but diminished explanatory power.

---

[2] Söilen (2004).
[3] Luhmann (1984).
[4] Boulding (1956).
[5] Boulding (1981).

This hyper-specialization often leads not to insight, but to intellectual dead ends. As Mats Alvesson and others have noted, large portions of the social sciences have become riddled with what he calls *functional stupidity*—systems where critical thinking is suppressed, originality is rare, and complexity is simplified away.[6] Researchers become experts on micro-topics so narrow that their findings have no practical application, no interdisciplinary relevance, and no value to society.

This is not just an academic problem. Public institutions are now filled with highly specialized experts whose contributions are increasingly difficult to distinguish from *bureaucratic inertia*. The phenomenon of "bullshit jobs," as explored in contemporary research, reflects a system that rewards specialization over usefulness, routine over relevance.

This fragmentation is still accelerating. Today, multiple disciplines may study the same phenomenon—such as environmental degradation—without ever engaging one another. Environmental economists, degrowth theorists, and sustainability scholars often work in parallel, each with their own journals, conferences, and methodological preferences. The result is duplication without dialogue, insight without synthesis. *Interdisciplinarity* has too often become a slogan rather than a practice, largely because genuine interdisciplinarity would require challenging the existing power structures embedded within established disciplines.

One root of this fragmentation lies in a mistaken lesson drawn from the natural sciences. In fields like rocket science or molecular biology, specialization works because the systems are closed, tightly defined, and governed by stable laws. In such domains, narrowing one's focus can lead to great breakthroughs. But social systems are open, adaptive, and historically contingent. They cannot be understood—or managed—by slicing them into ever-smaller pieces. In these systems, interconnections matter more than internal mechanics, and overspecialization becomes a liability, not an asset.

Social scientists are not rocket scientists. Treating them as such has produced a mountain of research with little impact, low relevance, and declining public trust. If the social sciences cannot reconnect to the systems they claim to study—real people, real institutions, real change—they risk marginalization, disinvestment, or outright collapse. The public will not fund disciplines it perceives as useless.

The solution is not to abandon expertise, but to reconnect it to purpose. And here, evolutionary thinking provides a way forward. Evolutionary logic—variation, selection, adaptation, and feedback—is not discipline-bound. It applies to economies, to political regimes, to cultural systems, to human cognition. It offers a framework for understanding real-world complexity without reducing it to formula.

The Evolutionary Social Sciences offer a shared foundation—not by inventing a new discipline, but by advancing a unifying logic of inquiry based on how complex systems actually evolve.[7] By focusing on the dynamics of change—rather than on disciplinary methods, academic traditions, or political leanings—we create space for real collaboration across fields. Using a common theoretical lens, like evolution-

---

[6] Alvesson and Spicer (2012).

[7] For a detailed overview and step-by-step approach, see Söilen (2025).

ary theory, encourages researchers to engage with the problem itself rather than defending turf. Without such integration, we risk fragmenting further into ever-smaller camps that—eventually, and we are nearing that point—speak only to themselves.

10.3   Bridging Disciplines for Evolutionary Integration

The previous section outlined the dangers of excessive specialization in the social sciences. As disciplines fragment, they often study the same problems—such as inequality or environmental degradation—without coordination, shared language, or mutual awareness. This weakens explanatory power and limits real-world relevance.

In contrast, evolutionary economics offers not only a theoretical framework but also a platform for integration. Its core logic—variation, selection, adaptation, and feedback—naturally aligns with concepts long developed in neighboring fields. Rather than reinventing the wheel, it invites collaboration.

Sociology, anthropology, and psychology help explain how norms, networks, and behavioral patterns shape economic behavior. History and political science offer insight into institutional change and policy dynamics. Geography and ecology draw attention to resource constraints and spatial interdependence. These perspectives don't merely supplement economic analysis—they are essential to understanding systemic evolution.

This kind of integration improves both theory and practice. It produces models that are more grounded, more adaptive, and more responsive to real-world complexity. It also shows that rigorous social science—across all disciplines—shares a commitment to empirical grounding, contextual awareness, and conceptual openness.

What follows is an overview of how different disciplines contribute to a richer evolutionary understanding of economic life:

As Table 10.1 illustrates, evolutionary economics already draws from a wide range of disciplines—but more deliberate integration is needed to turn parallel insights into cumulative progress. The challenge ahead is not to invent new bridges between disciplines, but to walk the ones already built. What's needed is a more deliberate integration—across curricula, research agendas, and public discourse—that moves beyond parallel academic workstreams toward cumulative, *cross-disciplinary learning*.

Importantly, the goal here is not to flatten all distinctions or turn everyone into a *generic social scientist*. We don't need to abandon specialization or leave our disciplinary homes. Instead, we can begin by aligning around a shared theoretical framework grounded in evolutionary principles. This common ground makes it easier to read and publish in one another's journals, attend shared conferences, and ultimately see the social sciences not as isolated silos, but as parts of a single evolving system. Such a shift doesn't dilute disciplinary rigor—it amplifies it by placing each perspective within a broader, more dynamic intellectual ecosystem.

Table 10.1 Interdisciplinary contributions to evolutionary economics

Discipline	Relevant theories/ concepts	Application to economics	Examples	References
Biology	Evolutionary theory, genetic algorithms	Models competition, adaptation, and survival in markets	Firms competing for market share resemble organisms adapting to environmental change	Nelson and Winter (1982), Metcalfe (1994)
Sociology	Social networks, institutional theory, cultural capital	Explains how norms, trust, and institutions shape economic behavior	Trade credit and access to capital often depend on embedded social networks	Granovetter (1985), Bourdieu (1986)
Anthropology	Cultural evolution, kinship theory	Highlights the role of culture and informal systems in shaping economies	Informal markets in rural or tribal communities governed by non-monetary norms	Boyd and Richerson (1985), Henrich et al. (2001)
Psychology	Behavioral economics, prospect theory	Explores decision-making under uncertainty, biases, and motivation	Investor overconfidence during bubbles; framing effects in consumer choices	Kahneman and Tversky (1979), Thaler and Sunstein (2008)
Ecology	Niche theory, coevolution	Examines how industries co-adapt within larger systems	Renewable energy firms evolving in tandem with environmental policy shifts	Boschma and Frenken (2006), Kauffman (1993)
History	Path dependency, historical institutionalism	Demonstrates how past trajectories shape current economic outcomes	Industrial legacy shaping modern labor markets and regulation	North (1990), Mokyr (1990)
Political science	Governance models, public choice theory	Investigates how power and institutions influence policy and economic structure	Lobbying efforts shaping subsidies and tax policies	Ostrom (1990), Acemoglu and Robinson (2012)
Mathematics	Game theory, chaos theory	Offers formal tools for modeling strategy and dynamic change	Predicting firm behavior via Nash equilibria in oligopolistic markets	Nash (1950), Schelling (1960)
Computer science	Agent-based modeling, machine learning	Simulates adaptive behavior and forecasts complex systems	Forecasting demand using machine learning and agent-based market models	Holland (1992), Epstein and Axtell (1996)

(continued)

Table 10.1 (continued)

Discipline	Relevant theories/ concepts	Application to economics	Examples	References
Behavioral biology	Altruism, dominance hierarchies, territoriality	Provides models of group dynamics and competition	Cooperative business alliances modeled on animal group strategies	Hamilton (1964), Dawkins (1976)
Philosophy	Ethics, epistemology	Questions the assumptions behind models and the values they encode	Debating ethical concerns of automating economic decisions via AI	Sen (1999), Rawls (1971)
Geography	Spatial economics, regional development	Studies how location and spatial proximity shape economic development	Industry clustering in tech hubs like Silicon Valley or Shenzhen	Krugman (1991), Glaeser (2011)
Law	Property rights, contract theory	Defines the legal frameworks underpinning markets and innovation	IP law driving R&D investment in biotech or software industries	Coase (1960), Williamson (1985)
Linguistics	Semiotics, discourse analysis	Analyzes how language influences economic behavior and perception	Investor sentiment shaped by tone in quarterly reports and financial news	Fairclough (1992), Lakoff (1987)
Geopolitics	Geoeconomics, economic warfare	Examines how states leverage natural resources, demographics, geography, and economic instruments to gain strategic advantage	The "SEPT golden formula" in geoeconomics emphasizes science, education, production, and trade as key drivers of national competitiveness in an interconnected global economy	Söilen (2012)

This shift is not without precedent. Foundational figures have long argued for a more dynamic and integrated economic science. Veblen (1898) famously asked why economics had not yet become an evolutionary science, pointing to the need for a historically grounded, behavioral account of economic life. Marshall, often regarded as a pillar of neoclassical thought, acknowledged the evolutionary nature of economic processes. More recently, scholars such as Nightingale and Laurent (2001), O'Hara (2001), and Hart (2013) have explored how Darwinian principles can be applied to institutional change, technological adaptation, and capitalist development. Mariolis and Tsoulfidis (2016), meanwhile, show how classical and spectral approaches can complement evolutionary models by capturing long-run structural imbalances.

Geographers have also contributed significantly. Evolutionary economic geography—a field now supported by major works such as *The Handbook of Evolutionary Economic Geography* (Boschma & Martin, 2012), *Evolutionary Economic Geography in China* (He & Zhu, 2019), and Kogler's (2017) theoretical synthesis—demonstrates how spatial patterns, institutional context, and innovation dynamics coevolve. These studies enhance economic analysis by embedding it within real-world contexts of geography, demography, and path-dependent development.

Interdisciplinary collaboration adds not only conceptual richness but also methodological precision. Biology provides analogies for competition, adaptation, and cooperation—useful for modeling markets and firm dynamics. Sociology contributes theories of trust, networks, and institutional norms. Anthropology sharpens our understanding of cultural evolution and informal systems. Psychology, particularly behavioral economics, brings deep insight into bounded rationality and cognitive bias.

Other disciplines help operationalize these insights. Political science examines power, governance, and institutional resilience. History offers longitudinal depth through concepts like institutional memory and path dependence. Mathematics and computer science contribute modeling tools—from game theory to agent-based simulation and machine learning. Ecology reminds us of the importance of co-adaptation and niche formation. Geography shows how spatial proximity shapes clustering and innovation. Philosophy interrogates the values and assumptions behind economic reasoning. Law defines the formal rules that structure markets, innovation, and institutional stability.

One final bridge has been one of my interests for more than three decades: geopolitics. As explored earlier, the tools of geoeconomics—such as resource competition, trade policy, and sanctions—are inherently evolutionary. They reflect processes of competition, imitation, learning, and institutional coevolution across nations. Frameworks like the "SEPT formula" (Science, Education, Production, Trade) demonstrate how strategic national development mirrors firm-level adaptation on a global scale.[8]

---

[8] This perspective is developed in *Geoeconomics* (Söilen, 2012), where both states and enterprises are analyzed as competitive, quasi-biological entities operating within a global evolutionary system. The central idea is that nation-states and multinational firms behave like living organisms—adapting, competing, and coevolving under systemic constraints. One practical outcome of this view is the "SEPT formula"—Science, Education, Production, Trade—a simple but powerful logic: investment in science leads to better education, which enables more advanced production, which in turn generates trade surpluses, creating new resources to reinvest in science. We describe it as the golden formula of competitiveness. The broader biological analogy has deep roots, going back to Rudolf Kjellén, the Swedish political scientist who coined the term *geopolitics* and proposed studying the state as a living organism.

10.4   Final Reflections: Evolutionary Economics as a Methodological Hub

What emerges from this chapter is not only a richer understanding of evolutionary economics but also a broader blueprint for reimagining the social sciences. The goal is not to build a new super-discipline, but to establish a shared methodological foundation—a project we and others have called the *Evolutionary Social Sciences*—rooted in empirical realism, conceptual coherence, and practical utility.

The three-layer model introduced earlier—behavioral and cultural foundations (Layer 1), methodological tools and models (Layer 2), and emergent patterns and institutions (Layer 3)—provides a scaffolding for this integration. Crucially, it does not impose a single method or ideology. Instead, it organizes inquiry around how real-world systems evolve—through variation, feedback, selection, and coadaptation. This is not just a logic for economics; it is a way to unify how we understand change across disciplines.

In practice, most social sciences already follow similar pathways. Whether in economics, sociology, anthropology, political science, or psychology, what we recognize as good science tends to rest on shared foundations: empirical grounding, transparent reasoning, and methodological consistency. There is no secret sauce unique to one field. Nor have the social sciences—despite centuries of effort—succeeded in establishing a unified theory of everything. Perhaps this is because the answer has been in front of us all along.

Yet evolutionary thinking has not always helped clarify the path forward. In fact, some of its early social applications, also mentioned earlier, did more to discredit it than advance it. Herbert Spencer's popularization of "survival of the fittest" was widely adopted as a justification for laissez-faire capitalism and social inequality—an interpretation more ideological than scientific.[9] Later, figures like Oswald Spengler used evolutionary metaphors to frame grand civilizational narratives steeped in cultural pessimism and conservative determinism.[10] These contributions, though intellectually stimulating, belong more properly to the *humanities*—and particularly to philosophy—than to the social sciences, as they lack empirical grounding and testable frameworks.

Our reluctance to embrace a *unified framework* has deep historical roots. After the irrationalities of Wilhelm II and the catastrophe of the First World War—followed by Nazi Germany's appropriation of cultural and geopolitical ideas—many scholars understandably became wary of grand explanatory theories drawn from biology. These reactions were not only reasonable; they were expected—much like the antithesis in a dialectical process. But while the pivot away from biology was emotionally and politically justified, it never produced a compelling alternative. The adoption of physics as a metaphor for social science did not deliver the theoretical clarity or predictive power many had hoped for.

---

[9] Spencer (1864).

[10] Spengler (1926).

As a result, the social sciences now find themselves in a kind of limbo—having distanced themselves from biology for the wrong reasons, while also recognizing that the physics-inspired paradigm has not worked. The result is a fragmented intellectual landscape in which each discipline largely defines its own standards—often without consistent adherence to scientific rigor, and too frequently relying on vague affiliations to "schools of thought" without the obligation to clearly explain their assumptions, internal logic, or empirical relevance. In this vacuum, ideology has too often filled the gap, with political agendas replacing the theoretical foundations that once defined academic inquiry.

As shown in some detail in this book, this is where evolutionary theory can help—not as a metaphor, but as a general framework for organizing knowledge about change. It offers structure to a field too often plagued by theoretical drift. Evolutionary theory provides clear criteria: a useful theory must explain variation, identify mechanisms of selection, and account for adaptation over time.

Still, many scholars remain wary. Part of this resistance stems from a persistent fear: that applying evolutionary logic to human behavior might reduce us to mere animals, stripping away our complexity, dignity, or moral agency. Some researchers recoil even at the biological classification of humans as animals—a resistance that says more about *romantic exceptionalism* than scientific reasoning. But acknowledging that we are part of the natural world does not diminish our humanity. On the contrary, understanding how we adapt, organize, and coevolve is precisely what allows us to build better institutions, policies, and collective futures.

Evolutionary economics, seen in this light, is not the endpoint—but a launch point. It can serve as a methodological hub, a center from which other disciplines can collaborate, share tools, and generate shared insight into how human systems function and evolve. What we need is not disciplinary purity, but intellectual courage: to move beyond legacy divisions, challenge outdated assumptions, and rebuild the social sciences on a foundation of dynamic, adaptive thinking.

In the next chapter, we explore how this interdisciplinary framework opens up new research pathways. We identify open questions, promising applications, and methodological innovations that can turn evolutionary thinking from a theoretical lens into a practical tool—for analyzing complexity and guiding strategic action in a world that refuses to sit still but keeps throwing us around.

References

Acemoglu, D., & Robinson, J. A. (2012). *Why nations fail: The origins of power, prosperity, and poverty*. Crown Business.

Alvesson, M., & Spicer, A. (2012). The stupidity paradox: The power and pitfalls of functional stupidity at work. *Journal of Management Studies, 49*(7), 1194–1216.

Boschma, R. A., & Frenken, K. (2006). Why is economic geography not an evolutionary science? Towards an evolutionary economic geography. *Journal of Economic Geography, 6*(3), 273–302.

Boschma, R., & Martin, R. (Eds.). (2012). *The handbook of evolutionary economic geography*. Edward Elgar.

Boulding, K. E. (1956). *The image: Knowledge in life and society.* University of Michigan Press.

Boulding, K. E. (1981). *Ecodynamics: A new theory of societal evolution.* Sage.

Bourdieu, P. (1986). The forms of capital. In J. Richardson (Ed.), *Handbook of theory and research for the sociology of education* (pp. 241–258). Greenwood.

Boyd, R., & Richerson, P. J. (1985). *Culture and the evolutionary process.* University of Chicago Press.

Coase, R. H. (1960). The problem of social cost. *Journal of Law and Economics, 3*(1), 1–44.

Dawkins, R. (1976). *The selfish gene.* Oxford University Press.

Epstein, J. M., & Axtell, R. (1996). *Growing artificial societies: Social science from the bottom up.* Brookings Institution Press.

Fairclough, N. (1992). *Discourse and social change.* Polity Press.

Glaeser, E. L. (2011). *Triumph of the city: How our greatest invention makes us richer, smarter, greener, healthier, and happier.* Penguin Press.

Granovetter, M. (1985). Economic action and social structure: The problem of embeddedness. *American Journal of Sociology, 91*(3), 481–510.

Hamilton, W. D. (1964). The genetical evolution of social behavior. I & II. *Journal of Theoretical Biology, 7*(1), 1–52.

Hart, N. (2013). *Alfred Marshall and modern economics: Equilibrium theory and evolutionary economics.* Palgrave Macmillan.

He, C., & Zhu, S. (2019). *Evolutionary economic geography in China.* Springer.

Henrich, J., Boyd, R., Bowles, S., Camerer, C., Fehr, E., Gintis, H., & McElreath, R. (2001). Cooperation, reciprocity and punishment in fifteen small-scale societies. *American Economic Review, 91*(2), 73–78. https://doi.org/10.1257/aer.91.2.73

Holland, J. H. (1992). *Adaptation in natural and artificial systems.* MIT Press.

Kahneman, D., & Tversky, A. (1979). Prospect theory: An analysis of decision under risk. *Econometrica, 47*(2), 263–292.

Luhmann, N. (1984). *Soziale Systeme: Grundriß einer allgemeinen Theorie.* Suhrkamp.

Kauffman, S. A. (1993). *The origins of order: Self-organization and selection in evolution.* Oxford University Press.

Kogler, D. (2017). *Evolutionary economic geography: Theoretical and empirical Progress.* Routledge.

Krugman, P. (1991). *Geography and trade.* MIT Press.

Lakoff, G. (1987). *Women, fire, and dangerous things: What categories reveal about the mind.* University of Chicago Press.

Mariolis, T., & Tsoulfidis, L. (2016). *Modern classical economics and reality: A spectral analysis of the theory of value and distribution.* Springer Japan.

Metcalfe, J. S. (1994). Evolutionary economics and technology policy. *The Economic Journal, 104*(425), 931–944. https://doi.org/10.2307/2234988

Mokyr, J. (1990). *The lever of riches: Technological creativity and economic progress.* Oxford University Press.

Nash, J. F. (1950). Equilibrium points in n-person games. *Proceedings of the National Academy of Sciences, 36*(1), 48–49.

Nelson, R. R., & Winter, S. G. (1982). *An evolutionary theory of economic change.* Harvard University Press.

Nightingale, J., & Laurent, J. (2001). *Darwinism and evolutionary economics.* Edward Elgar Publishing.

North, D. C. (1990). *Institutions, institutional change, and economic performance.* Cambridge University Press.

O'Hara, P. A. (2001). *Marx, Veblen, and contemporary institutional political economy: Principles and unstable dynamics of capitalism.* Edward Elgar Publishing.

Ostrom, E. (1990). *Governing the commons: The evolution of institutions for collective action.* Cambridge University Press.

Rawls, J. (1971). *A theory of justice.* Harvard University Press.

Schelling, T. C. (1960). *The strategy of conflict.* Harvard University Press.

Sen, A. (1999). *Development as freedom*. Knopf.

Söilen, K. S. (2004). *Wirtschaftsspionage in Verhandlungen aus informationsökonomischer und wirtschaftsethischer Perspektive: Eine interdisziplinäre Analyse* [Doctoral dissertation, Blekinge Institute of Technology]. Blekinge Institute of Technology Research Archive.

Söilen, K. S. (2012). *Geoeconomics*. Bookboon.

Söilen, K. S. (2025). *The researcher's journey: A guide to methodology and academia in social sciences* (1st ed.). Springer.

Spencer, H. (1864). *Principles of biology* (Vol. 1). Williams and Norgate.

Spengler, O. (1926). *The decline of the west* (C. F. Atkinson, Trans.). Alfred A. Knopf. (Original work published 1918).

Thaler, R. H., & Sunstein, C. R. (2008). *Nudge: Improving decisions about health, wealth, and happiness*. Yale University Press.

Williamson, O. E. (1985). *The economic institutions of capitalism: Firms, markets, relational contracting*. Free Press.

Further Reading

Cantner, U., & Graf, H. (2008). Interaction structures in local innovation systems. *Jena Economic Research Papers, 18*(2), 243–249.

Frenken, K. (2006). *Innovation, evolution, and complexity theory*. Edward Elgar Publishing.

Kjellén, R. (1924). *The state as a living organism* [Original work published 1916]. Verlag von S. Hirzel.

Luhmann, N. (1995). *Social systems* (J. Bednarz Jr. & D. Baecker, Trans.). Stanford University Press. *(Original work published 1984 as "Soziale Systeme")*

North, D. C. (2010). *Understanding the process of economic change*. Princeton University Press.

Mapping the Future of Evolutionary Economics

11

Abstract

This chapter identifies key directions for future research in evolutionary economics, focusing on how the field can respond to accelerating technological disruption, ecological pressure, and geopolitical shifts. It offers a roadmap for inquiry into long-term resource stewardship, institutional resilience, global interdependence, and the role of digital transformation—especially artificial intelligence—not only as a topic of analysis but also as a modeling tool. While some of the proposals draw on the legacy of Georgescu-Roegen and the post-growth tradition, this chapter presents that lineage as one among many viable pathways. The broader aim is to encourage a pluralistic and adaptive approach to economic inquiry, grounded in evolutionary principles such as variation, selection, coevolution, and historical contingency. Rather than forecasting the future, the chapter promotes methodological flexibility, systems thinking, and curriculum reform as tools for navigating—and shaping—an increasingly complex world.

Keywords

Evolutionary economics · Future research · Sustainability · AI · Institutional change · Digital transformation · Adaptive systems · Complexity · Foresight · Economics education

Understanding the future of economics requires more than trend-spotting or predictive modeling—it demands a shift in how we frame economic inquiry itself. This chapter explores how evolutionary economics can shape research agendas across

© The Author(s), under exclusive license to Springer Nature
Switzerland AG 2025
K. Solberg Söilen, *Applied Evolutionary Economics*, Management for
Professionals, https://doi.org/10.1007/978-3-032-03683-4_11

emerging domains—most notably *artificial intelligence (AI)*, but also *sustainability*, *institutional resilience*, and *intergenerational equity*.

At the center of this transformation is AI—the most consequential human invention since the wheel and fire. But unlike those past breakthroughs, AI is not simply a tool—it is a dynamic, learning system. It evolves, adapts, and interacts. Already, AI systems are beginning to absorb tasks once reserved for human cognition: pattern recognition, strategic modeling, and creative synthesis. Soon, a progression will unfold in stages:

- *Better AI* will continue to outperform human experts in narrow domains such as forecasting, market analysis, and pattern detection.
- *Autonomous AI agents* will begin acting independently in research, commerce, and policymaking—optimizing decisions, negotiating contracts, and generating new models.
- *AI integrated with robotics and sensor systems* will increasingly blur the line between digital intelligence and physical agency, allowing adaptive responses across both cognitive and material systems.

Each of these stages expands the reach of algorithmic decision-making—and each challenges the role of human judgment, including that of economists and social scientists. Evolutionary economics is uniquely positioned to engage with this shift, as its core concepts—feedback loops, variation, selection, and co-adaptation—mirror the very processes by which AI systems now operate and evolve.

AI will no longer just model economic behavior; it will become a participant in the system itself. This raises profound questions: What roles remain uniquely human? How do we govern and interpret hybrid human-machine systems? What becomes of theory in a world where machines simulate, test, and even refine economic models recursively?

This transformation also brings new attention to the domains least amenable to automation—care work, manual labor, and emotionally intelligent interaction—at least for now. But as AI evolves in tandem with robotics, these boundaries too will shift. Human relevance may increasingly lie not in outperforming machines at computation, but in asking meaningful questions, setting ethical boundaries, and interpreting complex outcomes in real-world contexts.

If the first chapters of this book made the case for evolutionary economics as a method and worldview, this chapter applies that logic to the near future. It argues that our primary economic and scientific challenge is not to predict the future, but to coevolve with it—deliberately, adaptively, and with attention to the institutions, ethics, and capacities that will shape what comes next.

11.1   Sustainability, Technological Change, and Networked Economies

The research pathways explored in this chapter begin with one influential—though by no means exclusive—line of thought: the work of *Nicholas Georgescu-Roegen*. His contribution is not presented here as canonical, but as illustrative. He was one of the first economists to link thermodynamics with economic processes, reframing economics not as the pursuit of perpetual growth, but as the science of survival—focused on long-term resilience, energy constraints, and intergenerational equity. His legacy helps clarify a broader truth: evolutionary economics is best understood not as a fixed model, but as an open framework for studying how real-world systems adapt under pressure.

This spirit of openness is especially important in a time of accelerating transformation. Technological disruption, ecological degradation, geopolitical fragmentation, and institutional fragility are not isolated problems. They are interlinked stressors that demand adaptive, forward-looking responses. Evolutionary economics is uniquely suited to this task because it focuses not on equilibrium or optimization, but on processes: on how systems learn, adjust, fail, and recover over time.

One practical outgrowth of this perspective is *post-growth thinking*. Unlike degrowth, which often emphasizes contraction, or traditional growth models that prioritize expansion at all costs, *post-growth economics* seeks dynamic balance. It envisions a system where prosperity, innovation, and improved well-being are decoupled from irreversible environmental harm. The goal is not to halt development, but to shift its foundations—toward sustainability, equity, and institutional resilience.

A real-world example of this logic is Norway's sovereign wealth fund, designed not just to manage resource revenues in the present, but to serve future generations. This kind of long-term planning reflects the evolutionary emphasis on institutions that adapt across time horizons. Yet most political and financial systems still incentivize short-termism: financial markets reward quarterly returns; democratic cycles pressure parties to promise immediate gains. Neither structure aligns well with the complex, delayed-feedback problems now facing humanity—from climate instability to AI governance.

This is where evolutionary economics offers a vital corrective. It encourages researchers to study how institutions, technologies, and value systems coevolve—not only descriptively, but normatively. The goal is to understand which mechanisms foster long-term adaptability and resilience and how we might design better tools, structures, and norms to guide economic and political evolution.

Yet our political and economic institutions remain poorly suited to these challenges. Financial markets reward short-term performance; political parties chase electoral cycles. Conservative platforms often focus on preserving accumulated wealth, while progressive ones emphasize redistribution—both reactive positions with limited foresight. Structural transformation rarely fits the incentive structures of modern democracies, which tend to be driven more by *media cycles* and personal political ambitions than by strategic horizons.

This is where evolutionary economics provides crucial leverage. It shifts attention from optimizing static models to understanding how institutions, technologies, and values coevolve over time. Future research should focus on the adaptive mechanisms that shape our systems—not only in theory, but in actionable practice:

1. *Long-Term Resource Allocation and Intergenerational Equity*: Building on Georgescu-Roegen's legacy, new models are needed to support institutional frameworks that prioritize the well-being of future generations. This includes *sovereign wealth funds*, *ecological accounting methods*, and the enforcement of planetary boundaries. Key research questions include the following: How do societies update their value systems over time? What kinds of narratives and mechanisms support long-term orientation?
2. *Environmental Sustainability and Systemic Adaptation*: The rise of *renewable technologies*, *circular economies*, and *biodiversity restoration* presents a real-time laboratory for evolutionary change. How do technological ecosystems evolve in response to environmental limits? What policies best accelerate this transition without imposing undue social costs?
3. *Strategic Governance and Institutional Innovation*: Evolutionary approaches can help us reimagine governance itself—not as a static set of rules, but as an evolving system. Research could focus on institutional innovations such as *citizen assemblies*, *long-term planning commissions*, *adaptive regulation*, or constitutionally mandated sustainability targets.
4. *Digital Transformation and Socioeconomic Restructuring*: The digital economy is not only reshaping work and consumption; it is altering the very structure of markets, knowledge, and coordination. Evolutionary economics can examine how digital infrastructures and AI interact with sustainability goals, inequality dynamics, and cultural adaptation.
5. *Global Interdependence Under Stress*: The COVID-19 pandemic, climate volatility, and geopolitical fragmentation have exposed the fragility of global interdependence. How do complex trade and financial systems adapt under pressure? What forms of regionalism, redundancy, or strategic decoupling are likely to emerge? What configurations support resilience without retreating into protectionism?

Taken together, these themes sketch a pragmatic research agenda—one that goes beyond critique and offers tools for shaping the future in more adaptive, inclusive, and sustainable ways. The goal is not to forecast a fixed outcome but to improve our capacity for *anticipatory governance*: to navigate uncertainty with wisdom, foresight, and institutional flexibility.

Studies of digital economies and platform dynamics can build on the work of Parker et al. (2016) and Brynjolfsson and McAfee (2014), who explore network effects, data-driven competition, and technological disruption. In the context of global trade and supply chain resilience, foundational insights from Ghemawat (2001) and Baldwin (2016) highlight how globalization adapts under shifting strategic and geopolitical conditions.

Environmental sustainability research has been significantly shaped by Rockström et al. (2009) on planetary boundaries, Mont and Plepys (2008) on sustainable consumption, and Stern (2006), whose influential work outlines the long-term economic risks of climate change. Innovation ecosystems and industrial clustering are addressed by Porter (1990) and Audretsch and Feldman (1996), who emphasize the coevolution of firms, regions, and institutions in driving innovation. Meanwhile, cultural evolution in economic behavior is enriched by Boyd and Richerson (1985) and Hofstede (2001), whose work underscores how norms and belief systems guide decision-making and institutional development.

Despite their diversity, these research efforts share a common thread—explicitly or implicitly—anchored in the evolutionary perspective pioneered by Georgescu-Roegen: economics as the science of adaptation, stewardship, and long-term planning. But this is only one trajectory among many. Evolutionary economics does not demand consensus or ideological commitment. Its value lies in its openness to complexity, its pluralism in method and scope, and its capacity to accommodate perspectives that emphasize not only progress but also breakdown, conflict, emergence, and experimentation.

Many of the challenges outlined in this section are not new, and substantial progress has already been made across domains—from green technology and digital markets to institutional resilience and behavioral economics. A crucial next step is to systematically gather, assess, and connect this growing body of work. What has been explored should be curated, categorized, and made accessible—not only to prevent duplication but also to help future researchers identify promising directions and overlooked questions.

One practical proposal would be to develop a structured bibliometric map or dynamic database of evolutionary economic research, organized along the dimensions outlined in this book: foundational principles, theoretical orientation, empirical scope, historical context, and methodological strategy. AI tools could play a vital role in this task, offering scalable ways to scan, synthesize, and visualize the state of the field. Such an effort would not only clarify what is known—it would sharpen our collective sense of what still needs to be discovered.

It is also important to stress that the methodologies outlined in Table 11.1 are illustrative, not prescriptive. Depending on the question at hand, many other approaches—such as grounded theory, ethnography, participatory research, or narrative methods—may be more appropriate. When studying open, adaptive systems, methodological flexibility is not just a virtue but a necessity.

The real strength of evolutionary thinking lies in its ability to explain how systems change, learn, and reorganize over time. In digital economies, platforms evolve in response to user behavior and market forces. In trade and finance, supply networks adapt to geopolitical shocks and environmental disruptions. Cultural norms shift rapidly in the face of new challenges, altering consumer behavior, labor practices, and institutional legitimacy. Innovation ecosystems like Silicon Valley thrive not just because of individual talent, but because they allow firms, regulators, and knowledge flows to co-adapt in real time.

Table 11.1 Future research directions in evolutionary economics

Main pathway	Research area	Proposed study focus	Key questions	Potential methodologies	Expected contributions
Long-term resource allocation and intergenerational equity	Intergenerational institutions	Study institutional mechanisms for preserving value across generations	How can societies build institutions that prioritize future generations?	Institutional analysis, comparative policy studies	Blueprints for long-term institutional design
	Ecological accounting models	Develop accounting methods incorporating ecological boundaries	How do we measure economic activity without encouraging environmental harm?	Systems modeling, sustainability metrics	Better integration of ecology into economic planning
	Cultural evolution and economy	Examine how values, norms, and beliefs shape economic behavior	How do cultural dynamics influence long-term economic change?	Ethnography, comparative cultural analysis	Deeper integration of cultural context in economic development strategies
	Behavioral evolution in markets	Investigate how consumer and firm behavior evolves under uncertainty	How do heuristics and learning shape market patterns?	Behavioral experiments, agent-based simulations	Better understanding of bounded rationality and adaptive market dynamics
Environmental sustainability and systemic adaptation	Green technology evolution	Track diffusion and performance of green technologies under selection pressure	What enables green technologies to scale and stabilize in markets?	Case studies, innovation diffusion models	Insights into market mechanisms that support sustainability
	Circular economic models	Examine how circular economic structures evolve in diverse settings	What drives the success or failure of circular economic initiatives?	Comparative institutional analysis, coevolutionary modeling	Design principles for regenerative economic systems
	Environmental sustainability	Explore economic adaptation to ecological constraints and limits	How can industries transition toward sustainable models?	Lifecycle analysis, coevolutionary modeling	Tools for integrating environmental limits into economic planning
	Innovation ecosystems	Understand how innovation hubs and clusters evolve	What drives the success or decline of innovation ecosystems?	Case studies, longitudinal cluster analysis	Identification of evolutionary drivers behind innovation sustainability

Strategic governance and institutional evolution	*Institutional innovation for sustainability*	Explore new forms of governance that prioritize long-term goods	How can political systems be redesigned for long-term planning?	Experimental governance trials, historical institutionalism	Policy tools for managing collective long-term interests
	Strategic foresight in democratic systems	Analyze systemic barriers to long-range policy planning in democracies	What governance models balance responsiveness with strategic foresight?	Scenario planning, political economy analysis	Frameworks for sustainable democratic reform
	Economic resilience	Analyze how systems adapt to crises and uncertainty	What makes economic systems robust against shocks?	Scenario planning, historical case analysis	Policy tools for managing disruption and improving systemic adaptability
	Global inequality dynamics	Explore long-run drivers of inequality within and across nations	What evolutionary forces sustain or reduce inequality?	Longitudinal analysis, multilevel modeling	Insights for designing redistributive policies grounded in systemic dynamics
Digital transformation and socioeconomic restructuring	*Platform economies and adaptive competition*	Model competitive dynamics of digital platforms over time	How do platform dynamics reflect evolutionary competition principles?	Agent-based modeling, network simulation	Models of competition and survival in digital economies
	Digital work, AI, and labor evolution	Understand labor market transitions under automation and AI integration	What adaptive strategies can prepare labor markets for digital disruption?	Longitudinal labor studies, machine learning	Guidance for workforce adaptation and education policy
	Digital economies	Apply evolutionary theory to digital platform competition and network effects	How do digital platforms evolve under competitive pressure?	Agent-based modeling, network analysis	Insights into platform dominance and digital market adaptation
	Blockchain and decentralization	Analyze how decentralized technologies reshape economic systems	How do blockchain ecosystems evolve under pressure and growth?	Network analysis, evolutionary simulations	Frameworks for understanding decentralized adaptation and coordination

(continued)

Table 11.1 (continued)

Main pathway	Research area	Proposed study focus	Key questions	Potential methodologies	Expected contributions
Global interdependence under stress	*Trade networks and systemic resilience*	Analyze how global supply chains adapt to disruptions and geopolitical shifts	What factors improve the resilience of trade networks in a multipolar world?	Evolutionary game theory; trade policy analysis	Improved tools for global economic planning under uncertainty
	Geoeconomics and climate-linked trade strategy	Investigate the interaction between trade policy, climate action, and national strategies	How does climate policy reshape strategic trade relations?	Mixed-method analysis, strategic modeling	New strategies for sustainable and competitive national trade policy
	Global trade networks	Study the adaptive dynamics of international trade systems	How do trade alliances and supply chains evolve over time?	Evolutionary game theory, comparative analysis	Improved resilience frameworks for evolving trade regimes
	Urban evolution	Study how cities adapt to demographic and technological transformations	How do urban systems evolve alongside economic needs?	Spatial modeling, evolutionary urban studies	Guidance for adaptive and sustainable urban development

We observe similar dynamics in economic resilience. National responses to the 2008 financial crisis or the COVID-19 pandemic reveal how institutions learn under pressure. Trends like the rise of plant-based diets or digital currencies illustrate how cultural and behavioral evolution continues to reshape markets. The emergence of blockchain, decentralized finance, and platform capitalism signals a broader transition away from centralized control—developments that evolutionary models are particularly well-equipped to interpret.

In the spirit of Georgescu-Roegen—though he never coined the terms—economics needs a new *Geist* that reflects the shifting *Weltanschauung* of our time.[1] As the intellectual center of gravity moves beyond Western traditions and the marginalist paradigm, the need for new, globally relevant scientific frameworks becomes urgent. Evolutionary theory, with its empirical depth and openness to complexity, offers exactly that: not a fixed answer, but a dynamic way of asking the right questions. And for an era defined by uncertainty, that may be its most essential contribution.

11.2 Concluding Reflections on Evolution and Economic Understanding

This book has advanced a simple but demanding proposition: economics must evolve into a science of evolution—grounded not in mechanical metaphors, but in models that reflect how real systems behave. Economic life is not static or linear. It is shaped by feedback, inertia, breakthrough, and breakdown. These are not anomalies. They are the rule. And they demand a scientific approach capable of tracking adaptation in all its forms—technological, institutional, cultural, and ecological.

The themes explored across this volume—from green innovation and digital platform dynamics to long-term governance and institutional resilience—illustrate just how broad the implications of this shift can be. But they also show something subtler: the value of reframing our questions. Evolutionary thinking changes how we approach complexity. Instead of looking for optimal states, it asks how systems learn, respond, and reorganize. It rewards researchers who study change, not control.

This is what makes evolutionary economics especially relevant now. As global institutions fragment, as the boundaries between markets and machines blur, and as cultural norms shift faster than laws can follow, we need tools that are empirical, integrative, and resilient. We also need a mindset that welcomes unpredictability—not as failure, but as a defining feature of the systems we live in.

This shift has geopolitical and geoeconomic consequences as well. The intellectual assumptions that dominated post-war Western economics—rational actors,

---

[1] The term *Weltanschauung* (worldview) was introduced by Immanuel Kant in the late eighteenth century and later developed in depth by Wilhelm Dilthey, who gave it its modern cultural and epistemological meaning. The concept of *Geist* (spirit or collective mind) was central to G.W.F. Hegel's early nineteenth-century philosophy, particularly in his dialectical account of societal development. See Kant (1790), *Kritik der Urteilskraft*; Hegel (1807), *Phänomenologie des Geistes*; and Dilthey (1883), *Einleitung in die Geisteswissenschaften*.

marginal equilibrium, frictionless systems—reflected a moment in history that is now passing. The rise of other economic centers, particularly in Asia, is also a shift in epistemology. The very questions economics is being asked to answer are changing. Evolutionary economics offers a vocabulary for this transition—one rooted in coevolution, historical specificity, and systems-level insight.

That insight must now extend into how we train economists. As argued throughout this book, no meaningful transformation in research will take hold without a parallel shift in education. Students should be taught not just how systems work, but how they evolve—and how to intervene with humility, realism, and strategic foresight. This requires more than adding topics to syllabi. It calls for rethinking the very purpose of economic education: not to produce formulaic answers, but to cultivate adaptive intelligence.

What matters, in the end, is not which school of thought prevails, but whether economics as a discipline can reestablish its relevance. That means showing a capacity not just to describe the world, but to help shape it—toward resilience, equity, and sustainability. Evolutionary economics, if embraced in full, offers the tools for that task. But the future of the field will depend on whether those tools are put to use.

In the next chapter, we turn directly to education. If change is inevitable, how do we prepare students not only to understand it—but to lead it?

References

Audretsch, D. B., & Feldman, M. P. (1996). Innovative clusters and the industry life cycle. *Review of Industrial Organization, 11*(2), 253–273.

Baldwin, R. (2016). *The great convergence: Information technology and the new globalization.* Harvard University Press.

Boyd, R., & Richerson, P. J. (1985). *Culture and the evolutionary process.* University of Chicago Press.

Brynjolfsson, E., & McAfee, A. (2014). *The second machine age: Work, progress, and prosperity in a time of brilliant technologies.* W.W. Norton & Company.

Dilthey, W. (1883). *Einleitung in die Geisteswissenschaften* [Introduction to the human sciences]. Teubner.

Ghemawat, P. (2001). Distance still matters: The hard reality of global expansion. *Harvard Business Review, 79*(8), 137–147.

Hegel, G. W. F. (1807). *Phänomenologie des Geistes* [Phenomenology of spirit]. Joseph Anton Goebhardt.

Hofstede, G. (2001). *Culture's consequences: Comparing values, behaviors, institutions and organizations across nations* (2nd ed.). Sage.

Kant, I. (1790). *Kritik der Urteilskraft* [Critique of judgment]. Lagarde.

Mont, O., & Plepys, A. (2008). Sustainable consumption progress: Should we be proud or alarmed? *Journal of Cleaner Production, 16*(4), 531–537.

Parker, G. G., Van Alstyne, M. W., & Choudary, S. P. (2016). *Platform revolution: How networked markets are transforming the economy—and how to make them work for you.* W. W. Norton & Company.

Porter, M. E. (1990). *The competitive advantage of nations.* Free Press.

Rockström, J., Steffen, W., Noone, K., et al. (2009). A safe operating space for humanity. *Nature, 461*(7263), 472–475.

Stern, N. (2006). *The Stern review: The economics of climate change.* HM Treasury.

Further Reading

Brynjolfsson, E., Rock, D., & Syverson, C. (2017). *Artificial intelligence and the modern productivity paradox*. NBER Working Paper No. 24001.

Florida, R. (2005). *The flight of the creative class: The new global competition for talent*. Harper Business.

Glaeser, E. L. (2011). *Triumph of the city: How our greatest invention makes us richer, smarter, greener, healthier, and happier*. Penguin Books.

Hanushek, E. A., & Woessmann, L. (2008). The role of cognitive skills in economic development. *Journal of Economic Literature, 46*(3), 607–668.

Holling, C. S. (1973). Resilience and stability of ecological systems. *Annual Review of Ecology and Systematics, 4*(1), 1–23.

Kahneman, D., & Tversky, A. (1979). Prospect theory: An analysis of decision under risk. *Econometrica, 47*(2), 263–292.

Nakamoto, S. (2008). *Bitcoin: A peer-to-peer electronic cash system*. Retrieved from https://bitcoin.org/bitcoin.pdf

Piketty, T. (2014). *Capital in the twenty-first century*. Harvard University Press.

Silver, D., Huang, A., Maddison, C. J., et al. (2016). Mastering the game of go with deep neural networks and tree search. *Nature, 529*(7587), 484–489.

Söilen, K. S. (2025). *The researcher's journey: A guide to methodology and academia in social sciences* (1st ed.). Springer Cham.

Tapscott, D., & Tapscott, A. (2016). *Blockchain revolution: How the technology behind bitcoin is changing money, business, and the world*. Penguin Books.

Taleb, N. N. (2012). *Antifragile: Things that gain from disorder*. Random House.

Reforming Economics Education: Building for Relevance and Complexity

12

Abstract

This chapter proposes concrete reforms to modernize economics education through the lens of evolutionary economics. Arguing that current curricula remain too focused on static models, it outlines how principles like adaptation, selection, and complexity can be embedded at all levels of instruction. It provides a roadmap for integrating interdisciplinary thinking, dynamic modeling tools, and real-world case studies into economics and business programs. These reforms aim not only to improve relevance but also to foster a new generation of economists equipped to address systemic challenges in a rapidly changing world.

Keywords

Economics education · Curriculum reform · Evolutionary theory · Interdisciplinary learning · Adaptive systems · Real-world relevance · Dynamic modeling · Future skills

Anyone following international assessments of educational performance—from PISA to university benchmarking studies—will have noticed a striking trend: several Asian countries have not only caught up with the West but also, in many cases, clearly surpassed it. This reversal is particularly notable given that the West not only shaped much of the modern university system but also originated the dominant strands of mainstream economics. Today, however, it is Asian students—trained in more rigorous, competitive systems—who increasingly outperform their Western peers across a range of critical competencies.

This is not a trend easily explained away, though many attempt to. A common response is to assert that Western societies offer more "balanced" upbringings, deeper cultural traditions, or superior values. And there may be some truth to that.

© The Author(s), under exclusive license to Springer Nature
Switzerland AG 2025
K. Solberg Söilen, *Applied Evolutionary Economics*, Management for
Professionals, https://doi.org/10.1007/978-3-032-03683-4_12

Life is not reducible to test scores. But if we truly believe these values are our competitive edge, we must ask the uncomfortable question: what exactly are those values doing for us? If they are not producing sharper minds, stronger institutions, or more innovative systems, then their practical significance must be reconsidered.

For younger generations to thrive in an increasingly complex and contested world, they will need more than inherited ideals. They will need better tools, broader perspectives, and the intellectual flexibility to adapt to rapid change. Any meaningful understanding of progress—economic, social, or scientific—depends on this.

Economics education is part of this broader reckoning. A growing number of employers now question the real-world usefulness of traditional business school curricula. Many report little return from hiring graduates steeped in conventional economic models. Were it not for continued demand from governments and public institutions, the professional standing of economics degrees might be significantly weaker. This does not mean the discipline lacks value—but it does mean we are overdue for serious reflection about what, and how, we teach.

Calls to reform economics education have grown louder in recent years, especially in the wake of financial crises, climate emergencies, and technological disruptions. Yet much of this debate remains superficial—focused more on appearances than substance. This chapter aims to move beyond critique and propose actionable reforms grounded in evolutionary thinking.

Drawing from the framework developed throughout this book, we advocate for a modernization of economics education—from undergraduate instruction to doctoral training—that reflects how real economies function: as adaptive, historical, and complex systems. The goal is not to make education more fashionable or marketable, but more relevant. In a world defined by uncertainty, systemic risk, and rapid transformation, relevance is no longer a luxury—it is a necessity.

Despite its growing appeal, evolutionary economics remains a marginal field.[1] A glance at Google Scholar citations shows a sharp drop from the most-cited scholars in this area, indicating both concentration and underdevelopment. Few graduate programs offer formal courses in the subject, and when heterodox approaches are included, they are often grouped together as brief survey modules rather than integrated into the core of the curriculum.

This final chapter argues for a structural shift. Evolutionary thinking should not be treated as a curiosity or elective, but as a foundation for training the twenty-first-century economists. Concepts such as adaptation, feedback, coevolution, and selection are not just metaphors. They have real analytical power and practical significance. Embedding these ideas in economics education would strengthen interdisciplinary integration—drawing from biology, anthropology, psychology, and systems science—and would better prepare students to understand and influence the dynamic systems they will encounter.

---

[1] Despite its promise, evolutionary economics remains marginal. Citation counts for its top scholars drop steeply—from around 88,000 to just over 13,000—highlighting its concentrated influence. Formal courses are rare in graduate programs, and heterodox approaches are typically covered only briefly, if at all.

In the few pages that remain, we outline concrete proposals to embed evolutionary thinking into economics education at three levels: pedagogical design, curriculum content, and institutional structure. The aim is not to replace existing models, but to enrich them—restoring realism, rigor, and relevance to a field that risks falling behind the world it seeks to explain.

12.1   Curriculum Shift: Embedding Evolutionary Thinking in Economics Education

To make economics meaningful in the twenty-first century, we must reform not only *what* we teach but also *how* we teach it—and most importantly, the assumptions we ask students to accept from the outset. A curriculum shaped by evolutionary economics moves beyond static abstraction. It equips students to understand economies as they truly are: dynamic, path-dependent, and continuously adapting systems embedded in history, institutions, and culture.

When I browse the old textbooks in my economics library—more than 1500 classic volumes on business and economics—I'm struck by what we've lost. A hundred years ago, teaching often focused on practical, concrete knowledge: the actual goods people traded, the logic of specific markets, and the institutional machinery behind them. Much of that has since been replaced by layers of abstract theory—often vague, redundant, and couched in language that obscures more than it reveals. If you studied business (or *handelsfag*) in Copenhagen a century ago, you likely left with a working understanding of how the stock exchange (*børsen*) functioned in practice. Today, I doubt most students could say the same.

This isn't a nostalgic complaint. It's a diagnosis of a growing mismatch between textbook economics and lived economic experience. From financial crises to environmental degradation, from AI-driven labor markets to geopolitical shifts, students increasingly sense that current models don't prepare them to understand—let alone influence—the complex systems shaping the future. Evolutionary economics offers a remedy. It trains economists to think historically, systemically, and creatively about change—and to treat real-world complexity not as a problem to be simplified away, but as a core feature of the systems they aim to understand.

But integrating this approach into curricula requires more than adding a few new readings or side lectures. It demands a deliberate redesign of educational goals. The aim is not merely to transmit knowledge, but to cultivate a new kind of economist—someone who is observant rather than doctrinaire, curious rather than compliant, adaptive rather than abstract. An economist who not only understands models, but also knows their way around the world's markets and institutions—who can think with theory, but who, above all, thinks practically.

Why Evolutionary Thinking in Education?
Because the economy does not stand still. Because reality is not in equilibrium. Because the problems our societies face cannot be solved by elegant formulas alone. Evolutionary thinking prepares students for a world in flux by offering five key shifts in perspective:

- *From Optimization to Adaptation*: Real economies are not about achieving ideal states but about adjusting to shifting conditions. Students should be trained to ask: *What works, and for whom, in a given context—and how might that change?*
- *From Isolation to Coevolution*: Economics must be taught as a deeply interconnected field. Technologies evolve, cultures shift, institutions adapt—and so do economic behaviors.
- *From Static Models to Dynamic Systems*: Educating through simplified diagrams of equilibrium leaves students unprepared for feedback effects, network dynamics, and emergence. We need tools that match the system's complexity.
- *From Acausal Theory to Historical Explanation*: Events have momentum. Policies have path dependencies. A good economist understands how yesterday's decisions constrain today's possibilities.
- *From Method Monoculture to Method Pluralism*: Students should learn to think with multiple tools—simulation, case study, qualitative interviews, and data analytics—based on what a problem requires, not what a discipline prescribes.

By embedding these principles, we equip students not only to interpret economic change but also to participate in shaping it.

But cultivating a new kind of economist also requires more than classroom reform—it demands a different attitude toward the world. Business students cannot succeed globally if they are not taught to be curious, mobile, and resilient. If they are unwilling to travel, to live uncomfortably for a time, or to step outside familiar *cultural bubbles*, they will struggle in international business.

Many Western companies today report a surprising difficulty in finding economics or business graduates willing to spend even a few years working in Africa or Southeast Asia. Why? Not because these students lack talent, but because they have internalized a *lifestyle expectation*—comfort, predictability, convenience—that was never truly their own idea. It is something they were taught to want. What we must revive in education is a kind of *missionary spirit*—an adventurous outlook that views discomfort not as a cost, but as a price worth paying for learning and impact. China has already succeeded in embedding this mindset in its business class. That is why, despite cultural affinities with Europe or North America, many African and Latin American economies are now increasingly tied to China through infrastructure, trade, and investment. The West may still win hearts, but it is increasingly losing contracts (Table 12.1).

While these reforms offer a strategic roadmap, their success depends on everyday decisions made by individual educators and departments.

Some institutions are already moving in this direction, too. For example, University College London (UCL) has developed interdisciplinary economics programs that integrate political science, data analysis, and behavioral theory. Maastricht University uses problem-based learning to train students in complex

Table 12.1 Educational reforms to integrate evolutionary theory into economics curricula

Category	Proposed reform	Explanation	Example of application	Potential impact
Core curriculum	Introduce "evolutionary economics" as a foundational course	Establishes the field as central to understanding economic change and dynamics	A full course on adaptation, selection, and coevolution applied to economic systems	Builds strong theoretical grounding for future economists
Cross-disciplinary modules	Integrate biology, sociology, and anthropology modules	Enriches perspectives using cultural, social, and biological evolution	Guest lectures on kinship economics or cultural norms and markets	Promotes interdisciplinary thinking and systems-level insight
Case study analysis	Use evolutionary case studies in teaching	Connects theory to real-world economic evolution	Analysis of the digital shift in retail or Silicon Valley's growth path	Encourages applied understanding and critical thinking
Modeling and simulation	Teach tools like evolutionary game theory and ABM	Introduces students to complex system dynamics and adaptive modeling	Labs using NetLogo or Python to model platform competition	Develops cutting-edge analytical skills
Policy implications	Add modules on adaptive policymaking	Shows how evolutionary theory guides responsive economic policy	Policy debates on carbon pricing or inequality mitigation via adaptive institutions	Trains students for real-world, dynamic policymaking
Mixed-method training	Combine qualitative and quantitative research approaches	Encourages integrated analysis of complex economic phenomena	Workshops blending archival research with simulation outputs	Prepares students for interdisciplinary research and publication

(continued)

Table 12.1 (continued)

Category	Proposed reform	Explanation	Example of application	Potential impact
Capstone projects	Let students apply evolutionary theory in final projects	Encourages innovation in addressing real economic problems	Projects on gig economy evolution, trade network adaptation, or firm competition	Fosters creativity and applied learning
Collaborative learning	Promote group and interdisciplinary teamwork	Encourages learning from varied perspectives	Teams with economics, biology, and sociology students tackling urban adaptation	Builds teamwork, communication, and integrative skills
Digital economy focus	Add content on tech transformation and evolutionary impact	Prepares students for fast-changing economic landscapes	Modules on blockchain, platform economies, and AI markets	Aligns curricula with digital-age realities
Lifelong learning	Develop ongoing learning pathways	Emphasizes continual skill renewal in evolving systems	Micro-credentials in adaptive economics via online platforms	Ensures long-term relevance of graduates in the labor market
Global perspective	Compare economic evolution across cultures and geographies	Highlights how context shapes economic adaptation	Courses on African, Asian, and European models of economic resilience	Expands global literacy and cross-cultural competence
Ethical considerations	Embed ethics of adaptation and systemic change	Encourages reflection on consequences of economic decisions	Debates on AI-driven markets, environmental trade-offs, or inequality amplification	Instills responsibility and moral grounding in future leaders
Integration of technology	Use real-time simulation and AI tools in instruction	Enhances learning through interactive and practical applications	Evolutionary simulations of pandemic-related supply chain disruption	Engages students with hands-on, scenario-based learning
Program structure reform	Establish joint interdisciplinary PhD and master's programs	Breaks down academic silos by training students across social sciences from the outset	PhD program co-hosted by departments of economics, sociology, and anthropology	Promotes deep, lasting interdisciplinary collaboration and systemic thinking

systems thinking, encouraging practical engagement from the start. In Japan, the Japan Association for Evolutionary Economics (JAFEE) continues to support research and conferences that bring together evolutionary economists from across disciplines. These cases demonstrate that the kind of curricular innovation proposed here is not only feasible—it is already underway.

12.2   Implementation Challenges and Faculty-Level Change

Transforming economics education won't begin with policy declarations or strategic frameworks. It will begin—quietly and incrementally—in classrooms. It starts when faculty revise a syllabus, introduce a case study, or allow students to run simulations based on real-world uncertainty. These small shifts are the real levers of reform. If enough educators take those risks, the system can change. But that change depends on recognizing a hard truth: our methods—and our disciplinary boundaries—are no longer adequate for the complexity of the world we are trying to understand.

The challenge is not simply to replace one theory with another. It is to redefine what we are trying to teach. Economics and business students must develop systems thinking, historical awareness, adaptability, and the ability to work across disciplines. A foundational course in evolutionary economics could introduce these skills, rooted in the core principles of variation, selection, coevolution, and adaptive fit.

These concepts must be paired with more applied and *experiential learning*. *Case-based learning* should become a default—not a supplement. Students should analyze platform economies, post-tariff supply chains, and green industrial transitions not just through lectures, but through simulations, fieldwork, and interactive modeling. Tools like agent-based modeling and evolutionary game theory offer intuitive access to feedback loops and nonlinear dynamics and should be introduced early and often—not reserved for methodological specialists.

Equally essential is reform in research training. *Mixed-method designs*—combining qualitative insight with computational tools—should become standard, helping students learn how to study complex adaptive systems in real-world settings. *Capstone projects* should be grounded in current business or social problems and preferably structured to cut across disciplinary boundaries.

One of the most powerful learning experiences we can offer students is the challenge of *hands-on entrepreneurship*. Every business student should be encouraged—or even required—to start a small company during their education. Not as a hypothetical classroom exercise, but as a live project with real stakes. Whether it's a group initiative, a solo venture, or a locally rooted service, the goal is not commercial success but practical immersion. Accounting, marketing, finance, and strategy come alive when they are applied in practice. The outcome might be a business that is shut down, scaled, or passed on to new students as a form of "learning legacy." University incubators can support this process—but it must be embedded in the curriculum, not offered as an extracurricular bonus.

Such projects reconnect theory to practice. Students don't just acquire knowledge—they test it. They learn judgment, resilience, and how to distinguish between useful tools and empty abstractions. This hands-on experience bridges the growing disconnect between business education and business reality.

The deeper benefit, however, is cultural. Students who have tested their own ideas, failed and adjusted, or perhaps even succeeded leave university with a different mindset. They are less likely to be passive recipients of *management jargon* and more likely to think independently, question assumptions, and act with agency in complex situations. That is precisely the kind of economist—and citizen—the twenty-first century needs.

Yet this disconnect also reflects a deeper problem—one rooted in the faculty themselves. Many instructors in business schools have never set foot in a company, managed a budget, sold a product, or made decisions under market pressure. Today, it is not unusual to find accounting professors unfamiliar with actual bookkeeping or marketing scholars who've never worked with customers. This isn't a critique of academic research; it is a critique of *professional insulation*. We cannot teach business from behind a wall of theory—especially when that theory is not only detached from practice but may also rest on flawed assumptions.

To restore credibility to business and economics education, we must rebuild the foundations. That means hiring educators with practical experience—like we still had in many business schools when I began teaching some 25 years ago—creating clear pathways for professionals to enter academia, and rewarding faculty who bridge theory and practice, not just those who publish in abstract journals. The professor of the future must be both a thinker and a practitioner. The days of teaching markets without understanding them must end.

Finally, *institutional reform* must support this cultural shift. Joint master's and doctoral programs across economics, sociology, anthropology, and political science should be built to foster interdisciplinary fluency. These programs require *cross-departmental supervision*, *co-taught courses*, and *shared methodological toolkits*. Research grants and career incentives must be redesigned to reward collaboration across fields, not penalize it. None of this will work unless faculty are trained—and meaningfully encouraged—to step outside their disciplinary silos.

These changes are not about rejecting academic depth. They are about restoring relevance. Education must reconnect with the world it claims to serve. The next section turns to this question of academic legitimacy: how relevance earns trust—and how trust, in turn, can enable lasting change.

12.3   Reclaiming Purpose and Legitimacy in Economics Education

The central problem facing economics today is not that it is unethical or ill-intentioned. It is that, in many crucial respects, it no longer works. It no longer explains the systems we live in, nor does it guide decision-making in a way that supports long-term societal health. It was remarkably effective in the decades immediately following the Second World War, helping to structure recovery and growth. But over time, its assumptions—particularly its short-term focus, individualistic logic, and abstraction from real-world institutions—have proven increasingly out of step with the economic realities they claim to model.

Nowhere is this clearer than in the experience of the middle class in many Western countries. Far from being empowered by modern economic policy, it has become progressively burdened—by debt, by stagnating wages, and by the erosion of social mobility. This trajectory could have been foreseen. A discipline built on models that emphasize *individual maximization* over *collective resilience*, consumption over conservation, and short-term incentives over long-term outcomes was bound to struggle with generational transitions, systemic inequality, and ecological degradation.

This is not a failure of values. It is a failure of function.

And it is increasingly visible. Businesses question the relevance of academic economics. Policymakers rely on private consultants rather than university departments. Students gravitate to disciplines that seem better suited to understanding real-world complexity. When public trust fades, *institutional legitimacy* becomes difficult to sustain.

This is the quiet legitimacy crisis now confronting the field. It cannot be solved by slogans or incremental adjustments. What's needed is a clear, constructive reorientation toward realism, long-term thinking, and systemic relevance.

Evolutionary economics can help lead that shift—not by claiming to be the final answer, but by offering a more adaptive and integrative framework. It emphasizes change, feedback, coevolution, and historical context. It focuses on how institutions form and dissolve, how behaviors emerge and spread, and how societies adapt—or fail to adapt—to external pressures.

But for such a framework to earn its place, it must prove itself useful. That means showing how it helps us understand financial instability, technological disruption, and institutional decay. It must provide tools that work not only in theory but also in the hands of practitioners—tools that guide decision-making under uncertainty, support long-term policy design, and reflect the structural challenges of interconnected global systems.

Legitimacy also requires a shift in how academic work is evaluated. Universities must reward real-world engagement, interdisciplinary collaboration, and policy relevance. Applied work, field-based research, and cross-sector partnerships must count—not only for career advancement but also as central to the mission of economics itself.

In business education especially, the disconnect has grown stark. Many faculty have little or no experience in the domains they teach. This isn't a matter of ethics—it's a structural mismatch. The models they use are rarely tested against operational practice. The result is a growing gap between what is taught and what is needed.

Students, meanwhile, are increasingly aware of the limitations. They seek more than lectures and exams. They want tools they can use, frameworks they can apply, and opportunities to learn through experience. Requiring every student to launch a small business—not as a simulation but as a real venture—would offer a way to reconnect economic theory with market reality. Incubators already exist. What's missing is their full integration into *pedagogy*.

At the same time, evolutionary economics must avoid replicating the insularity it criticizes. It should not claim exclusivity, nor marginalize other approaches. Its strength lies in openness—in its capacity to explain diverse phenomena and link insights across disciplines. It must earn legitimacy by performance, not position.

History offers cautionary lessons. Scholars such as Georgescu-Roegen and Peter Drucker made substantial contributions that were largely sidelined by mainstream economics—not because they were wrong, but because their insights didn't fit the dominant paradigm. Georgescu-Roegen's thermodynamic logic and Drucker's management science proved enduring, but neither was institutionally embraced at the time (even though Drucker was immensely popular in corporate boardrooms).

That kind of *intellectual myopia* is no longer sustainable. In some countries, departments are being closed or consolidated—not because economics has been discredited, but because it has ceased to meet the needs of its constituents. Employers, students, and policymakers all seek relevance—and are often finding it elsewhere.

This challenge is compounded by disciplinary fragmentation. While some regions, such as the United Kingdom, have retained integrative perspectives grounded in *political economy*, others—most notably the United States—have moved toward increasing specialization and methodological orthodoxy. The result is a proliferation of narrow studies, often disconnected from one another and from real-world impact.

If economics is to regain its role, it must reconnect—not just internally, but across the social sciences. Evolutionary economics can help enable that integration—not by asserting dominance, but by offering a flexible, empirically grounded framework that treats economics, sociology, political science, anthropology, and psychology as branches of the same inquiry: understanding how human systems evolve.

The United States, long the intellectual center of economic theory, is now at a crossroads. In some circles, a reassessment is underway. Whether this rethinking results in genuine reform or merely a reshuffling of the status quo remains to be seen. What is clear is that global legitimacy now rests not on historical prestige but on relevance, responsiveness, and results.

In the end, any discipline that seeks public support must deliver public value. That value is no longer measured solely in publications or citations. It is measured in insight, utility, and trust. Economics must once again become a tool for understanding the world as it is—so that we might shape it as it could be.

12.4 Final Reflections: The Future of Economic Thought in an Uncertain World

A paradigm shift—from neoclassical to evolutionary economics—may not unfold through grand declarations or institutional mandates, but rather gradually, as the inadequacies of existing models become impossible to ignore. Such transitions often emerge from the friction of lived reality: from crises, contradictions, and the inability of dominant frameworks to explain or respond to unfolding events.

We may speculate that triggers could include a collapse of the USD-based financial system, the continued erosion of the Western industrial base, or the widespread social consequences of climate instability. Whatever the catalyst, the transition itself would illustrate the evolutionary logic of adaptation under pressure.

Several plausible forces could accelerate this shift:

- *Environmental degradation* may force societies to abandon growth-centered models that ignore ecological limits. This could renew interest in resilience, systems thinking, and adaptive policy—concerns central to Georgescu-Roegen's pioneering work, to whom this book is dedicated.
- *Social unrest*, whether from geopolitical conflict, deepening inequality, or economic disruption, may expose the shortcomings of static and idealized models of rational behavior. This could strengthen demands for frameworks that reflect actual social dynamics and institutional realities.
- *The rise of alternative schools of thought*, especially in emerging economies, may further challenge Western academic orthodoxy. Japan, for instance, has long been a center for vibrant research in evolutionary economics.[2]

Unlike past shifts—such as the abrupt rise of neoclassical economics after the Second World War—an evolutionary turn may develop more organically, driven by:

- The accumulation of compelling empirical evidence that highlights the limitations of equilibrium models and linear thinking.
- Intellectual openness in academic communities, particularly outside the traditional centers of economic thought.
- The practical relevance of evolutionary approaches in addressing real-world challenges such as innovation, complexity, sustainability, and digital transformation.

---

[2] Recent contributions by Yagi (2024), Shiozawa (2024), Aruka (2024), and Nishibe and Isogai (2024), along with the ongoing efforts of the Japan Association for Evolutionary Economics (JAFEE), reflect a deep and sustained commitment to the field. This intellectual momentum is not limited to Japan; similar interest has been cultivated for more than a generation in Germany and parts of the United Kingdom, where evolutionary approaches continue to shape debates in economic theory and policy.

Yet any meaningful transition must also reckon with its intellectual foundations. As discussed in this book, Georgescu-Roegen offered one of the most ambitious attempts to ground economics in the life sciences. His application of *thermodynamic principles* and evolutionary theory provided an essential critique of growth-centered economic thinking. However, while his theoretical insights remain valuable, his proposed program was ultimately too radical and unrealistic to gain wide traction. The responses that followed—particularly the rise of *Ecological Economics* and the *Degrowth* movement—have had the virtue of keeping parts of his legacy alive but often suffer from similar limitations: a tendency toward political advocacy, insufficient engagement with empirical micro-level behavior, and a lack of actionable models that connect individual decisions with systemic change.

The proposals made in this book aim to contribute something new. Rather than replacing one sweeping macro framework with another, it is suggested that we develop two focused, complementary fields at the micro level: *Biological Behavioral Economics* and *Physiology Economics*. These perspectives integrate evolutionary and physiological insights directly into economic analysis, helping us understand how embodied, historically shaped human beings actually make decisions. The former emphasizes long-term adaptive traits such as reciprocity, in-group preference, and fairness. The latter examines the short-term influence of bodily states like hunger, stress, or hormonal variation on economic behavior. Together, they offer a more realistic, grounded approach to understanding choice—not in idealized markets, but in lived, biological experience.

For such a paradigm to take root, however, it must be reflected in how we educate economists. As we argued in the opening chapter, reconceptualizing economics as an evolutionary science requires not only better models but also better learning environments. Students must be trained to think historically, biologically, and contextually. Students must learn to engage with uncertainty and contradiction, not shy away from it. Occasional failure should be normalized—even encouraged—as part of the learning process. Just as importantly, the willingness to dedicate years to focused, often stressful work must be recognized as a virtue, not a flaw. The reforms proposed in this chapter are, in that sense, not just pedagogical updates, but part of a larger intellectual transition.

We must also remain open to the possibility that the next economic paradigm may come from somewhere else entirely. Depending on geopolitical developments and the rise of new cultural powers, alternative frameworks—perhaps rooted in *Confucianism*, systems metaphysics, or other traditions—may gain traction.

What is certain is that the current economic model cannot remain intact—because it has failed to serve the long-term interests of the Western world, and arguably, much of the rest of the world as well. The United States experienced a relatively brief period as the world's undisputed superpower, a position that, rather than being used to build lasting national strength, often fuelled unsustainable debt, offshored its industrial base, and hollowed out its middle class. As Thomas Piketty has shown, wealth concentration increased dramatically during this time, while large segments of the workforce were left behind—turned into *precarious laborers* in a service economy that prioritized shareholder profits over national resilience.[3]

Meanwhile, many Asian nations—first the Tigers, and later China—invested heavily in education, infrastructure, and long-term industrial policy. Today, they lead in many of the world's most critical technologies. According to the Australian Strategic Policy Institute (ASPI), China now holds a dominant position in 37 out of 44 key technology fields, while Europe leads in almost none.[4] If life in Europe is to remain prosperous, safe, and attractive, this trajectory must be reversed. As the Draghi Report on EU competitiveness clearly warns, Europe's future depends on serious rethinking—not only of its institutions and strategies but also of the economic paradigm that guides them.[5]

If we hope to shape a generation ready for complexity, we must first reimagine how we teach it. The next paradigm in economics may not arrive by consensus, but by necessity—and education is where that transformation must begin.

Throughout this book, we have argued that economics is, at its core, an evolutionary science. Drawing on insights from biology, anthropology, sociology, and complexity theory, we have tried to show that human behavior and institutions are shaped by the same adaptive processes we observe in nature. This perspective reconnects economics with the rest of the sciences—and with the realities of human life in all its richness, variability, and contradiction.

If this book has helped even a few readers see those connections more clearly, ask better questions, or imagine a more grounded and adaptive economics, then its purpose has been fulfilled.

References

Aruka, Y. (Ed.). (2024). *Evolutionary foundations of economic science: How can scientists contribute to policy dialogue?* Springer.

Australian Strategic Policy Institute. (2023). *ASPI critical technology tracker: Key technology fields and global leadership.* Australian Strategic Policy Institute. https://www.aspi.org.au/report/critical-technology-tracker

Draghi, M. (2024). *Report on the future of European competitiveness.* European Commission.

Nishibe, M., & Isogai, A. (Eds.). (2024). *Diversity and transformation of Asian capitalisms: Evolutionary and institutional perspectives.* Springer.

Piketty, T. (2014). *Capital in the twenty-first century* (A. Goldhammer, Trans.). Harvard University Press.

Shiozawa, Y. (2024). Reconsidering evolutionary economics in East Asia. In Y. Aruka (Ed.), *Evolutionary foundations of economic science* (pp. 145–163). Springer.

---

[3] Piketty (2014).

[4] Australian Strategic Policy Institute (2023).

[5] Draghi (2024).

Further Reading

Boyer, R., Uemura, H., Yamada, T., & Song, L. (Eds.). (2018). *Evolving diversity and interdependence of capitalisms: Transformations of regional integration in EU and Asia.* Springer Japan.

Cantner, U., & Hanusch, H. (2010). *Volkswirtschaftslehre 1. Grundlegende Mikro-und Makroökonomik.* Springer.

Söilen, K. S. (2024). *Digital marketing: Tools, techniques and best practices for graduate students and managers.* Springer.

Appendix A: A Summary of Tools for Evolutionary Economics

In Table A.1 summarizes how foundational concepts from biology can enrich our understanding of economic behavior, particularly in areas such as market dynamics, resilience, innovation, and competition. By adopting an evolutionary lens, economists gain tools to better explain adaptive behavior, systemic change, and long-term economic sustainability.

Table A.1 Applying biological concepts in economic analysis

Biological concept	Definition	Economic analogy	Applications in economics
Natural Selection	Traits that enhance fitness survive over time	Firms with better strategies outcompete rivals	Explains dominance of adaptable firms (e.g., Amazon)
Adaptation	Organisms adjust to environmental change	Firms responding to policy shifts or market disruptions	Analyzing innovation in response to crises
Variation	Genetic diversity within a population	Diversity in products, strategies, or firms	Studying innovation pipelines and competitive differentiation
Mutation	Random genetic changes introducing novelty	Disruptive innovation or unexpected market shifts	Role of radical innovation (e.g., blockchain, AI)
Fitness Landscapes	Visual map of adaptive peaks and valleys	Strategic optimization under constraints	Identifying high-performance business models
Genetic Drift	Random fluctuations in gene frequencies	Market shifts due to chance events	Explains sudden firm success/failure independent of merit
Punctuated Equilibrium	Long stability punctuated by rapid change	Technological or regulatory shocks causing disruption	Explains industry upheavals (e.g., shift to digital photography)

(continued)

© The Author(s), under exclusive license to Springer Nature Switzerland AG 2025
K. Solberg Söilen, *Applied Evolutionary Economics*, Management for Professionals, https://doi.org/10.1007/978-3-032-03683-4

Table A.1 (continued)

Biological concept	Definition	Economic analogy	Applications in economics
Speciation	Formation of new species in different niches	Emergence of new firms or sectors	Niche development in emerging industries
Coevolution	Mutual adaptation between species	Interdependent evolution of firms and technologies	Platform ecosystems (e.g., iOS and app developers)
Survival of the Fittest	Only the most adapted organisms endure	Competitive markets filter out inefficient actors	Core logic of free-market survival
Ecological Niches	Roles species occupy in ecosystems	Market segmentation and specialization	Analyzing consumer targeting and product differentiation
Carrying Capacity	Maximum sustainable population for an environment	Resource limits to growth	Modeling environmental and economic sustainability
Resource Allocation	Distribution of nutrients and energy	Capital and labor distribution across firms	Studying efficiency and trade-offs in production systems
Competition	Organisms vie for limited resources	Firms compete for market share	Models of pricing, entry barriers, and monopolistic behavior
Cooperation/ Mutualism	Species benefit from mutual collaboration	Strategic alliances and shared platforms	Understanding collaborative innovation (e.g., open source)
Altruism	Sacrificing individual gain for group benefit	CSR and contributions to public goods	Explains non-market contributions to welfare (e.g., social enterprises)
Predator–Prey Dynamics	Interaction of dependent species—one benefits, one risks loss	Disruptors vs. incumbents; firms exploiting dependencies	Analyzing competitive asymmetries (e.g., Uber vs. taxi industry)
Entropy	Tendency toward disorder or energy dissipation	Waste and inefficiency in production and systems	Explains diminishing returns and energy constraints (cf. Georgescu-Roegen)
Sustainability	Maintaining system processes over time	Long-term resilience in economic systems	Green economics and resource-conscious growth planning
Kin Selection	Favoring genetic relatives in cooperation	Trust and cooperation in family firms or local economies	Studying informal trust economies and social capital
Sexual Selection	Traits evolve for attractiveness rather than survival	Branding and consumer appeal	Luxury goods, status signaling, and marketing psychology
Red Queen Hypothesis	Continuous adaptation to keep pace with others	Constant innovation to remain competitive	Highlights treadmill dynamics in tech and finance sectors

Table A.1 (continued)

Biological concept	Definition	Economic analogy	Applications in economics
Symbiosis	Long-term beneficial interspecies interaction	Platforms and supplier networks	Apple–app ecosystem, Salesforce–third-party integrators
Keystone Species	Disproportionately impactful organisms in ecosystems	Core firms that stabilize or destabilize markets	Understanding the systemic role of dominant actors (e.g., Google, Amazon)
Ecological Resilience	Ability of ecosystems to recover from shocks	Economic recovery after crises	Studying systemic robustness post-recession or disruption
Cultural Evolution	Transmission of learned behaviors and norms	Institutional change and policy evolution	Path dependency, labor market shifts, regulatory inertia
Niche Construction	Organisms modify their environments to suit themselves	Firms reshaping markets to their advantage	Tesla redefining auto and energy sectors simultaneously

Index

Zeitfracht Medien GmbH
Ferdinand-Jühlke-Straße 7
99095 Erfurt, Deutschland
produktsicherheit@kolibri360.de